When Good Kids Do Bad Things

When
Good Kids Do
Bad Things

A SURVIVAL GUIDE
FOR PARENTS

Katherine Gordy Levine

W·W·Norton & Company
New York   London

"Funky Winkerbean" cartoons, which appear on pages 23, 46, 62, 101, and 170, are reprinted with the special permission of North America Syndicate.

SAD PERSONS scale, which appears on page 168, was developed by William M. Patterson, M.D.; Henry H. Dohn, M.D.; Julian Bird, M.R.C.P., M.R.C.; and Gary Patterson, M.S., and was first published in "Evaluation of Suicidal Patients: The Sad Persons Scale" in *Psychosomatics*, Vol. 24, pages 343–49, a journal published by the American Psychiatric Press. Used by permission.

"Rescuer's Quiz," which appears on pages 238–40, is reprinted from *Recovery from Rescuing* by Jacqueline Castine, copyright 1989, with the permission of the publishers, Health Communications, Inc., Deerfield Beach, Florida.

Printed in the United States of America.

The text of this book is composed in Garamond #3, with the display set in Garamond Bold Condensed. Composition and manufacturing by the Maple–Vail Book Manufacturing Group. Book design by Margaret Wagner.

First Edition.

Library of Congress Cataloging-in-Publication Data

Levine, Katherine G.
When good kids do bad things : a survival guide for parents / Katherine G. Levine.
p.   cm.
Includes index.
ISBN 0-393-03019-9
1. Parent and teenager—United States.   2. Adolescent psychology—United States.   I. Title.
HQ799.15.L48   1991
649'.125—dc20   91-8580

W.W. Norton & Company, Inc., 500 Fifth Avenue, New York, N.Y. 10110
W.W. Norton & Company, Ltd., 10 Coptic Street, London WC1A 1PU

1 2 3 4 5 6 7 8 9 0

This book is dedicated to all of my foster children. David and I may not have really liked each one of you every moment of every day, but we did love you in a very special way. We still do. You will never leave our hearts or our prayers.

Contents

Preface

████████████████

It has been nearly five years since our last foster child left the suburban New York house where my husband David and I cared for almost four hundred foster kids in little more than a decade, as well as raise two boys of our own. Our biological sons were entering their teens. The time had come to live a more normal life.

Our twelve years of foster parenting were challenging, exasperating, and often wrenching emotionally. They were also fun and funny, at times, but trying to take care of four or five unrelated teenagers at a time, *and* raise our own two boys, was never an easy job.

This book is the book David and I needed during those years, especially when the foster kids were "acting out" their teenage problems and doing other things that got them into trouble.

Instead, we could find only the "Pollyanish" books, with few exceptions. As we racked our brains and hearts because of some draining conflict or another, the parenting books did little but unrealistically put the ball in our corner. If we did such-and-such, success would quickly follow. We would do such-and-such . . . and rarely get relief, much less success.

The most prevalent, and annoying, assumption of these blithe books could be stated this way: when your child does something you, the parent(s), don't like, changing the situation is entirely up to you. Many seemed to suggest that parents should behave and speak like therapists. These were the years when Parent Effectiveness Training

(PET) peaked in the public consciousness: ideally, parents were to refrain from judging their kid's actions and serenely allow life to provide the consequences for misbehavior. In our special situation, we had neither the time nor the patience for this technique. Soon, the gospel of "tough love" swamped PET. The parents who had restrained from criticizing now tried desperately to transform themselves into Marine drill sergeants. For better or worse, neither David nor I has what the military calls "command presence."

How does my book supersede these other approaches? Well, for some parents, it may not. Nowhere in these pages do I insist, or even hint, that the Levine way is the one true, right way. No one approach will work at all times for all kids and all parents. Quite frankly, I never learned any magic tricks for keeping my several hundred or so "good kids" (who were, as you will see, no different from your own teenagers, for the most part) from doing "bad things." And our own sons gave their father and me many a sleepless night, many a gray hair. The basic lesson we learned in our foster parenting years can be learned in many other areas of life: easy answers to some problems simply don't exist.

Why, then, this book? Because I did learn something very valuable from our experiences: a way of effecting real change in an adolescent's behavior.

Our success as parents evolved from a growing understanding that behavior would not change until we were able to win the kid's active cooperation. I knew, of course, that parents have to sustain a caring relationship, no matter what. But that did not seem possible when I had reached my wit's end . . . or David and I were on the verge of murdering each other . . . or either one of us wanted to strangle a kid. Sustain a caring relationship, no matter what?

Well, with much practice, I eventually learned and developed a number of caring ways of responding to unacceptable behavior. Ultimately, those ways turned into a planned response to bad behavior I call the Caring Response. This process, which is really the heart of this book, can be recycled in many different ways until it achieves your goals, or until the need for professional help is definitely established.

During the past five years I have been teaching this process to parents in my consulting practice, Parent Tactics. Most of the time, I've found, the Caring Response helps parents who are in conflict with their kid. Even when it does not immediately result in a change in misbehavior, this process has helped parents focus on themselves, then move on to concentrating on figuring out what to do next.

Finally, let's not forget that the only expert on how to parent a particular child is, and always will be, the person actually parenting that child. As a parent, you know better than anyone else what you can and cannot do, and what works best with you and with your child.

Certainly, I believe that strongly. This book is my attempt to define, explain, and share options that are bedded in a process, the Caring Response, which can help you explore alternative answers to almost any problem you face with your "good kid." Skip over the passages that don't apply to you and take what you find helpful. And let me hear from you. If you have any suggestions or comments about this book or would like to share your own experiences, you can write to me in care of W. W. Norton, 500 Fifth Avenue, New York, NY 10110.

As parents, we all have much the same concerns and insecurities. From my experiences with hundreds of teenagers, and with our own two sons, and from my many sessions with worried parents, I believe I can point a pathway, if not set down precise answers that apply across the board.

Author's Note

The stories in this book are based on my personal experiences as foster parent, parent, workshop leader, and therapist. But the stories are composites of many similar tales. I have blended and masked identities to protect the privacy of the children and parents involved. The only story in this book that has not undergone some sort of transformation is my account of Zachary's joy ride, which I have his permission to share.

Acknowledgments

$\mathbf{T}$his book is the creation of many. I hope my thank you note mentions them all.

First, there's Brutus. Difficult dog, snarling rambunctious boxer, he'd been kicked out of his third home just before he adopted David. After they'd lived together for a year, dog decided it was high time man put an end to bachelorhood. Brutus picked me up at the beach, completing a threesome.

Without David, my husband, this book simply could not have been. It was his idea that we become foster parents, for he saw the challenge and felt the children's pain. I was frightened, but, as has often happened in our life together, he showed me how to do more than I believed I could. That is a remarkable talent. Often, he has nurtured my successes without considering the cost to his own—a rare and generous trait. In every way, this book is his as much as mine.

It is also the creation of our many children: our two wonderful biological sons, our very special foster children, the teens I've helped in my private practice, and the kids whose parents have taken my workshops. Those parents and others have also influenced these pages, including the parents of our foster children, my friends who are parents, the parents of my children's friends, and the many parents who also happened to be students of mine. First among all of these parents is my mother, Katherine Broomall Gordy, who taught me to take time out for sunsets, for wishing upon a star, for listening to the songs of birds. Most of all, she taught me the importance of caring about others. My father, John Denard Gordy, had lessons that were just as valuable: I learned always to value honesty between people, and to let go of the things I could never change.

Other people helped create this book by helping me become who I am. Aunt Dot gave me a strong faith in myself. Lloyd Trout and Thomas Hardy inspired me to take up horseback riding, thus indirectly teaching me that life isn't a matter of mistakes and accidents, but of lessons that have to be repeated until they are learned.

Finally, I have learned some lessons in schools, for I've been lucky in having had some very gifted teachers. Mr. Snavely, for one, gamely kept throwing theorems at me until I learned enough to pass geometry. Mr. Davis, though driven by my unique spelling and punctuation to tear out what little hair he had left, nevertheless had enough faith to appoint me editor of our high school yearbook. Mr. Flagg taught me how to drive when my father couldn't. Miss Porter, who never succeeded in teaching me to sing, did teach me to love music. At the University of Delaware, I was privileged to have a class under Bernard Phillips, a Zen Buddhist-Quaker-Jewish philosophy professor who taught me the difference between religion and spirituality. I was also fortunate to study with Charles Bohner, Janney D'Armond, and Edward Rosenberry—English professors who taught me that, even if I couldn't spell, I could still think and write. Later, at Bryn Mawr College's Graduate School of Social Work and Social Research, I was shown how to turn compassion into actual helping by Ricky Ross, Jean Haring, and Calvin Setledge. Also, in my career Charlotte Hamel, Muriel Gayford, and Naomi Gitterman became very important role models.

During the years we were foster parents, many professionals were assigned to help as well as monitor us and the children in our care. Special mention must go to Susan Langer, who helped us decide if we really wanted to take on the job of being "special need" foster parents; Joan DiBlasi, who set up the systems within the Department of Social Service that made possible our financial survival; Jeanne Quatroni and Jack Garrity, who stood by us those first difficult days; Debbie Beals, who was not only a support for us but also stayed with our children more than once, giving us several very necessary breaks; and also Patty Gross, Joyce Remkus, Lionel Oliver, Kim Smith, Carol Korn, Sheryl Blau, Joan Cuppiola, Jim Hoffnagle, Don Kimmelman, Adele Rigano, and Jim Bishop. Each of these people went well beyond the call of professional duty. In fact, without their support, David and I could not have survived as foster parents, and this book would have been greatly diminished.

To move from my head to the printed page, my book has needed a great deal of help, beginning with the advice and suggestions given by good friends. Donna Santora Vovcsko, the sister I never had, was the initial sounding board for my theories, while her husband, Jerry, introduced me to the word processor and the ins and outs of computer networking. Cathy Agar and Jane Bloomer helped me find just the right title for the book. Jane Persons Handley, Barbara Burris Machemer, and Virginia Lanier Biasotto—along with others from the Henpecker Group—added wisdom and support. Rob Colby Pierce became my private grammarian. Gerry Wallman, who was writing her own book long before I began, shared with me the blazing of her path.

In time, Ruth Wreschner became my literary agent: she understood the message of the book. She helped shape it and found it a home at Norton, with Mary Cunnane as editor. Mary patiently taught me what it takes to turn ideas and knowledge into a book. I am also grateful that, in her wisdom, she introduced me to Charles Flowers, who joined our efforts to bring about the final transformation of my work. Behind the scenes at Norton is a host of helpers who also made this book possible; one of the best is Rebecca Castillo.

Finally, I believe a Higher Power guides us all. I am grateful to that power for blessing me with the help I needed to write this book.

When Good Kids Do
Bad Things

ONE

The Basics

"Have you gone crazy?"

"Oh, Mom . . ."

"You've never done anything like this before. . . . I can't believe it! It must be that new friend of yours."

"Oh, sure."

"Don't talk back to me, young lady, and wipe that smirk off your face. What's got into you? I don't recognize you any more."

"Get real, Mom."

"You don't even sound like yourself. What happened to the little girl who never did anything wrong? How come you never smile the way you used to? How could you get yourself into trouble this way?"

"Do I really have to hear this?"

Meet three "good kids" I've known well: Terry, who doesn't stop smiling even when you ask her to do the pots and pans; Jon, shy but always the first to comfort a younger child who gets hurt; and then Jennie, so successful and well liked in school that she's regularly featured in the campus newspaper. "Good kids" every one—but if your own child, or children, is anything like they are, you may be heading for trouble, because these "good kids" do very "bad things." And they won't stop, they can't stop, unless their parents learn the difference between bad behavior and "bad kids."

Take Terry, a blond, twelve-year-old girl-next-door dressed in full Middle America Mall: Levi 501s, Benetton sweatshirt (two sizes too large), UBU sneakers. Her braces gleam as she unself-consciously pops gum. Still very much a child but sensitive to adult demands, she is indeed her mother's joy, her father's pride, the bane of her nine-year-old brother's existence. She makes friends easily in her sixth-grade-class, and because one of them has just made a dare, Terry is about to be arrested for shoplifting.

Jon is not such a standout. An average student in the eighth grade, son of middle-class parents who own a nondescript tract house, he is unusually short but has always compensated with energetic behavior, a real verve for living. Lately, something has soured. On several occasions, the energy has exploded, and devil-may-care Jon has raged against his parents, screaming curses and hurling objects. Once, he smashed through a plate-glass window; twice, he's broken chairs by throwing them against the wall. His parents, who have always enjoyed their son's unusual vigor, are stunned. Most of the time, he is still their delightfully lively child, curious and fun-loving. Why these occasional outbursts of violence? They can't see any pattern, but that's because they haven't discovered one basic fact. Jon's moodiness always strikes about a day after he's smoked a joint. This good kid cannot handle his secret substance abuse.

Jennie would look down her nose at Terry and Jon. She would never steal, or even cheat, because she is proud of the good grades she earns in her junior year of high school. She would certainly never smoke cigarettes, much less pot, or drink alcohol, because she trains her body hard for track and is state high jump champion. Her whole life right now is focused on getting accepted by Stanford University. For that reason, she has been carefully storing up a supply of sleeping pills, enough to kill herself. If Stanford rejects her, she is ready.

Not one of these kids, or hundreds of thousands like them, can be called "bad," but they are behaving "badly"—that is, illegally, anti-socially, self-destructively. This book is intended as a handbook, a guide, for dealing with our good children when they do bad things. It is also full of the warning signs that indicate the rare worst-case scenario for any of us parents, the kid who is really "bad"—in other words, the kid who desperately needs professional help.

What You May Need to Learn

Jon and Jennifer are already embroiled in adolescence; Terry is on the brink of that fascinatingly difficult time. What about your own kids? If they are between the ages of ten and sixteen, this book is for you, because I discuss the challenges you and they will face during the years of early and middle adolescence.

Of course, many children can say goodbye to childhood and march along the road to adulthood with scarcely a misstep. But change is upsetting to many other teenagers, and they may stumble or even fall. Some wander down crooked lanes, vanish from sight, turn up in unexpected places, do uncharacteristic things. They worry and grieve their parents.

You are such a parent, or you would not feel the need to read what I have to say.

Maybe you think you're overreacting. The child you love came home one night smelling of something like peach brandy. (For some unfathomable reason, that's the initiation drink of choice where we live.) He seems hurt when you question him. Don't you trust him? Can't you believe that a friend's older brother spilled a drink on him? You say you do, but doubts linger. He protested just a little bit too much.

Or maybe you have even less to go on. Quite often, the young teenager becomes less communicative, even secretive, no longer sharing stories about her friends or telling you where she goes after school. You want to respect her growing independence, but her few responses have created a web of lies. And you definitely did not buy her those expensive new boots or that designer blouse. What's going on? How can you find out?

Or maybe you can't sleep nights because your child's attack of "teenage blues" looks a lot like serious depression to you. How can you tell? Falling grades, loss of interest in old buddies and favorite activities, far too many hours spent asleep—you know that friends' children have gone through this kind of "phase" and recovered their own personalities. But you aren't sure. You've read in the paper about the rise in teenage suicides all over the country.

These are the kinds of problems we can explore together in this book. I teach prospective social workers how to deal with them, I work with severely troubled teenagers in a crisis intervention program, and my husband David and I have two sons in their late teens. They are strong, loving individuals, and they have given us, to paraphrase the ancient Chinese curse, "interesting times."

But much of the experience I have drawn upon was earned during a period of draining, exasperating, occasionally joyful, foster parenting. Teenage assault, drug and alcohol abuse, attempted seductions, thefts, property destruction—my family lived with them for twelve years in a large, rambling house we rented outside New York City. This situation was so unusual, even crazy, that I'm still not sure how we all survived. (And TV producers have considered making our lives the basis for a situation comedy!) I had to learn, sometimes on the spur of the moment, how to put theory into practice.

How I Know What I'm Talking About

Over a period of twelve years, David and I cared for 367 children in our own home. We have only two biological children, Zachary and Daniel, but when they were growing up, we decided to become foster parents in a special program set up by our local Department of Child Welfare. The youngsters involved could not live with their families or get along with regular foster parents. Four to six of them lived with us at a time—some lighting for only a few days, others moving in for months on end. Almost all had been accused by someone of doing bad things.

Of course, I anticipated fierce challenges, but I was confident that my professional background gave me an edge. As a licensed therapist and college professor with an advanced degree in social work, I had specialized in the study of adolescent behavior. I knew what is and is not normal development. I expected that I would analyze any behavior problem or conflict with a coolly academic eye, reason out a solution, and briskly put it into effect. One day at a time. . . .

I was wrong. Within weeks, I was emotionally strung out and physically exhausted. My husband and I were taking out our frustrations and fears on each other; our marriage seemed to be in serious trouble. Sleepless nights, property damage, confrontations with the authorities—I lost every shred of self-confidence. Books, lectures, studies, therapy sessions? Like a nonswimmer who tries to learn by reading a Red Cross manual and then leaps into the Atlantic during Hurricane Hugo, I suddenly faced the chilling realization that I had a lot to learn—and very little time left to do so.

First, as you would expect, I ran to other professionals for help. Blaming myself, as most caring parents will, I assumed that I had not learned my subject well enough or had had inadequate training in social work. Perhaps I had been wool-gathering during the lectures on practical aspects of real parenting. Perhaps, as a specialist in social work, I was not familiar with the special parenting tricks known only to psychologists and psychiatrists.

Wrong again. A gifted, experienced psychotherapist can help a patient work on personality changes over the long term, when such changes are needed. Their expertise is not geared toward solving practical problems or dispensing advice, especially to parents.

What I discovered, after flailing about, was that the most practical, useful, and lifesaving advice on specific problems came from experienced parents. The parent of a teenager has a young lifetime's worth of on-the-job experience, earned at the rate of twenty-four hours a day, seven days a week. Certainly, professional counseling will often help a troubled teenager, but sometimes, to get through the day, you need something more like a Household Hint from Heloise. That's the moral of the story about my mother and the therapist.

When twelve-year-old Kerry lived with us for about three months, she went regularly to a very good therapist who understood her emotional needs well. She was a somewhat dreamy, feckless child, her face still pudgy with baby fat in a halo of naturally blond hair. Her family life had been appallingly difficult. I was sympathetic with her problems, though she was not very communicative. She was a quiet, unassuming kid. And she had a very bad habit that soon drove me up the wall.

Wherever Kerry sat, she would unconsciously pick at loose threads. Her own clothes, a throw pillow at her side, the arm of a chair or couch—she simply could not sit still for any extended period of time without picking, picking, picking. Buttons fell off, hems came undone; still, she picked. And since nerves as well as edges fray, I went to her therapist.

"When she can talk about her anger toward her father, the picking will stop," he said. "But she has a lot of anger, so don't expect sudden magic." A sound professional analysis, no doubt, but I couldn't afford to wait until every piece of furniture in our house was picked down to the bare bones.

Next, I tried a behavior modification expert. Rather than explore the reasons behind a bad habit, behaviorists work to change the habit by changing behavior.

This particular behaviorist agreed that I was right to come to him. "Yes, picking is just the same kind of problem behavior modification can help with," he said. "I can see the both of you in two weeks." In the meantime, Kerry and I were to keep separate diaries noting down when, where, and under what circumstances the picking took place.

This advice is standard in behavior modification. The diary-keeping establishes a baseline for measuring change. It may also uncover some of the factors that reinforce the unacceptable behavior.

Unfortunately, Kerry had been placed with us because she hated school so much she had run away from home, school, and anything that resembled school work. I suspected there would be no diary-keeping, but I asked, anyway. She just laughed. (Eventually it was discovered that Kerry suffered from a very specific learning disability. Once she received help, she did just fine, but that is another story.)

That left the ball in my court. I love to write and I had faithfully kept a personal journal of my thoughts and observations for years—before I became a parent. Zach was not yet four years old, Daniel was six months, and our six foster children at the time ranged in age from nine to fourteen. I was lucky to find a minute to jot down a grocery list. Yet and still, succumbing to the crazy parental need to bend over backward, I tried. Within a few days, my sanity was restored and I admitted that my life had no room at the time for behavior modification record-keeping. I canceled our appointment with the expert.

Enter now the most fabled and maligned of experts. Mom. For all the usual reasons, I had never thought to ask this particular experienced parent for advice. When she came to visit for a few days, however, she quietly watched Kerry's picking for a few hours and then came up with a practical approach: turn the bad habit into an asset. She taught my idler a type of embroidery that requires pulling threads and fraying edges. By the time Kerry had pulled and frayed her twenty-fourth napkin, she had had enough. Our furniture was safe again.

Let me be clear: I'm not saying that professional help is not useful in many situations. When it comes to understanding and dealing with the buried feelings that can create problems, a good therapist is often a parent's best friend. But for parents living with good kids who do bad things, experienced parents can often provide the best advice. In this case, I discovered afterward that our behaviorist, unmarried and still in his twenties, had never been responsible for raising an actual child. His skills had been honed while watching caged rats. As a lab scientist, he had learned the value of accurate records; hence his faith in diaries for Kerry's problem. No parent would have thought it practical to ask the mother of seven kids to keep a diary.

This book was conceived and written in the knowledge that actual parenting is demanding, time-consuming, difficult. I talk about some of the reasons kids behave badly, but I focus on the practical advice David and I had to learn. The kind only mothers and fathers can give.

But *Your* Kids Are Different?

Your kids, of course, are very different from the troubled teenagers that government brought to our house because no one else could or would take charge of them at the time.

Not on your life.

As a matter of fact, most of our foster children came from families like yours. They were the sons and daughters of physicians, police officers, attorneys, plumbers, teachers, salespeople, computer programmers, truck drivers, small businessmen, secretaries, clergy, and clerks. They came from intact families, separated families, and single-parent households, and they represented all socioeconomic levels—the very rich, blue collar, professional class, working poor, middle-class, welfare-dependent.

As human beings, they differed not at all from your kids. Most were good kids, and many had done nothing really wrong. Some had super-strict parents who overreacted when their youngster rebelled by violating a curfew, hanging out with the wrong crowd, skipping school, or running away from home for a day or two. Other kids had also done these kinds of things, even though their parents were much too easygoing. And believe it or not, some of our foster children had been raised by parents who did everything just right. Who said life is fair? Even the best parents can have good children who do bad things.

Welcome aboard.

Of course, a few of our foster children were indeed bad children.

They did things your kids would never dream of doing. Yet, even as we breathed a sigh of relief to see them go, we often realized that they had taught us something new. You'll see what I mean as we get into the details of helping your youngster find a pathway through the difficult years of early adolescence.

What We'll Talk About

Some things are worth worrying about. Others aren't. I'll teach you the difference.

Even when worrying is legitimate, you have to recognize that a parent can't always control a child. You've probably seen the books that promise overnight miracles: Just make the right moves, say the right things, and harmony is yours. Well, that can be true some of the time. It simply will not be true all of the time.

I'll make clear which situations you can control and which you cannot. These are important distinctions, tough to accept, but they are essential to the well-being of your family. When doing nothing is the right course of action, I'll tell you how to help yourself survive the necessary ordeal of waiting and hoping for the best.

But when it's sensible to "do something," I'll have a full Chinese menu of suggestions. Try one idea from list A, and if it doesn't work, choose something from list B. After all, even if your self-confidence about your parenting has been rocked a bit lately, you're still the expert on what you can and can't do, and you're still the best judge of what might work with your youngster. I promise you a wide variety of options.

One technique I'll explain is the Caring Response, my six-step plan to help parents confront and negotiate a change in their child's unacceptable behavior. The Caring Response combines the much-publicized "tough love" approach and a kind of communication I've dubbed "soft love." Both kinds of love have a lot to offer teenagers and their parents.

When the Caring Response isn't enough, you will want to learn about the Caring Intervention, a process that draws on the strategy of the Caring Response but involves other people who care about your child and have also experienced the unacceptable behavior. They can learn to become partners with you in confronting your badly behaving good kid and negotiating change.

When both of these techniques fail—and that is rare—you may need to go for outside help. You'll learn how to use the Caring Response and the Caring Intervention as ways of convincing your kid to participate in therapy. Drawing upon scores of experiences with our foster children, I'm going to give you frank advice about making sure that you find the best help available.

Finally, we will get to a subject you have probably not thought about enough, if at all: taking care of yourself. The adolescent years of your children can be dangerously wearing on you. If you ignore your own needs and wounds, you will be helping nobody, and you could be sowing seeds of resentment and misunderstanding that will flower disastrously in the years to come.

But before that essential final chapter, let me warn you that none of my suggestions is meant to be a "quick fix." Family life may look easy on TV sitcoms, where even the most disturbing problems are recognized, confronted, and solved between two commercial breaks. But you don't have Roseanne Barr's or Bill Cosby's scriptwriters. Your life is complex, ever changing, unpredictable, and your children are not precocious young actors hired for their charm. Nor are they puppets or robots. They, too, are complex, ever changing, unpredictable.

But you and I can pool our knowledge to find practical solutions to most of the problems that worry you. It's really possible, as I've learned from living with our biological children and our foster children. Read on. Help is here.

T W O

Good Kids or Bad?

"Did you throw that hard snowball at Mrs. Geraghty?"

"Sure."

"What were you thinking of? She's a frail old lady. Didn't you know she might get knocked over and hurt herself?"

"I won't do it again."

"That's not the point. She's not going to be able to walk around for the next week or so. Is that what you wanted?"

"No."

"Do you have anything else to say for yourself? How did you feel when she fell down?"

"Well . . . she really went flying. It was funny!"

How do you tell whether your kid is good or bad? Even in our morally pluralistic age, the answer is as simple as it is ancient.

We all hear a lot of cynicism about values: "Whatever feels right is right." "You do your thing, I'll do mine." Your kids already know that U.S. presidents have lied, rock stars and athletes do heavy-duty drugs, business executives get caught in monumental frauds. They may feel that society believes now that the stuff of conscience is individually determined.

Not so. Good people know that it is wrong to hurt others or to be

30

dishonest. If we cheat on April 15, we explain to ourselves that it is okay because we work so hard, because tax rates are unfair, because everyone else cheats, too. If we tell someone a lie, we argue inwardly that it was to protect her feelings. Who are we really trying to fool? Our conscience. Truly bad people have no reason to make these kinds of self-serving justifications. They don't care.

What is true for adults is true for adolescents. Perhaps even more so, because they are often trying so hard to decide for themselves what to believe and how to live. The kid with a conscience is a good kid, no matter what he's just done to cause you worry.

Bad Kids I Have Known

At thirteen, Carl robbed a younger boy, beat him up, and pushed him into a river. The victim drowned. Caught and confronted, Carl blithely said, "It's not my fault he couldn't swim." After serving two years in a state training school, he returned home meaner and tougher than ever.

He was nineteen when he first visited our house to go out on a date with our foster daughter Nancy. Tall and slender at fifteen, she had arrestingly beautiful almond-shaped eyes, a model's prominent cheekbones, and a sadly misplaced faith in the redeeming power of love. To her, Carl was a romantic desperado who could be reformed by the right woman. I could see only a surly hulk, electric with menace.

I was not alone. Nancy's parents and the courts had placed her with us in hopes of cooling off her relationship with Carl. Before the month was out, however, she ran away with him to Georgia. After her parents and juvenile authorities tracked her down, Nancy was sent to a locked facility. She escaped. By this time she was sixteen, and the court could do nothing. She moved in with her lover, had his baby, and kept the relationship afloat for two years. Her romantic illusions were eventually shattered by harsh reality, however, and Nancy took an apartment on her own.

A good kid herself, she never seemed to learn that Carl simply did not have a conscience. About three years ago, she agreed to meet him in an empty parking lot, hoping he would begin to help supporting their son. He beat her to death. The bad kid had become an evil man. The intuitions of Nancy's parents and the authorities were cruelly proved right.

Ginny was just as obviously bad, though in a very different way. A muscular, angry-looking sixteen-year-old with brassy hair, she wore heavy eye makeup and acted the lout. She befriended some of my foster daughters, who were fascinated, but I disliked her from the first. As it turned out, she was concentrating her charms, whatever they were, on our teenage girls. Her boyfriend, a member of a Satanic group, wanted her to find "fresh meat," i.e., young girls who would agree to the club "gang-bang." Ginny succeeded with one of our foster daughters, who willingly shared her body with the membership. Soon she realized that this was not enough. The gang was into rape and physical abuse. She escaped and made it back home to her parents. Like Nancy, she was a basically good kid who was mesmerized by someone bad, a mistake in judgment she was lucky enough to survive.

Not every bad kid is quite so malevolent as Carl and Ginny, but they share the absence of conscience.

Thirteen-year-old Jimmy, who lasted with us only a few weeks, was short, overweight, unpleasant, slovenly. We had to force him to take a shower or change his overripe clothing. One day, another foster child happened to look out a window and saw him hurl our cat against a garage door. He picked up the stunned creature and slammed it against the door again. When we stopped him, he just shrugged. His explanation: he was bored. He felt no guilt, just annoyance that he had been caught and would be punished.

The very different-appearing Cliff—neatly dressed, courteous, socially poised at fifteen—turned out to be bad, too. He thought it was hilariously funny to roll drunks. He also enjoyed snatching purses from "old ladies." As he explained to us without a trace of embarrassment, "the older the better, because the slower she runs and the easier she is to knock down."

Somehow, Sally of the china blue innocent eyes was even more horrifying to me. She spent her allowance on gerbils, set them loose in our house, and shrieked with delight as our two cats attacked and killed them. "My conscience is clear," she insisted, when I tried to talk with her. It was her money, she earned it, she was just "having a good time." She was as glacially calm as when, later, she slammed a car door on another child's hand. "Accidents happen," she remarked with a smirk.

Bad Kids: How to Tell

The lack of conscience is, in large part, the inability to care about others. Carl's nonchalance about murder shows that he has no bonding to anyone else, no sense of empathy or even awareness that others can feel and be hurt, and no conviction that others have as much right to life as he does.

Bad seeds? Psychopaths? The terms change over the years, but you can recognize the truly bad kid, whatever the label, by acts or characteristics like those I've listed below:

BAD-KID GIVEAWAYS

- Doesn't show genuine affection
- Has no empathy
- Knows the difference between right and wrong but could care less
- Hurts others for no reason
- Even if superficially charming, actually cares only about his or her own needs
- Acts cruelly toward animals, small children, anyone weaker
- Never feels guilt
- Doesn't know the meaning of remorse
- Believes that it's best to be bad
- Believes that the only wrong is getting caught
- Worships the devil or witches

The last point may have brought you up short. Perhaps you consider devil worship or the serious practice of witchcraft a little bit daft, but that is not necessarily so. Some people worship Satan as sanely as most of us worship God. To some, devil worship can be an expression of a sane person's need to explain away bad behavior.

The devil-worshiping teenager, however, could well be a bad kid who lacks a conscience. She might also be psychotic, having lost touch with reality. The psychotic is not "bad" but diseased, and she may even retain the ability to distinguish right from wrong. Only a trained psychiatrist can tell whether your Satan-obsessed youngster is merely trying to rationalize bad behavior, or lacks a conscience, or is psychotic.

Some time ago, I was reminded of the difference between the bad kid and the psychotic in a group home program I directed for New York City. Our adolescent girls were one step away from jail, state training school, or psychiatric hospital. In order to qualify for this home of last resort, they had to be thrown out of at least seven other settings. Some were bad kids, but many were emotionally disturbed.

Take well-built, tall Sherry. The other residents called her "Vanessa" because she looked so much like one of the daughters on "The Cosby Show." Her mother was addicted to crack, her stepfather often beat and sexually abused her, and she was so emotionally disturbed that she sometimes heard voices and believed she could tell what was going on inside other people's heads. She was what most people mean when they say "crazy," and when she got really out of control, the psychiatrists diagnosed her behavior as psychotic.

When the home first opened, the girls harassed me and the rest of the staff during a rough period of testing. Could we be trusted? Would we become like the other people in their lives and beat them when they misbehaved? Sherry's tactic was to whisk off my glasses and run away with them. We'd be sitting quietly talking, and suddenly her hand would dart out and off she'd go. If I waited patiently, though steaming inside, she would soon be back to return my property.

On a particularly trying day, Sherry's petty teasing was the last straw. Waiting for her to return with the glasses, I began to cry. When she walked back in to find tears streaming down my face, she was astonished.

"Why are you crying, Miss Katherine?" she asked.

"Sherry, staff and I are trying so hard to help you, and some days it is very hard. On a day like today, your taking my glasses was more than I could bear."

"I'm sorry," she said. "I didn't mean to make you cry. I'll never do that again." And she never did, for, despite her emotional illness, she was a person of conscience. She even learned that she should go for help if the voices in her head told her to hurt someone. She was definitely not a bad person.

But enormously strong twelve-year-old Sophia, built like a Chicago Bears fullback, was entirely a different matter. Once, when told she'd have to wait her turn to do laundry, she hefted the washing machine and threw it three feet across the room. During her stay in the group home, she attacked staff, kicked in doors, pushed other residents down the stairs. She didn't hear voices. She simply wanted what she wanted when she wanted it and didn't care who got hurt in the process.

When staff worked frantically to restrain a desperately suicidal resident, Sophia dissolved in laughter. "I hope she kills herself," she explained. "Then I can take her clothes."

Not one of the several psychiatrists who examined her thought she was psychotic. "She is as sane as I am," one told us, "but she has no conscience. If she were older, she'd be considered a career criminal." All of his colleagues echoed that opinion. Eventually Sophia was moved to a juvenile detention center. She probably will end up in jail.

These lurid tales are, I hope, far outside your experience with your kid. But they are extreme enough to make the point. Except for the rare case of psychosis, the difference between a good kid doing bad and a bad kid is one word: conscience.

Let's summarize.

If your child is genuinely affectionate, cares about other people, feels remorseful after hurting someone, thinks that bullying is bad, protects weaker children or animals, wants to do what is right and thinks that hurting others simply to hurt them is wrong—you needn't worry. Your child is a child of conscience.

And if he is not? If you cannot recall a time when your youngster showed genuine concern for others, displayed remorse for doing a bad thing, or rationalized a wrongdoing, then you should worry. Other characteristics would indicate that you should do more than worry. If you hear from the school or from other parents that your kid is a bully, if you find her hurting smaller children or animals or starting fires, or if you have good reason to suspect that she is seriously involved in Satanism, you have to consider the possibility that she is a bad kid. Professional help may be needed.

Don't pause. If the foregoing paragraph hits home like M. C. Hammer, turn immediately to Chapter 16 and the Appendix, which explain how and where to find the professional help your family needs, and to Chapter 15, which will help you to persuade your child to go along with your decision to take her to a professional. Read them and set up an appointment with all due speed.

When Conscience Gets Misplaced

Are you still unsure?

Usually that means your good kid's conscience has been temporarily mislaid. Perhaps he used to tell the truth, no matter what, but lately has been lying now and then just for the sake of lying. Perhaps you've just recently been shocked to realize that you can no longer trust him to do the right thing, although you always have in the past. Once caring, he has not been showing remorse after hurting someone.

Clearly something is going on. During adolescence, more than a few good kids change and seem to lose all sense of right and wrong for a while. That may well be the case with your child. Whether or not the problem is more serious, only time will tell.

Sandy, fourteen, was nothing but trouble when she came to live in our home. She even looked like a storm brewing—dark clouds of swirling Cher-like hair, straight black brows accentuating glowering eyes, a mouth permanently twisted into an angry scowl.

"I can't explain it," her worried mother said to me on the phone. "Until last year, my Sandy was the easiest kid in the world to live with; we had a really great relationship. Now I find it hard to believe she is the same girl. She lies to me, she's stolen from me. Last week, she hit me. I just don't understand what happened."

As it turned out, most of what happened was adolescence.

Added to the expected storm and stress of these years, moreover, was the hurt of an unexpected divorce that became very messy and painful. This maelstrom of emotions was more than she could handle. Previously, Sandy, like other children, had handled hurt by blaming herself and trying to be extra good. No longer. Adolescents, when hurt, tend to focus on what others have done wrong. They blame others for their pain. And they blaze with anger.

The child still present in Sandy may have thought that the divorce and its disruption were her fault, but her adolescent self, testing new perspectives every day, blamed her mother. Her bad behavior was retaliation for the suffering she felt. Perhaps something similar has happened in your household. Childhood hurts often become the volatile angers of adolescence, sending your youngster's conscience deep into cold storage.

Drugs, too, can make conscience disappear. About one in ten of our foster children were serious abusers, and the pattern was clear: the heavier the drug use, the dimmer the conscience. I particularly recall one boy, a sincerely caring individual who was especially devoted to his aging grandmother. When she was rushed to the hospital for treatment of pneumonia, he was alarmed. He also took advantage of the occasion to steal and pawn her jewelry. Drug abuse had swamped his conscience.

Turning on turns conscience off. So if you suspect your caring child has become noncaring because of drugs, turn immediately to Chapter 12, which goes into drug use and abuse. The sooner you know what you are actually up against, the sooner you can find the appropriate kind of help.

But perhaps you've been feeling pretty lucky during the last few paragraphs because you can honestly say, "Yes, my child is a child of conscience." Fine. You've got good reason to feel relief.

When you've finished savoring this moment of faith in your youngster, read on. It's time to figure out why this child you love so much is doing something bad.

T H R E E

The Gotcha Wars

MOM: "You know you aren't allowed to go driving with that crowd."

GOOD KID: (being bad) "But Dad said I could."

DAD: (to Mom) "Wait a minute. He said you said he could go."

MOM: "I did no such thing."

GOOD/BAD KID: "You said, 'See what your father says.' That means you don't mind if he doesn't."

MOM: "Give me a break. I thought you had to be kidding around. What I said was, 'Try that one on your father and see what he says.' You know I did not mean that I was changing the rules."

GOOD/BAD KID: "That's not fair. You lied to me."

DAD: "Sounds like you just weren't listening—"

GOOD/BAD KID: "You're making fun of me. You know I want to be with my friends, and you pretended I could go. That's mean. I don't have to take this!" (Exits, slamming door.)

When you are drawn into the peculiarly insidious teenage ploy I call the Gotcha War, you may soon become convinced that you are a failure as a parent. That's a typical reaction. Or you may yearn to give up the struggle and make a weak truce, accepting the horrible truth that your okay kid has become bad. That's another typical reaction.

Both are nonsense.

38

Gotcha Wars will keep you on your toes, but parents can win them. The alternative can be disastrous. You can't just walk away. This chapter gives you the order of battle that will lead to D-Day. And you'll learn to achieve victory that is not a defeat for your kid.

Gotcha Wars are as natural to adolescence as overwrought sebaceous glands and refrigerator raids. The basic premise is simple: after years of following parental advice and orders, the teenager is suddenly eager to fight back. It doesn't matter that you won Parent-of-the-Year awards all along the way. The point of the Gotcha Wars is not to get revenge but to earn adulthood. You represent the adult world; your kid has to prove herself . . . and there you are. The key word to remember is "contrariness," or what Edgar Allan Poe called "the imp of the perverse."

Here's how it goes. You make a reasonable suggestion. Your "imp" will have nothing to do with it. You make the alternative suggestion. She is unmoved. You are calm and pleasant. Your kid snarls. You snarl back. Your kid shouts or weeps. And so forth, on and on. Is there any sense to be found here? Well, yes. You have to understand that your kid, consciously or not, wants to wage war, wants to put you in the wrong, wants to win! She's looking for an excuse to fight. If you don't supply one, she'll create one by herself. This chapter is a wartime guidebook.

Gotcha Night

It was frigid outside, but the atmosphere in my office was steaming hot. This was another Gotcha Night at Parent Tactics, the parenting workshop I created.

"I don't know if I can take it," shouted Tom, a burly man who had always reminded me before of the young John Wayne, slow to anger, riding herd on his emotions. Recently granted custody of his thirteen-year-old son, he soon found himself locked head to head, horn to horn, in a Gotcha War. He was, as George Bush likes to say, about to go ballistic.

"Last night was typical. We were going to go to a movie. Mark came in from sledding with his clothes all wet and I told him to change. He mumbled that he didn't have any clean clothes. We went to his room and there was plenty of clean stuff, but he didn't like any of it. Two pairs of pants and three shirts were brand-new. Mark picked them out himself two weeks ago, but now he can't stand them.

"I got angry. He refused to change, I refused to let him go to the movies. What was supposed to be a good family time became just another damned run-in. It drives me crazy. I pride myself on being in control of myself, but when I spend any time with my son, I'm ready to kill. He loves to make me angry."

Everyone else nodded sympathetically. They were all fighting Gotcha Wars at home.

Anne, the willowy blond mother of twelve-year-old twins, complained about the "nothing-to-eat" song she heard every day.

"It happens as soon as I come in from shopping. I've caved in to all of their junk food fantasies. There's food everywhere! But it never fails. One of my kids slouches into the kitchen, opens the refrigerator door, and moans, 'There's nothing to eat, there's nothing to eat.' Over and over again. When that doesn't get a rise, he'll turn and ask, 'What's there to eat?' And like a fool, I list the contents of all the kitchen cabinets, the refrigerator, the storage cellar, the cookie jar. I'll even mention the hidden stash of candy. Finally, when I've given up all hope of finding anything that might pull him back from the brink of starvation, his face lights up with a little smirk and I know he's won again."

"Yes," chimed in Joan, the normally cheerful mother of three teen-agers, "I know that smile of victory and I hate it. At our house these days, the rule is, Don't Ever Agree with Mom. If I say 'Good Morning,' I get growled at. I say 'night,' one of them says 'day.' I say 'black,' I hear 'white.'

"But what bothers me most is when they've done something wrong. They've all learned how to take a mild reprimand and turn it into a federal case. And when I finally begin to feel that I must be the guilty party and the only thing to do is apologize, there's that wretched smile again. Well, at least now I have a name for it. The Gotcha Smile."

We laughed to relieve the tension, but everyone in this Parent Tactics group was very worried. The Gotcha Wars can be frightening: daily battles over trivial issues, provocative behavior, the child's need to be angry or make her parents angry.

If the Gotcha Wars are being waged in your home, you probably have two main worries. Can this sudden tendency to pick fights lead to trouble? How can a youngster who can't take criticism ever make it in the real world outside?

Believe me, your child will not savage her way through life, provoking rather than trying to get along. The way you're treated is no measure of the way people are treated outside the home. Most good kids are at their worst when dealing with their parents. They know that no one else would put up with some of their provocative ways. Parents are a convenient safety valve for anger. Nevertheless, you want these disturbing conflicts to end.

Well, like me at one time, you may be wasting a lot of time trying to find the answer that will bring lasting peace. Believe me, this is one of those areas where there isn't much you can do to change your child's behavior.

I've learned that peace is sometimes possible, and truces can be made, but most of the time life with a teenager, any teenager, means being on one side or the other of the Gotcha War.

You may find that an unpleasant truth, but there it is. No matter what you do, no matter how carefully you listen, no matter how sensitively you respond, the war will continue. But don't lose hope and give up. I'll get to some tactics that will help you through the dark days. First, though, you need to focus on your attitude toward the behavior.

Why Is This Happening?

You'll suffer less from the Gotcha Wars when you realize that you aren't personally responsible for the attacks. We are talking about generalized adolescent behavior that just comes with the territory. Most commonly, the teenager needs to provoke parental anger in order to deal with his own uncomfortable feelings.

It's not so different from how very little kids deal with their fear of monsters under the bed. When Zach was two, we couldn't get him to sleep because ogres lay in wait everywhere, ready to pounce. No amount of loving reason could convince him otherwise. But if I lost patience and yelled at him, off he went to the Land of Nod. Worrying about Mom's anger, which he knew and could handle, was easier than dealing with the eerie dangers of the monsters lurking out of sight. Once I caught on, I tried pretending to be angry. No good. He knew the difference. Only my authentic boiling anger was sufficient to keep those monsters at bay. He was provoking my anger to help him deal with his fears.

The Monsters Within

For adolescents, the monsters hide within. The irresistible act of growing up is often not just difficult but downright frightening. The desire to remain a child can be very strong and can turn into one of the subconscious monsters that your kid has to fight against.

In my first semester at college, I disliked my roommate, longed for my high school boyfriend, and generally felt lonely and bereft. One night I called my mother and bitterly complained about my loneliness. She could not have been more understanding.

"Why not come home?" she said. "You don't have to stay there if you are unhappy. Lots of kids don't go to college. Come on home and work for your father."

Forget loneliness. I instantly became one live bolt of anger. I couldn't believe that my own mother wanted me to give up, come home, and become a child again.

"You don't understand," I said with as much disdain as I could muster and hung up. Thereafter, whenever I felt overwhelmingly homesick, I would call home and maneuver my mother into telling me to give up and come home, and the whole scenario would play out again until I slammed down the phone. I was using my anger with her to fight the temptation of returning to the dangerously appealing comfort and safety of home.

That anger kept me in school, although I did not know or suspect at all that I was using it to cover feelings that were even more painful. Part of me felt that growing up was too hard and wanted to go home, have my parents take care of me, and wait patiently until my boyfriend returned from the service to claim me as his bride. But giving in to this fantasy was unacceptable to another part of me. Torn, I handled my scared feelings by periodically provoking my mother.

Forbidden Feelings

Another cause of Gotcha Wars is the teenager's confusion when loving feelings toward a parent begin to get mixed up with newly emerging sexual impulses. Since sexual feelings toward a parent are taboo, they must be hidden. Anger is an effective cover-up.

When I was a foster parent, teenaged Jane sometimes babysat Daniel and Zach. I had first met her and her father, Sam, at a Little League game when she was eight years old; she covered first base. A sweet girl with a round, solemn face, Jane had luminous eyes and a smashing grin. An only child, she had been put in Sam's custody when her parents divorced; her mother was an alcoholic. Her father wasn't a handsome man—his nose was too big, his hair was vanishing, he was bulging in the middle—but he was friendly and outgoing, with a smile that made you feel warm and comfortable.

At that time, father and daughter had a close, loving relationship. When early adolescence hit Jane, however, she began to pull away. Sam was philosophical about her sudden refusal to go anywhere with him. He was deeply hurt, however, by her new rudeness and even nastiness, by her refusal of any physical contact.

"We used to have such a good time together," he told me. "Now we can't spend five minutes sitting on the living room couch watching TV without her getting into a huff. When I go into her room at night to tuck her in, she is at her worst. That used to be a loving and close time for us."

Not long afterward, when Jane was babysitting one of my sons, she began complaining bitterly about her father.

Suddenly, I had a flashback that explained it all. When I turned twelve or thirteen and began to think of myself as a woman, I couldn't stand to have my father hold my hand or kiss me. To him, I was still the little girl who was his pride and joy, who always gave him hello and goodbye hugs and kisses. Like Jane, I felt too old for "such stuff," although I couldn't exactly explain why. I didn't understand that my changed attitude was related to my growing sexual awareness.

For both Jane and me, puberty's rush of strange new feelings was terrifying to Daddy's Little Girl. The door was opened on forbidden territory. Unable to handle any longer the physical closeness that had been so natural before, both of us hurt our fathers' feelings in ways neither of them deserved.

I knew that, just like me, Jane still loved Sam very much. Also like me, she was using anger to deal with her less acceptable feelings. As in other versions of the Gotcha Wars, there was nothing that our fathers could do but wait for the stormy years to pass. Eventually, they did.

You Made Me Do It

Provoking parental anger can also be a good way to justify doing what you want.

For some of my foster children, this you-made-me-do-it anger generally surfaced on weekends. No mystery about the timing. Weekends meant thinking about going to see hometown friends or being with people the courts had ordered them not to see. Because these children did not lack conscience, they needed to have an excuse for doing the bad thing they wanted to do. A favored tactic was to provoke David or me into a fight.

One weekend, Jon-Paul had been invited to a Sweet Sixteen party in his hometown, but his probation officer refused to let him go. On the morning of the day of the party, this kid began literally following me around the house, room to room, telling me every bad thing he had ever seen me do. When I tried to escape by locking myself in the bathroom, he continued this tirade, pounding on the door.

Finally, I broke down. I came out and yelled at him to get away and leave me alone.

"Well, if that's the way you feel, I'll get away," he replied. "Far away. No one would expect me to stay somewhere I'm not wanted." Yes, the victory smile of the veteran Gotcha Warrior lit up his face.

I was reminded, as I often am, of a wonderful line from the baseball movie, *Bull Durham*. "Some days you win, some days you lose, and some days it rains."

That day with Jon-Paul, I lost.

Ducking Guilt . . . Avoiding Temptation

Provoking you to anger can help your kid deal with temptation or guilt that is deeply troubling to her.

Carrie, one of the loveliest foster kids ever placed with us, had a Sophia Loren voluptuousness at thirteen that had the boys swarming. She wasn't interested, and most took the hint. But seventeen-year-old Peter was persistent and finally managed to work his way into her affections. "He's not all over me," Carrie explained. Her match in good looks with his blond hair, sea-green eyes, and shy smile, Peter had treated her with respect.

For a time, they dated casually: he walked her home from school, they met at the mall on Saturdays, they went on group dates to the local cineplex. After about two months of this, Peter took Carrie to the Junior Prom, pulled out a ring, and announced to all within hearing that they were now going steady.

Enter Carrie, Carrie Quite Contrary. She was no longer sweet and unfailingly cooperative. She cut three classes within three days, which earned her Saturday detention and automatic grounding at our house for the weekend. She and Peter could make contact only by telephone from Friday through Sunday.

On Monday and Tuesday, she seemed to be her old self again. She made it to school on time and didn't cut any classes. We gave her permission to have an evening study date with Peter at the library for a couple of hours, but she came home flushed, flustered, and an hour late. The minute she walked in the door, she began yelling at David and me about how unreasonable our rules were. By the end of this flare-up, she had lost all school night study-date privileges.

And so it went on, for days. For the rest of the week Carrie was calm, but on Saturday morning she refused to clean the kitchen, her usual chore of the day. We made her cancel her Saturday night date with Peter. The next week was halcyon again; they were allowed to go to a well-chaperoned party Friday night. But once again she came home flushed, flustered, and eager to fight. On the alert, David and I were able to evade her invitation to verbal fisticuffs and got her to hop off to bed. The next day she came home two hours late from a mall foray with some girlfriends and was grounded. She had to break her Saturday night date with Peter.

The pattern was now clear, so I took the frontal approach. I suggested to Carrie that she was picking fights and breaking rules so that we would help her limit her relationship with Peter.

"Are you crazy?" she snapped. "I love him. I can't stand it when you ground me and I can't see him."

"Well," I replied, "I just thought that going steady might mean he wants more from you than you are comfortable giving."

Her response: an angry look and hostile silence. The pattern of breaking the rules, fighting, and losing privileges continued. Eventually, handsome Peter asked for his ring back. Carrie cried pitifully, saying much about the fickleness of men, and once again became Sweet, Sweet Carrie Uncontrary.

My attempt to have her understand the motivation for her Gotcha

Wars had gone nowhere. Patience—and sticking to our house rules—was the answer. But knowing what Carrie was doing was helpful to me. Although she could never acknowledge that she needed outside help to keep her relationship with Peter from becoming sexualized, I saw that she needed to be grounded in order to avoid temptation.

Forgive My Sins

At times, a teenager manipulates you into punishing him for his sins, be they real or imagined. A Gotcha War gets precisely the results he wants.

In *Between Parent and Child,* Haim Ginott describes such an episode. As a family drives peacefully toward Disney World, the mother praises her son for playing so well with his younger brother. Immediately, the older kid explodes in a fit of anger. Ginott explains that, belying the surface calm, the boy had actually been thinking about how much he hated his younger brother and imagining ways of giving him pain. The mother's praise created guilt for these bad thoughts, and the boy sought punishment.

Our foster children mastered the art of seeking punishment. David and I found that one of our trickiest jobs was suiting the punishment to a child's conscience, not to her crime. If the punishment was too light for the individual conscience, trouble would brew. If too heavy, things would get just as bad.

One girl raced out of the house in a temper tantrum and didn't return for an hour. It was raining hard, and she was soaked through when she came back in. That seemed punishment enough to me, but she disagreed. She decided she should lose all privileges for a month—no allowance, no phone calls, no leaving the property. I commuted this Draconian sentence to loss of privileges for a weekend, but she would have none of it. She rigidly followed her own punishment schedule for the entire month.

In this case, the need to be punished was satisfied without harm to David and me. Other children could earn punishment only by picking fights, escalating a Gotcha War, or hurting themselves physically.

Dangerous Waters: Single Parents in the Gotcha Wars

It's hard enough to survive Gotcha Wars with your adolescent warrior when you have a spousal ally living in the same house. If you are single, separated, divorced, or a stepparent, however, the order of battle can become even more complicated. The less affection remaining between separated parents, for example, the more dangerous the position of the parent living with the child.

Central to the adolescent's rules of Gotcha Warring is the tactic of playing one parent against the other, even when one parent is, and always has been, unknown to the child. The unknown parent, after all is the Perfect Parent. You are right there, perfectly positioned to be blamed, criticized, resented, and manipulated. Your "faults" are plain as day. The absent parent never does or says anything wrong. Uninvolved, out of the daily picture, she never has to say no, never has to nag, never loses her temper, never makes a mistake or presents an obstacle. Why should she? She does not share your responsibility for socializing the unsociable. You are the "heavy."

Moreover, when you are the parent who lives with the teenager, you're the parent who sees him at his worst, making it even harder for you to avoid conflict. Just being more aware of the inappropriate behavior around the house is going to lead to more frequent involvement in Gotcha Wars.

Finally, we all know that—despite the preaching of the experts—the much-admired, much-desired consistency of approach to be shared by ideal parents is hard to come by.

Most parents back each other up on some things; rarely do two parents support each other's position on all things. Think back to your own childhood. Most of us were able to get what we wanted, in at least some situations, by playing Mom against Dad, or vice versa. This can be normal family politics—or, if you and your child's other parent spend more time dealing with your anger toward each other than working together to deal with your child's latest Gotcha War maneuver, it can be destructive for everyone.

What does all of this mean? First, that the best kid in the world can't resist the martial advantage of playing one parent against the other in the Gotcha Wars. Second, that parents who do not live together need to work together as allies. Third, that when parents become victims of a child's skillful divide-and-conquer tactics, they may need to seek a professional ally.

Strategic Retreat

One particularly distressing tactic a teenager can use against a single parent is the cruelly effective device of running away to the other, "better" parent. Or she may just drive you bonkers by continually begging to be allowed to live in the other household. You, of course, are likely to feel deeply hurt by this rather dramatically expressed criticism, and your position of parental authority is threatened.

Curiously, your best response may be to arrange a change of custody, or, at the minimum, increase the amount of time your child spends in the care of the out-of-home parent. Is paradise to be found elsewhere? Let your child find out for herself. Of course, this is not a decision to be made on the spur of the moment, when you've suddenly had enough and feel like kicking your kid out of the house. And you certainly don't want to send her to live with a criminal or dangerously manipulative parent.

Still, the option is worth exploring, particularly when your child steadfastly insists that she wants to live with her other parent. Before agreeing with her, both parents should discuss the problem with a qualified professional. Your child may not really know her own mind, or she may be staking out a tactical position without fully realizing the potential consequences, or she may need to explore for herself. Some of our foster kids went back and forth between one parent and the other, then to a relative, then to our house, and all the way round again before they learned an essential lesson: they were getting nowhere by acting out their problems against someone else. Gradually they realized it was time to stop waging high-intensity Gotcha Wars and settle down to work on their own problems for themselves.

Meanwhile, as you stay alert to your teenager's tactical maneuvers, don't lower your guard in another critically important area—your own

THE GOTCHA WARS 49

sphere of action. All too often, parents, whether single or living with the other parent, begin using the kid as a weapon. Here's a clue: when you are more concerned about the actions and reactions of the other parent than about what's going on with your kid, you have crossed the danger line. You are beginning to use him in skirmishes with his other parent. These are side actions that should not involve him at all. He did not create these problems, whatever they are, and can only be wounded by your struggles. Whether you resent or respect, love or loathe your child's other parent, you should stay well away from that parent's relationship with your child—except in matters that unarguably involve life, limb, and physical safety. By the same token, that other parent should not meddle in your relationship with your kid. Like all ideals, this one is hard to attain, but both parents should recognize the need to try. It's not the end of the world if you can't always hold your tongue when it comes to cracks about your former husband's skill at boiling water, but that kind of thing is a warning signal, no matter how witty you think you're being. Whatever goes on, has gone on, or may still go on between you and the other parent, the two of you must work to maintain an alliance when dealing with your child. Every possible alternative is emotionally dangerous to the kid you love.

Granted, sometimes a well-meaning parent may not actually recognize that she's turned her offspring into artillery, so it's always a good idea to sit back and take stock. Yes, you may think you are acting only in your child's best interest . . . but think again. Is is possible you have used your good kid as a weapon against his other parent, even once or twice? Has his other parent accused you of doing so? Has someone else mentioned the possibility? If you are warring with the other parent, you may be inclined to discount his comments, but don't make that mistake. Whatever his motive, he may have sniffed out the truth. In your child's best interest, consider the possibility and get an unbiased opinion from someone who is knowledgeable about your situation. If you find that you have been using your child as a weapon and don't know how to stop, discuss the problem with a skilled professional. The phenomenon is not at all rare, and a good therapist will have useful strategies for dealing with it.

I hope I'm not sounding as if I think this problem is easily handled. You will have to work hard, especially when you're the single parent. Quite reasonably, you might resent the other parent or envy her relationship with your child. After all, your daily burden of parenting is much more onerous than it would be if you and the other parent were living together in peace and harmony. The more adults in the vicinity of a teenager, the greater the likelihood that problems will be shared between the grownups and duly solved.

Instead, as we've discussed, you tend to suffer by comparison with the out-of-house parent, and you have to fight many a battle all by yourself. Perhaps worst of all, it is the in-home parent who often becomes the scapegoat for the hurt and anger your good kid feels because both of his parents don't live with him.

These are additional burdens. Recognize them, deal with them, but don't become obsessed with them. In other words, don't exacerbate your difficulties by carrying excess emotional baggage. Don't blame yourself for the divorce or separation. Don't think yourself flawed because you are a parent alone. Don't look for shortcomings because you aren't your child's biological parent.

Despite the many additional problems, the job of the single parent is precisely the same as that of the parent who lives with his kid's other parent: to feel and act as a caring parent in every possible way. When the Gotcha Wars heat up, it doesn't matter that you and your child live in a family situation that may not be strictly traditional. What matters is your pursuit of the wartime goals addressed throughout this chapter.

Sad, but True

By now you can recognize that the different kinds of Gotcha Wars share a motivation that is based on a sad truth about human nature: often we make ourselves feel better by making someone else feel bad.

Usually your Gotcha Warrior is not attacking you for something you did or did not do as a parent. Instead, you've become your adolescent's scapegoat. In the child's unconscious, you are supposed to bear the burden of his painful feelings.

A Gotcha War makes you feel bad. It can make you want to chew the radiator. Often, however, it will make your adolescent feel much, much better.

When to Worry

If teenager provocation of parents is normal, is it always okay?

No.

There are exceptions that cross the line of expected adolescent development. If a Gotcha War ever results in physical harm to you or your child, seek professional help and find it fast. Don't be fooled by the apologies and promises to do better that generally follow a physical assault in a family. For the moment, everyone is shocked into remorse. The accompanying sense of shame makes it hard to look for help.

But provocation that has turned physical once is likely to do so again. Err on the safe side. If necessary, use a Caring Intervention (see page 197) to persuade the physically violent person in the family to enter therapy.

Another warning is continuous destruction of property. Often such destructiveness is a prelude to physical assault. Deal with it by seeking professional help immediately.

Chances are, however, that your child's provocations have not reached either of these two extremes. But what about the possibility that you may need help? It's normal to feel anger during a Gotcha War, but too much anger on your part may be a sign of deeper trouble. Think carefully about the items in the following checklist of responses to your child's anger.

PARENTAL ANGER CHECKLIST

1. Are you angry all of the time?
2. Do you find it hard now to see anything good about your kid?
3. Are you afraid of losing control and hurting your teenager physically?
4. Are you afraid that your youngster will hurt you?

If number 1 is true, worry. Worry even more if the others are also true.

If you are angry all the time, it is clear that you need to talk with someone. A trusted, loyal friend may be the answer. Whoever you choose, don't stay locked in a cell-block of hostility. That brooding silence harms you and harms your kid.

When talking with a friend doesn't ease the constant anger, find a Parents Anonymous group or visit a professional therapist. You are a ticking time bomb.

Nine Steps for Handling Anger

In the majority of cases, professional help is not necessary, but you have some hard work ahead of you. To handle the anger in your household, you have to analyze the specific problem and select the appropriate response. You can't always be right, but you can often improve the atmosphere. I've set down nine suggestions that have been helpful to David and me. They are not cure-alls in exact dosages, but they point the way:

1. **Assess the legitimacy of your kid's anger.** If you aren't certain it's unreasonable, sit down with a sensible, straight-talking friend and talk out the situation. If your friend thinks that your teenager is angry for a good reason, acknowledge that with the child and negotiate a change.

2. **If the anger is not legitimate, make yourself disengage.** Don't take the anger personally or wallow in guilt. Remember that Sam was a reasonable father but Jane had to attack him anyway because of necessary angers that sprang from her growing up. He felt better when he learned to disengage, but she continued to bitch and act out. Meeting with my Parent Tactics support group helped him keep his perspective.

3. **Disengagement of feelings does not mean that you ignore provocative behavior.** When the Gotcha War goes beyond a dirty look, some artful dawdling, and a few slammed doors, it is time to respond with vigor. In our innocence as neophyte foster parents, David and I thought it wise to ignore provocative words. Therefore, to get our full attention and our help in dealing with their feelings, the children had to punch holes in walls, smash windows, throw punches at us. When we learned to respond to squalls before they became hurricanes, life in our house became much calmer. Ignore the dirty looks but not inappropriately verbalized anger. Ignore the hastily slammed door but not the irate slam that rattles the door frame.

4. **The first response should be kept low on the burner.** Anne of the "nothing-to-eat" game learned to ignore her twins' complaints and respond to direct questions about the food supply by raising her

eyebrows and shrugging her shoulders. This approach did not bring a complete halt to the grumbling, but she began to feel less upset because she was more in control.

To minimize your involvement when a kid itches to pick a verbal fight, it helps to remember five words and phrases suggested by Tom Alibrandi, an author, counselor, and lecturer:

Yes.
No.
Oh, really.
Wow.
Whatever.

To his list, I've added five more:

Uh-huh.
Hmm.
Tell me.
I see.
Well.

These can be varied with such nonverbal responses as:

Raised eyebrows
Shrugged shoulders
Dirty looks of my own

Warning: These tactics may be hazardous to your mental health. All too soon, your kids will learn from your example. Zach got me less than a week after I began using them. His "Whatever" and "Wow" can still get to me, and Danny is following in the tradition. Annoying, yes, but the level of discourse, such as it is, does not become dangerously overheated.

5. Measure the effectiveness of your response by what happens next. If your child is still steaming after you've tried one short angry retort or a few rounds of Alibrandi's magic words, call time out. Say something like, "If you still feel the same after you've calmed down, we can talk about this, but I need a break right now," and walk away. If she returns with the complaint, listen and try to negotiate a resolution. If she doesn't, relax until the next outbreak. When the war continues, raise the level of your response. Be prepared to get nastier, but first try a few skirmishes of a different nature. You will see what I mean in my explanation of the Caring Response (see page 173), which will help you very much with all of this.

6. **Be quick to laugh at yourself.** But remember that trying to defuse a tense situation by laughing at a teenager is tricky. Stealing a recognizable line from a TV parent can sometimes help. I cite my source to lighten the mood: "As Dr. Huxtable would say . . ." or "Here comes a Barrism." Roseanne Barr's "Noooo, really, you poooor thing" has served me very well in "Let's fight" situations. (Of course, Danny uses that one on me, too.) But be careful. Watch the child's response. If he's getting angrier instead of joining in the joke, apologize and back off.

7. **You have flaws, faults, foibles.** Be ready to admit them in the Gotcha Wars. I'm always astounded at how quickly a sincere confession of my part in the problem brings about a truce. But if admission of fault, like humor, fails to allay the anger, don't give in out of pure frustration. Happiness is not mandatory; standards of decent behavior are. Hence, the next tactic.

8. **Stick by your rules.** During my junior year in high school, I was the only one in my group who had a midnight curfew on the weekend. I complained bitterly, but deep down I loved that limitation. It kept me safe.

But how soon we forget. Just the other day, I was feeling very understanding. Earlier in the week, David and I had told Zach he could have no overnights for two weeks, but when he called to ask to spend the night at a friend's house, I gave in. He sounded so sweet on the phone. When he came home the next morning, he was growling like Bart Simpson. It seems that he hadn't wanted to stay over because he thought there might be some trouble. To save face, he had joked that I would laugh him off the phone if he called for permission. So, when he called, his friends were listening on the extension, expecting to hear someone's parent "freak out." There I was, being "reasonable" and, according to Zach, letting him down.

9. **Finally, remind yourself frequently to continue having patience and faith in your good kids.** Most Gotcha Wars are here one day, gone the next. Adolescent anger is a stage that passes. Before you know it, that argumentative, spiteful, disrespectful good kid of yours will grow up, pack her bags, and fondly kiss you goodbye. When that time comes, you will be nostalgic even for the Gotcha Wars.

TO SUMMARIZE:

If your good kid tries to provoke a fight, it's okay to let your own negative feelings show.

React. At the same time, don't feel guilty, and don't feel personally attacked, but do not suffer in silence. Feel free to express your opinions about the things that annoy you, and do so loudly and strongly. Just keep it short, use humor if you can, don't get sucked into long-winded battles.

Always remind your child that your love for him will survive all Gotcha War battles.

Once you have set a punishment, do not waver.

Finally, if the Gotcha Wars are causing someone to get physically hurt or if property is being destroyed, it is time to do a Caring Intervention.

Reading through this chapter once has been the beginning of successfully handling your own reactions to the Gotcha Wars, I hope. You may not stop the provocations, but you can avoid escalation into serious conflict. You may not receive the understanding you want from your child, but you can at least begin to understand the motivations behind her sudden change in behavior. And you will probably want to return to these pages more than once in the coming years, if your good kid has just become a teenager. No one perpetrates adolescence; it just happens to you. Remember? Calm down, and look once more at the suggestions and wartime tactics that begin back on page 52.

FOUR

Nose Rings, Tattoos, String Bikinis . . .

"You are not going to walk out of the house dressed like that!"

"What's wrong now?"

"Just look in the mirror! Are you trying to get arrested?"

"Oh, come on, Dad. Everybody dresses this way."

"In Times Square, maybe, but not in this neighborhood."

"Dad, this isn't the Middle Ages or something. I'm just wearing the style. There's nothing wrong with this."

"The hell there isn't!"

"What, then?"

"Well, you know what I mean."

"No, I don't."

"Yes, you do."

"I don't *believe* this."

"*I* don't believe this."

The kids in our neighborhood, and parents, too, think Mona overdoes it. Her family enjoys a comfortable life, and her three teenagers never get into serious trouble. But Mona is an Olympic-class worrier. Her large brown eyes have the slightly haunted look of a woodland creature being stalked by a predator, the enemy she can't see but knows is there, ready to pounce.

She worries constantly, and imaginatively, about her children's safety, what they eat or don't eat, where they're going, who they're with, what they're doing, what's happened and what hasn't happened, what might still happen. She's concerned about the clothes they wear, the way they cut their hair, the music they listen to, the TV shows they watch, the movies they go to, the books they bring home, the slang expressions they pick up . . . and, of course, the rest of us tease her a bit.

But Mona's obsessions are no fun for her kids, and they can be the cause of some pretty serious Gotcha Wars. More often than not, the kids win these battles—conflicts that should never have been started in the first place.

Last year, to take an ironic example, her thirteen-year-old son Brian was to receive an academic award in a ceremony before the whole student body. He was afraid of looking like a show-off, but she insisted that he dress up in gray flannels, Oxford cloth button-down shirt, traditional rep tie, and navy blue blazer. After a stormy scene, he agreed. Backstage, however, he went overboard in the opposite direction, quickly changing into tattered jeans and a Grateful Dead T-shirt. When he came out to claim his award, his friends cheered and hooted. Not only had Mona lost the Gotcha War but worse, everyone was distracted by this side issue from the real point—her "good" son's achievement.

In most cases, although we may have to bite our tongues, it really doesn't matter when our kids decide to wear high-tops to a formal dance or overalls to church. In fact, more preteens and teens benefit from learning to decide for themselves how to style their hair or decorate the room they live in. They are learning about themselves in the music, books, TV, and movies they choose.

But there are exceptions.

Occasionally, a Gotcha War over a nose ring, a tattoo, or a teenie-weenie yellow polka-dot bikini is no joke. Extreme style choices can make dangerously antisocial statements, and sexually provocative dress may be indicative of serious emotional problems.

Bikini Battles

In 1954, my father was not grateful that his only daughter had grown sophisticated enough to follow the latest trends of fashion. Or, as he put it, "No daughter of mine is going to be seen in public in that!"

All summer I seethed in my old one-piece swimsuit. The offending new two-piece would look like a smock in today's *Sports Illustrated* swimsuit issue. Perhaps an inch of waist was exposed, if that, and the top revealed less than most one-piece suits, but Dad was adamant.

He had not softened months later, when I tried to wangle permission to wear a strapless gown to the Senior Prom. My flag of surrender, as captured in my photo album, was a demure, slightly off-the-shoulder dress that could be worn at a christening.

You can guess what I vowed: Never, when I became a parent, would I be so Victorian, so stodgy, so ignorant about the real world.

Naturally, about three quarters of my Gotcha Wars with my foster daughters have been disagreements over what they want to wear in public.

And not just the girls. One year, our foster sons of all races wanted to out-stallion Sly Stallone. The skintight sweat shirts were okay with me, but not the groin-revealing sweat pants. Worse, the fad was to wear belts at least eight or nine inches too long, letting the overlap point to the crotch. Our objections to this presentation might well be stodgy or Victorian, but they were not based upon ignorance of the real world, by any means. This fad was squelched in our house.

The issue of sexually provocative dressing is not always that easy. Sometimes, a style that looks whorish to an adult carries no explicit sexual meaning to a preteen. She's just trying to look like Madonna, or like everyone else at school. In our multicultural society, different ethnic groups have different attitudes toward proper dress. Some first-generation parents are horrified that American teenage girls shave their legs or bare their arms, assuming that these are indications of sexual promiscuity. Even sections of the country have different values. The bleached-blond hairstyle that seems sporty, outdoorsy in a Southern California beach community may be thought cheap, or worse, in a Northeastern small town.

Perhaps you feel, as many parents do, that provocative dressing in itself isn't necessarily bad. Or perhaps you are the kind of parent who believes firmly that it is. Because provocative clothing may not be intended as a come-on, but can be taken for one, I find myself in the middle on this issue. I want my kids to have the fun of experimenting with their image, I want them to feel comfortable with their peers, but I also think it's wise for all of us to keep a gently wary eye on the outfits that sail out of our houses.

To help, I've devised a rating system, with apologies to the Code of the Motion Picture Association.

LEVINE'S TEENAGE CLOTHING CODE

GA: General Audience
This category includes all garb, however eccentric, that is nonetheless likely to be considered acceptable by grandparents, school principals and deans, priests, nuns, and rabbis. The General Audience label indicates that most reasonable grownups will not be provoked to make a disparaging or outraged comment. Let your kids wear this category without adding any remarks of your own. Let it be.

PG: Parental Guidance required
Clothing worthy of the Parental Guidance label matches the general community standard. That is, admittedly, a vague definition, but, as former Supreme Court Justice William Brennan said about pornography, "I can't define it, but I know it when I see it." You know, and so does your teenager, what your community considers to be extreme in terms of length, tightness, decolletage, or bulge revelation. PG outfits will require your gentle monitoring, but, generally speaking, you can downgrade them to the General Audience category by making some minor adjustments.

X: No Way, José
Clothes that do not meet the above standards because they make it impossible to think of anything but sex are X-rated. You do not allow them to be worn, no matter what arguments you get.

In Bikini Battles, you never surrender. Actually, I have found that saying no to X-rated attire rarely leads to a seriously protracted conflict. Kids may grumble, but they get the point. Your reaction indicates that they may have gone dangerously overboard, and that's not their aim. Most adolescents want help deciding what is proper and will abide by parental censorship that is reasonable.

But what about the teenager who insists upon wearing X-rated clothes?

First, be sure that you are using my rating system fairly. Try to find an independent judge to help you decide. Obviously, your friends are likely to agree with you, and your child's friends are likely to agree with him, but it should be possible to find some clear-eyed observer—

perhaps a teacher or guidance counselor or a style consultant at a trendy boutique where adolescents shop. None of these people can tell you what's "right" for your child, but they can tell you what is considered stylish and acceptable.

For maximum effect, you might want to get your teenager to cooperate in a kind of fashion show. You invite your independent judge to come over and rate the various offending outfits. Taken in the right spirit on all sides, this show might end your worries. Your daughter might laugh at some of her sexiest clothing, when seen in the cold light of day. You might realize that some of her outfits are more innocent than you thought. If you can both accept the judge's ratings, your child will be set on a less provocative course and you are less likely to become a professional Mona.

The fashion show might flop, however, and your child refuse to accept the judge's ratings. If you've got the stamina and courage, your next step could be a "reversal." Flip-flop completely . . . and let your teenager dress as smuttily as he pleases. You could even go so far as to suggest clothes that are even steamier than the ones he's used to wearing. This is not a course for the faint-hearted or impatient, but I know several parents who have been able to pull it off. It's a shock treatment, all right, having a parent encourage you to show a little bit more skin.

Understandably, you might be uncomfortable with that kind of ploy, so you could try a "half-reversal." You back off for a while, pretending to give up most control of your child's selection of clothing while remaining on the alert.

A mother in one of my Parent Tactics groups sat down with her daughter and made her "half-reversal" explicit:

"You know I don't like the clothes you wear. To me, they make you look cheap, and because I love you, I find that hard to deal with. But I'm bowing out, because you seem determined to keep on like this. From now on, you can buy what you want with your own money and wear whatever you want in front of your own friends. But don't expect me to like the way you look. I don't, and I won't. You think it's the 'in thing,' but it's vulgar to me."

For the next several months, belying this firm statement, that mother relied heavily upon the support of others in our group. As should be expected following a "reversal" or "half-reversal," her daughter explored new depths of sexy dress, no doubt certain that Mom would blow her cool. The mother kept on course, however, and eventually the tide turned, as it generally does in these situations. Ever since, the young woman has chosen outfits that make the Nixon daughters look like floozies. She is the epitome of girl-next-door wholesomeness.

How much should you be willing to go through if you try this technique? As a good general rule, six months of flamboyantly X-rated dressing is long enough for you, your child, and the community to endure.

All of us convey messages by the way we dress. Basically, choice of clothing reveals how we feel about ourselves. Your X-rated dresser is, at the very least, confused about something. It is time to seek professional help. Does she have such low self-esteem that sexual advertisement seems to be the only way to get admiration? Is he on the road to becoming a sexual addict? Is he getting the wrong message about relationships between men and women? Rather than harry yourself with the awful possibilities, consult the appropriate counselor.

Nose Rings, Tattoos ... Chartreuse Hair

Aside from come-on garb, any extremely unusual styles—the kind that turns heads at the mall or could cause traffic accidents—might be cause for concern.

That's "concern," not necessarily "alarm."

Frequently the adolescent search for self begins with the desire to be different from everyone else in sight. Some kids need only to be slightly different; others go in the other direction, dressing more conservatively than the local norm. Your child might go through a bewildering series of style changes, trying on different personalities for size: over several months, the black sweatpants are cast off for stone-washed jeans, which are thrown aside for white cords, surfer pants, bike tights, skater's jams . . . and ever onward.

But what about the nose rings, which are considered conservative adornments among the beautiful Fulani women of Mali but don't have quite that meaning in Raintree County, Ohio? Or the triple-pierced ears?

In our house, the foster-child years brought purple hair, shaved heads, punk jewelry, and four-inch-high Mohawks. Some kids dressed only in black or only in scarlet. Others stuck strictly to a complete uniform: motorcycle gang look, say, or pile of walking rags. Like you, probably, we were advised by the experts to ignore these stylistic statements.

Because the styles are in fact just that, however—very individual statements—it is not always wise to ignore them. To pay no attention to the outrageous costume is to pay no attention to the person who chooses to wear it. A moderate response is more helpful than no response.

As with provocative dress, you will have to decide what's appropriate by balancing your own taste against the child's legitimate needs and the prevailing styles of the school and community settings. This may be another time to check with the school guidance counselor or with an objective friend. But the stakes are not so high. Look for compromise, if you are really offended. Accept three earrings in one ear if the nose ring goes. Agree to the streak of chartreuse dye when your son is trying for the full war bonnet of teased mauve hair.

Or just be prepared to give in gracefully on this kind of issue. You don't control everything your good kid does. Sometimes she will shave her head without your approval because she believes (and it's true!) that you don't understand.

A little well-aimed humor won't hurt. David and I developed quite a repertoire of wisecracks, although you'd have to hear his snappy delivery to get the full effect of lines like these:

"Fine, but don't get too near me in public when you're dressed like that. I've got a reputation for good taste."

"Green hair is essential to your happiness? Then go for it. But don't blame me if sheep mistake your head for a meadow."

"Yes, you have a right to set trends, but this trend is blatantly bizarre. Still, you know that I will always care for the person more than for the trend. Just please try to call before bedtime if you get picked up and taken to Bellevue."

You don't have to be as clever as George Carlin. Your kid will get the point: your respect for his right to dress exotically does not include respect for his taste.

But while you gamely allow these excursions into new ways of being, you must not forgo your right to impose sensible limits. For example, a reasonable child will understand that she must dress appropriately for family affairs, religious ceremonies, and dinners with the boss. You should not have trouble with her on such occasions; if you do, there's a serious problem afoot.

Also, your tolerance does not have to include disbursements. Against our wishes, both Daniel and Zach had their ears pierced, but they paid for earrings and earholes. Parents cannot always control everything kids do, but we can control what we pay for.

Parental Alert: If the compromises I've outlined don't fit the situation in your home, if there is unbearable tension over this issue, if your child is dressing in ways that are acceptable only to a fringe element of your community, you probably need help. Are serious problems on the boil? Or is this only a passing, if unappetizing, phase? If your worries are shared by friends, teachers, or counselors, get help from a pro.

Pig Pen

Obviously, our house was never a serious contender for the white-glove test. Early adolescents do not see dirt as an enemy. They do not want to restrict the freedom of their clothes and possessions by confining them to drawers and closets. Boys, particularly, resist washing, in part because dirt keeps girls away. That will change overnight, of course, when girls suddenly become interesting, and clouds of Brut may suffocate the whole house. When I look at my water bill, I feel a distinct nostalgia for the early adolescent stage.

At ten, our son Danny feared that a shower would dissolve him like the Wicked Witch of the West. Two years later, he was Dapper Dan, every pore scoured. One of our foster children earned the name Dirt Bags, even from the other boys his own age. And girls go through the same stages, and eventual transformation. Ring-Around-the-Neck was a foster girl who had to be forced to bathe.

When does dirt become filth? Many educated, sophisticated visitors from Western Europe think Americans are foolishly obsessed with personal hygiene. Many think it unhealthy to bathe more than once a week, believing that daily showers lower the body's resistance to germs. In other words, your child's resistance to external applications of soap and hot water every day is not the worst problem in the world. This culture may be a bit nutty about natural body odors, and you may have the kind of child who thinks the use of deodorant is hypocrisy. Still, and even allowing for sociopolitical statement in the form of stale sweat, you have the right to insist on cleanliness that approaches the accepted cultural norm. Your child can dress like a compost heap, if she chooses, without having to smell like one. In my view, you should be concerned about underlying emotional problems if, when you vigorously pursue the issue, you are unable to get your kid to bathe twice weekly. Once a week may be enough, in your eyes. Fine. But don't expect an invitation to dinner at our house toward the end of the week.

Even less serious is the adolescent's typically messy room. A friend's recent experience may strike a chord:

"With three teenagers, it's all I can do to keep the kitchen and living room moderately neat," she says, "and sometimes they succumb to the mess, too. The last time we went on vacation, I didn't have time to pick up the house like I usually do, and while we were gone, the burglar alarm went off. Probably because some of those gym socks lying around could walk about by themselves. The police got a neighbor to let them in and leapt to the conclusion that we had been ransacked and burglarized. Our neighbor knew better, of course. He has teenage kids, too."

Unlike you, David and I had overseers from the state, and our foster home was subject to inspections. It was never easy. Would your child's room pass muster with an officer of the court? With our own two boys, we merely shut the bedroom doors and decided to interfere only when a foul smell began to drift through the rest of the house. I sometimes try the excuse of fire safety to get a path cleared through the rooms, but it rarely works. Perhaps one good reason for the mess is to keep unwanted grownups out. The messier the room, the happier and more private the adolescent.

As you know, some parents do have kids who keep their rooms neat and clean. Is this the result of some canny trick of parenting? I don't know, but if you have the answer, please write me the secret. It will be featured in the very next edition of this book.

Meanwhile, I've found that parents should not grind their molars over messy rooms. Just consider them a part of adolescent lifestyle that will vanish along with acne and cries of "Oh, Mom!"

At the other extreme, there is the rare kid who is compulsively neat. One teenage girl I know quite well is unable to ignore messes or dirt when she visits a friend's house. Unmade bed, scattered clothing, dust bunnies hiding under a desk—it all gets cheerfully spritzed. Not surprisingly, some of her friends take offense; others just roll their eyes. In certain moods, I think I would love to have this natural born charlady living in our house, but I'm also aware of the possibility of an unrecognized problem. This young lady's behavior is acutely unusual, and she should probably consult with a professional.

Definite Dress Alarms: Drugs, Cults

Sexy clothing, weird styles, dirty messes—these three exceptions to my rule of not worrying about teenage style are not as frightening as the fourth: clothes that advertise serious interest in drugs or Satanic cults.

And that includes the cutesy products that beer companies license these days. Chris, a tall, well-built fifteen year old when he came to live with us, seemed to have it all together. His aquiline features, green eyes, and glossy black hair could have seemed arrogant, but he had gentle, winning ways. His first load of laundry had ten T-shirts, each and every one of them decorated with a beer ad. As soon as he unpacked, he set out a display of empty beer cans on the windowsill. His gentle manner was strained when I insisted that both collections go home immediately.

Had I overreacted? You be the judge. During the six weeks Chris was placed with us, he reeled in roaring drunk three times. He wasn't mean; he wasn't uncontrollable. He was ill. He was an alcoholic—a truly good kid suffering from a terrible disease . . . and the T-shirts and cans were a tip-off. Four years after leaving our care, Chris's disease proved fatal. Driving home under the influence, the good kid spun off the road and crashed into a tree.

By the time Chris came to us, I had learned the difference between casually wearing a beer-blast T-shirt and the kind of behavior that is meant as an advertisement to "party." Almost every one of my kids with a serious drinking problem made a habit of wearing shirts, caps, or buttons promoting beer brands.

I may sound hard-line on this subject, but too many kids are dying. If I had my way, I'd ban all gear that advertises beer or partying. Your kid may be able to buy a sweatshirt praising party animals at the local card shop, but that doesn't make it right. The wise parent will not let a child wear clothing that promotes the use of drugs and booze. To me, this is a case where parental discretion definitely overrules the child's right to self-expression. (And I believe parents should protest to beer companies and retail outlets about the manufacture and sale of these licensed products.)

The best approach is not to raise the roof, even though you must not take no for an answer. I begin by joking: "Pay me, and I'll advertise anything . . . anything except lethal weapons. And I believe that beer in the hands of a teenager is as lethal as an assault rifle. I won't wear those shirts, and you won't either." Your child can have only one reason for rejecting this line of reasoning, I'm afraid. If she does, perhaps you should turn right now to page 148, where I begin a discussion of drug and alcohol abuse.

Drug-related clothing requires a sharper eye and some informed assessment. The Grateful Dead have popularized tie-dyed shirts, and some kids may feel that the random splashes of color are innocent art. Perhaps, but the policy of most drug rehab centers is to ban the shirts; for many users, they have acted as a badge of solidarity with the drug culture.

Or take Kira, a short, stocky fifteen-year-old whose heavy-lidded blue eyes and thick eyeglasses made her look like a stereotypical bookworm. Her chief interest did not lie on the printed page, however, as her advertisements proved. One was a gold marijuana leaf suspended from her neck on a gold chain. Then there were the cannabis leaves embroidered on the breast pocket of a denim jacket as well as on the back pockets of all of her jeans. Not subtle, except to her very caring parents, who thought that she simply liked (I'm not making this up) the decorative qualities of palm leaves.

Kira was outraged when I insisted that the jewelry and embroidered jeans had to be sent home. When I explained my thinking to her father, he threw the clothes in the trash. Kira's mother took a different view. She decided that the marijuana leaves were just an innocent attempt to become part of the school's most popular clique, not an advertisement of a desire to get stoned.

Maybe. Maybe not. I think of Chris and I err on the side of caution.

Satanic Chic

Many adolescents pass through a phase of fascination with the occult. Consider the success with teenage audiences of movies about the supernatural. Your kid's searching questions about the meaning of life might lead her to experiment with seances, tarot cards, or a Ouija board.

When does this normal interest become dangerous? An answer can sometimes be found in a teenager's clothing. Like druggies, people who are seriously involved with Satanism or witchcraft identify themselves to each other with symbols. Most parents will not recognize these occult signs. I didn't until one of my foster kids disclosed that he was a practicing warlock, or male witch. A recent recruit and proud of it, he was not as guarded as more experienced cultists. He explained some of the signs, and I made it my business to find out more.

Here's a list of the symbols I found to be most commonly used, but it may not be exhaustive:

- "666," the three-digit number used in the Book of Revelations as "the sign of the beast." (Former President Reagan is wryly welcomed as a colleague by Satanists amused by the number of letters in his full name, Ronald Wilson Reagan.)
- Upside-down crosses.
- "Satan Rules."
- "Natas," or "Satan" spelled backward.
- The ancient mystical symbol of the pentagram, or five-pointed star within a circle, sometimes accompanied by the head of a goat.
- A devil's face.
- Candles, because they serve important functions in Satanic rituals.
- Goats, a common symbol of Satan.
- Hearts that are bleeding, torn, pierced.
- Figures clothed in robes of black or red.

Now, remember that such symbols may be suggestive but are not necessarily hard-and-fast evidence. Doodling kids may quite innocently draw dripping candles, blood-smeared knives, and bleeding hearts, just as they get a kick out of the violence in kung fu and Rambo movies. By themselves, such drawings are not worrisome, but

I'd be on the lookout for any connection to the symbols on my list. That's the time to ask direct questions:

"That's a pentagram. Do you know what it stands for?"

"Why are you drawing a goat's head? Does it mean anything special?"

"The numbers '666' have a specific meaning. Do you know what it is?"

Most kids are ignorant of these symbolic meanings. Usually they will be interested in your explanation of the link to Satanism but happy to stop using them. I always began to worry when a kid continued to make such drawings or, worse, could readily answer my questions about the symbolic meanings. Either could be a signal that a child is exploring Satanic belief or is already deeply involved.

Consider this possibility carefully. On the one hand, despite all the media attention currently given to cult activities, very few people go down this path. On the other, you must not ignore the persistent appearance of Satanic slogans and signs in your child's clothing, posters, doodles, jewelry, or tattoos.

For once, however, it is not a good idea to share your concerns with your teenager. In this one area, I feel that you need to talk with an expert before sharing your fears with a kid who may be heavily involved in Satanism. Find someone who has had experience with children who have been attracted to cults. The professional observer can help you determine whether or not your fears are soundly based. She will understand the possible relationships between a child's emotional problems and Satanic worship or witchcraft. She will know how to begin to deal with the problem without making it worse. You will need her guidance.

DRESS CLUES: A SUMMARY

If your child dresses so provocatively or bizarrely that people turn to stare, intervene. If the intervention fails, go to a professional for help.

If your child's lifestyle includes an entrenched love of dirt and you cannot dispel this enchantment, don't hesitate to seek professional guidance.

Don't allow clothing that promotes alcohol or drug use. If the Gotcha Wars heat up, turn to Chapter 12, on drugs.

Finally, if you suspect your child is involved in the occult to an unhealthy degree, say nothing to him, but do find an experienced professional who can offer guidance to both of you.

RECESS

Some of the problems I've discussed in this chapter have their humorous side, but it's been a downer nonetheless. Don't, don't, don't. . . . Will you ever be able to relax? Unlikely as it might sound, your teenager at her worst may not be all that different from the Dalai Lama, who is today the most revered spiritual leader of Tibet and one of the most admired of world figures for his courage and wisdom.

Chosen in infancy as the reincarnation of his thirteen predecessors, the young Dalai Lama underwent rigorous instruction to prepare him for his sacred and political duties, watched over by his teachers. Even so, as a young teenager he could not resist sneaking down to the palace garage and taking one of the country's four automobiles for a joy ride. And he got caught because he drove the vehicle into a tree.

A good kid who did a bad thing, he turned out all right, as the world knows.

There's hope. Keep reading.

FIVE

In with the Out Crowd

"You can't fool me, young lady. You've been out with that rude little creep again, haven't you?"

"How can you talk about him that way? He's the only person who really cares about me."

"Oh? And that's why he stole that twenty-five dollars out of your pocketbook last week?"

"I already explained that. He wanted to get something and surprise me."

"Uh-huh."

"You'll never understand. You just hate him because his parents don't have a lot of money."

"You know that's not true. I judge him based on his behavior and it's been pretty slimy where you're concerned."

"That shows how much you know. He really loves me. We love each other."

"So why were you crying when you came in the door just now?"

"Shut up. He loves me."

I was driving Zach and three of his friends to a movie when they started playing a very revealing game of one-upmanship, rapping snappy like Vanilla Ice: Whose parents hated which of the other kids the most?

Tom's parents, it turned out, could not stand my Zach (What?), and Dick's mom and dad loathed the sight of Harry. Tom made Harry's parents gag, and Jack's parents couldn't decide which they liked least, Dick or Harry. Every parent in this chorus of disagreement did agree on one thing, however: their own child, when astray, had been led there by someone else's kid.

I laughed out loud, because I had been doing the same thing all week, blaming Harry because Zach had not been keeping curfew. The boys laughed, too, when I suggested that they create an imaginary new boy in town and blame him whenever they got in trouble.

Blame Harry or not, I had learned long before, from my foster children, that trying to sever teenage friendships is about as simple as separating egg whites from yolk after you've beaten the eggs into the batter.

Friends Like These . . .

If you looked closely at twelve-year-old Cathie you could see the baby fat beneath the piles of makeup. Most people just looked at her early-blooming figure and saw a nineteen-year-old. Friends her own age fell away, as often happens when a child looks mature early, and she felt she had no choice but to join an older crowd in town.

Today, these kids are settled, hardworking citizens, but back then they were a wild crew. "I'm Bad! I'm Bad!" their sweatshirts proclaimed. This was truth in advertising.

Naturally, Cathie's parents despised this crowd, but they couldn't stop her from hanging out with them. When she was grounded, Cathie would just wait until her parents were asleep and then sneak out on nightly forays. These adventures came to light only when Mom and Dad were roused by the police early one morning. Cathie had been caught joyriding with her older friends in a stolen car.

The incident seemed to be a watershed. Two of the joyriders were sent away to a detention center, Cathie looked chastened, her parents breathed a sigh of relief. Everything seemed fine for about two months, when there was another predawn arrest for the same offense. The cops warned Cathie's parents that the next joyride would bring her to family court.

The school year had just ended, so Cathie's mom and dad sent her to camp for the summer, hoping she would "come to her senses." Instead, her friends came to her, causing her to be expelled. Shipped to a relative's house, Cathie contacted her crowd and ran off with them to follow the Grateful Dead's summer tour. It took the police three weeks to find the wandering crew. Cathie was brought home, and some of her older friends were arrested for endangering the welfare of a minor.

Because her parents had pressed charges, Cathie refused to speak with them and asked for placement. After two weeks with us, she ran away with her friends yet again. Ultimately she would wind up spending two years in a treatment facility, where everyone was just like the friends her parents had hated so much.

What could they have done differently? After the second late-night joyride, they should probably have ceased and desisted in their efforts to separate their daughter from her friends. Instead, they should have concentrated on what Cathie was doing wrong. She should have been held accountable for her actions. By blaming the friends, these parents did not get to the real source of their problem: Cathie's tendency to do bad things.

The Influence of Friends

Folk wisdom has always made the message clear, whether in plain language—"Lie down with dogs, get up with fleas"—or in more eloquent diction, "Evil communications corrupt good manners."

Yes, friends do influence your child. They can sometimes influence him to do bad things. Peer pressure is powerful. In a group, even the best-behaved teen is likely to do something he would never dare do on his own, or even consider. Still, like Cathie's parents, you will probably achieve little by trying to separate teenagers who feel loyal to each other. In fact, you will probably jeopardize your relationship with your child. Besides, as I found out so unexpectedly, your child may seem like the bad influence to the parents of the friend whose influence you consider so harmful.

Your aim should be to worry about your child's acts and behavior, not to worry about his friends and their behavior. Keeping quiet about the supposedly dangerous friends is hard enough to do. When the bad influence appears in romantic form, however, your job will be even harder.

Not with My Kid

As I've noted before, I often look back in astonishment at the innate good sense my parents showed in difficult situations.

If a kid like Frank, my first true love, showed up to take out one of my foster daughters, I'd be in fits. A high school dropout from a dysfunctional family, he was on probation for stealing a car radio. He was Romeo to me, but he was a "hood," by the standards of those days, to my friends and my parents. He seemed to be on an antisocial track.

My parents let me know they disapproved, but, wisely, they did not interfere. They waited and waited and waited. After three years that must have seemed very long to them, Frank and I finally broke up. If they had tried to separate us before then, when our romance had run its natural course, we would have eloped.

In the long run, Frank did well. Probation was enough of a shock to straighten him out. But we grew apart for reasons that had nothing to do with his being a bad kid. What a disaster it would have been if we had run off and married because my parents overreacted. Instead, they made sure that I followed their rules, and they always blamed me, not my boyfriend, when I fell short.

December–May Romances

Age differences in teenage romance set parental alarm bells ringing. Won't the older partner lead the younger into wicked ways? Isn't there always some sort of exploitation involved?

Consider tall, lanky, sweet-faced Jim. The headmaster of his prestigious prep school said he was the brightest boy ever to grace their halls, but he was modest and mannerly to a fault. When he came to us at fourteen, he could have passed for nineteen, and therein lay the problem. His parents had tried to break up his romance with a twenty-one-year-old woman but failed. They went to court, charging the girlfriend with statutory rape and insisting that Jim be placed. The judge ordered the romance ended.

Following court guidelines, we monitored Jim's comings and goings, his mail and phone calls, but that wasn't enough. The lovers were discovered meeting at school during lunch hour, so the court sent Jim out of town to a residential treatment center for the rest of his school years. Love not only survived; it thrived. So did the boy's hatred of his parents and the judicial system. Today he is married to his older woman. Perhaps that is as it should be. Or perhaps things would have worked out differently if his parents had been as patient as mine.

Usually, of course, the boy is the older partner in these December–May alliances. With some frequency, girls were placed in our care in the hope that separation would bring an end to a relationship with a disturbingly older boy or man. Of all those attempts, I cannot recall a single time when parents and the court were able to end a romance that a child wanted to keep aflame.

But what about a couple like my Nancy and her homicidal lover Carl? You can't just give up when, as proved to be the case, his pathological behavior could lead to her death. When you are convinced that your child is dating someone who is dangerously unsavory, you must act fast.

Refuse to allow the boyfriend in your house, and stick to your decision. Acknowledge that you understand what your daughter finds attractive, then give your specific reasons for objecting to the relationship. Meanwhile, try to arrange a separation that seems to have nothing to do with the problem. Is there a church trip, or soccer camp, or family reunion that will get her out of town for a while? If you don't have a rich Uncle George who can take her to Europe, as in nineteenth-century novels, maybe you can secretly subsidize Cousin Alice to take your kid with the family to Disney World. If things are bad enough, parents have gone so far as to arrange a job transfer to another part of the country. It is important to come up with a ploy, no matter what it is, that will put some miles between your child and the loved one.

If that is not possible, ground her. Try three rounds of grounding, if the relationship continues. When those fail, use a Caring Intervention and try to negotiate a separation.

But if the Crazy Glue bonding the lovers still holds, there is only one option left: a reversal. You will have to accept the relationship. The most important aim in these situations is to maintain a caring relationship with your child, even if the hated other has to be invited to your house. It is better to lose this particular battle than to lose the entire war, as Jim's parents did.

If the situation is painful to you, don't try to go it alone. In a parental support group, you will meet people who can share your pain and help you learn how to handle things. A professional counselor can ease your burden and help you sustain a caring relationship with your child. Above all, that line of communication has to remain open.

Check Out the Behavior, Not the Friends

So do you always just back off?

Not quite. Sending Cathie off to a camp was a good move, for example, but her parents had waited too long to take action. The batter was already in the frying pan and sizzling.

To make any headway, you have to act early. Make it a point to meet all of your kid's new friends, especially heartthrobs, as soon as possible. Lure them with a well-stocked refrigerator and a humming VCR. Offer the original *Night of the Living Dead.* Thrill them with the legendary "ghost" in *Three Men and a Baby*—or the most recent equivalent. Volunteer to chauffeur the gang. (When kids loosen up and start talking to each other in the car, you might as well be the fifth wheel; you'll be amazed how much you'll learn secondhand about their friends and attitudes.)

I'd start worrying if your child doesn't want to bring his friends around. After some normal adolescent self-consciousness, most kids are comfortable with bringing home friends they know their parents will like. Few will show up with someone they suspect their parents won't like. If you know that your child is seeing someone you never get to meet, find out why.

I not only made every effort to get to know my sons' friends, I went after their parents, too. Most of the time, they wanted to know me as much as I wanted to know them, and we happily commiserated with each other about the difficulties of raising our children in today's world. It helped a lot and probably forestalled some misunderstandings. Of course, Zach and Danny were not initially pleased with my approach, but they relaxed when they realized that I was following a rule of criticizing their friends as little as possible.

No, I wasn't going to fall into that trap, like Cathie's parents. If friends can sometimes help a kid land in trouble, rarely can a good kid consistently be forced by friends to do something she knows is wrong.

Though I myself was a teenage Miss Straight Arrow, I ran with a rough crowd because I admired their derring-do. I guess I wanted to have the best of both worlds, but I knew there was a line between them.

One gorgeous spring day, my "bad" friends talked me into cutting school to go see Johnny Ray in concert. I would never have done that on my own. More important, I felt so guilty I never cut a class again. I kept my friends, and they kept cutting classes and teasing me about the good times I missed. But I had learned what worked for me and my conscience. The gain, even if it had been Elvis, was not worth the pain.

My beloved Frank, too, learned that he could not get me to do things I thought were bad. So I knew an important truth when I was dealing with foster children: unless part of the youngster is eager to go along, neither friends nor lover can lead a good kid down the primrose path.

Twice, though, I've encountered kids whose influence over others was exceptionally strong and dangerous. They weren't just bad friends; each was, in his way, an entrepreneur with my kids as prey.

Mickey, whose clever wit put Andrew Dice Clay in the shade, meant every nasty crack he made. Much as I disliked his delight in cruelty, some of his jokes made me laugh despite myself, for he brilliantly summed people up. He charmed my kids and manipulated them, instinctively guessing their weaknesses. These gifts were invaluable to him, because Mickey was one of the local pushers.

Another skillfully manipulative kid, a veritable walking hormone, saw our house as a kind of sexual convenience store. As each new girl arrived, he hotly pursued. Soon, I knew all of his best lines. I could repeat them to his latest conquest and list the girls whose hearts he had broken, though she was rarely deterred.

Mickey and the Hormone were dangerous enough to be exceptions to the rule, and I had to declare them off-limits to some of my foster kids. But that didn't always work. I had to take another approach. "I'm not willing to lock you up or send you to live somewhere else," I'd say to my charges, "but if you get in trouble when you're with Mickey, I will double any of the consequences to you. If you're late coming home, you'll be grounded four days instead of two. If you cut school with him, you'll be grounded eight days instead of four. Understood?"

With your child's friends, who are unlikely to be as dangerous as these grade-A sleazes, you'll have to admit that the glue is set and the friends are joined forever . . . or for as long as they want to be.

Try to soft-pedal your criticisms of the friend you dislike or distrust. Be tentative and casual about your negative remarks. Have as much regard for your child's feelings as if she were an adult friend who likes to hang out with someone you can't abide. Remember that a frontal attack will only rouse your child to defend the friend (The one time my father blew his cool and spouted off some nasty remarks about Frank we came very close to eloping.) And don't repeat your criticisms or concerns. Your child does not have to be reminded that his mother or father does not like his friend or romantic interest. He'll remember.

Don't say, "You'll have to stop hanging around with Rob. He has a drinking problem." This gets you nowhere, even if Rob drinks and drives and has had two serious accidents under the influence. Besides, as I've noted, Rob is not your priority problem. Your job is to focus on your child's bad behavior.

Rather, what you say should be addressed directly to your child and his sense of responsibility for his own actions, no matter what Rob does. "I feel so strongly about your safety," you might say, "that if you are getting into cars and riding with someone who has been drinking and I find out about it, I'll ground you for a month."

This approach leaves Rob out of the picture. It lets you deal with the main issue: your determination that your child understand and follow the rules, knowing that you hold him responsible for his own actions.

Keep Caring

By criticizing a bad friend so much that you alienate your child, you can fall right into the trap laid by someone who is a really evil influence.

To control Nancy, Carl set out to separate her from her parents and friends, one by one. He earned their hate and broke their ties to Nancy. Eventually, as a consequence, she became completely dependent on the man who would kill her. Her parents gave up, stopped talking to her, decided that she was no longer their daughter. Perhaps, had they not cut her off, Nancy would have left Carl long before she had his child. Even when she tried to leave him, long afterward, she felt she could not return home or contact her mother and father.

Don't let distaste for a kid's friend ruin your relationship with the kid herself.

Fortunately, the relationship you worry about will probably involve a friend who is basically good, not a sociopath like Carl. The friend might have serious problems. He might be contributing to your child's problems. But your question should be: Why does my son need this particular friend, or group of friends, or romantic interest? What is the attraction?

TO SUMMARIZE:

When your child joins a crowd that gets into trouble with the law or delights in taking risks, or when she falls in love with someone you can't stand, don't blame the friend(s) for the problem.

Recognize that the problem is the behavior of the kid you care about. That's where you need to focus your energies.

Work on the problem, but learn patience.

Keep caring about the kid, no matter what.

Repeat: Keep caring.

RECESS:

This chapter started off on a high note, but I'm afraid that all of these stories about bad relationships could bring you down.

Let's not make the mistake the newspapers make of concentrating only on the bad things that happen. Sure, the point of this book is to address problems. Naturally, I have to talk about a lot of experiences that have been unpleasant, and not all of them have turned out well for the families involved.

But let's not forget the good things. Adolescence is a wonderful time of opening doors and windows, even when in the process some walls get knocked down. Oh, yes. Even with all the tussles, the minor setbacks, most of you are having the time of your lives. Not perfection, but constant change and challenge. And somewhere in that gawky teenage body is the child you cherished and the adult who will be one of your best friends in the years to come.

Now, back to work. . . .

SIX

"I Did It in Study Hall"

"How come you aren't doing your homework?"

"I did it already."

"Hey, that's good. I'd be glad to check it over for you."

"Well, thanks, but that won't work."

"Why not?"

"Uh, it's not here."

"Oh?"

"I mean, I did it in study hall."

"Okay, that sounds good. Now you can use tonight's homework time to study ahead. That can help bring your grades back to normal."

"Yeah, sure, but I left all my books at school."

"I see. Then I guess you're not worried about the geometry test tomorrow. . . . You're all prepared."

"What?"

"Tomorrow's Friday, right? You always have a geometry quiz on Fridays."

"Oh."

David agrees. At least half the gray hairs I earned during our foster-parent years came from fussing, fuming, worrying with my "ten o'clock scholars." We went to school so often to deal with academic problems that some students thought we were on the faculty. We were on intimate terms with the principal, assistant principal, dean of students, school psychologist, social worker, librarian, guidance counselors, most teachers, maintenance personnel, and, of course, the attendance officer.

There were two separate kinds of academic problem: getting the kids to go to school; and getting them to study. In the second category I place vandalism, horsing around, getting into fights, because cutting up at school is just another way of cutting out.

In this chapter, when I talk about failing grades, I am talking about other school problems. All share the same causes.

Broken Promises

College is the passport to success, we all say. Work hard, make good grades, the world is yours.

For some of my foster kids, this inspiring message became the Big Lie. Realistically or unrealistically, they decided at some point that, no matter how hard they worked in school, they would never be able to go to college. Their disappointment, their disillusionment, broke my heart. I could not bear to see them give up.

Sheneque came to us at twelve because, in legal parlance, she had been present at the commission of a crime. With no parents to care for her, she had been living with a sister in a house of prostitution, though she was not turning tricks herself. Sweet-faced, skinny, poorly dressed, and terrified about living in such a "fancy" town, she did well with us. A wonderful mimic, she sparkled in Whoopi Goldberg routines. And she had a dream. Because she loved younger kids and they loved her back, Sheneque wanted to become a nursery school teacher.

Unlike most of our foster kids, she was eager to be registered in school from Day One. Every night she joined the faithful few at the kitchen table doing homework, checking and rechecking it, reading ahead, asking for help when she didn't understand something. She was determined. Although quite possibly brighter than most kids her age, she was a grade behind. Our school was the tenth she had attended in seven years. But it was the best, and that gave her hope.

After six months with us, she was moved to a long-term foster home. Eventually, we lost contact, but this was usually a sign that all is well. When our foster children bonded with someone else, we rarely heard from them again.

Then one day I got a call from Sheneque's former probation officer. Would we consider taking her again? "She's not sweet Sheneque anymore," she warned.

We said yes, but I was devastated. At sixteen, sweet Sheneque had become sexy Sheneque. In the three months she stayed with us, she turned a trick or two in our staid, middle-class, "fancy" town. In due course, she was moved to a group home. Soon, she was selling herself on the streets of Manhattan, hooked on drugs. I assume she's overdosed by now or died from AIDS.

One night, this new Sheneque sat with me at the same kitchen table where she had worked so hard only four years before.

"I studied hard, didn't I?" she asked wonderingly.

"Yes, you certainly did. What happened to the dream?"

She laughed away a momentary look of sadness. It was the old Whoopi Goldberg hoot.

"Kathy, a black girl like me with no money, no family? The only college I'm going to get into is the one on the streets."

Nothing I said in the ensuing weeks would convince her otherwise. I even promised that David and I would help pay out of our own pockets, but she had lost faith in her dream. Not just minority kids but bright, able, middle-class students also give up in school when they lose faith in their ability to fulfill their expectations for themselves. They might put the blame on society in general, on their teachers, on unruly classmates, but they have actually lost faith in their own capacity for learning and achievement. If your kid is falling behind, he may share Sheneque's disillusionment.

Darrell, a gentle but monumentally stubborn son of hard-working professionals, was sent to us at fifteen. His troubles had begun at school the year before. A good student who wanted to become a physician, he didn't make the high school honors track. Convinced he was shut out of medical school, embarrassed even more because his two older sisters were pulling down A's in college, Darrell the outstanding student became Darrell the outstanding truant.

After he had skipped forty-five days in a row, his frustrated parents sought help from family court. Placement with us changed nothing. He'd get up, have breakfast, and head out with the other kids . . . and skip. When I started driving him to school, he'd wave goodbye at the front door, enter with his classmates . . . and skip. He was determined that no one was going to tell him what to do. I could almost see the ice forming on his eyebrows when he became set on having his own way. He was convinced that, for him, school had nothing to offer. The promise had been broken.

After six weeks of truancy with us, Darrell had stretched the limits of the court's patience. He was sent to a "residential treatment" center, a cross between boarding school and psychiatric hospital. Even when forced to go to class, he did not improve—until an insightful counselor discovered that the boy loved animals. This story ended happily. Today, Darrell is successfully studying zoology at a state university, on course for a career in animal ecology. The secret: his counselor found a way to show him that the broken promise could be mended.

Overdosing on School Worries

You, like your child, are probably not immune to the effects of the promise. One danger, therefore, is that you can become too deeply involved in her school performance. An overdose of parental pressure can create or exacerbate problems in the classroom.

Ariel, so shy she hid behind the long brown sweep of her hair, was sweet, loving, always trying hard to please. Night after night, she cracked the books at our kitchen table, trying as hard as she could to do the right thing.

One night she asked me to help her concentrate by sitting with her. After about ten minutes of staring at a single page, she looked up with tears streaming down her face.

"I can't do it," she wailed. "I want to so much, and I just can't."

"Were her grades abysmal? No, she was an above-average student who passionately loved art, but her parents wanted academic perfection. When she dropped to a B+ in a highly competitive English honors course one semester, they made her drop out of an extracurricular art class. Although Ariel loved her parents and wanted to please them, the pressure became too much for her. A downward spiral began. She began to have trouble studying, her grades fell further, and she finally ran away. When her parents brought her to us, their parting remark said it all: "Call us when you get your grades in shape."

By this point, of course, she couldn't perform no matter how hard she tried, but her parents never learned to understand. Today, Ariel attends a local community college, and she produces artwork that others find gifted and sensitive. Her parents do not share in her success. They rarely speak to her. She is not achieving what they demanded.

Fortunately, few parents pressure their kids to that extreme. But that does not mean that youngsters, including yours, don't feel intensely pressured to perform and to fulfill your expectations of the American promise.

Failing with Straight A's

Remember Jennifer, the straight-A top athlete who was saving sleeping pills to kill herself if she didn't get into Stanford? Well, Stanford turned her down, but she was accepted by an Ivy League school. She didn't take the pills, but she became so seriously depressed that she had to be hospitalized.

In this case, low-keyed parents had urged their daughter to relax. In fact, Jennifer's father, whose parents had pressured him to get into a high-powered college, felt that he had been robbed of some valuable living time in his teen years. But Jennifer could not listen. In today's competitive society, inhuman pressures to succeed are constant, quite apart from parental influence.

A young client in my private practice tried to do away with himself when he discovered that his IQ was only 111. Somewhere, he got the mistaken idea that law schools don't accept applicants whose IQ falls below 126. To him, life was not worth living if he could not someday practice law.

This is insane. Somehow, you have to protect your child from falling prey to such distorted values. Every kid is endangered when we measure personal worth only by academic performance—bright kids like Ariel just as much as the average and less gifted students.

Without "making a big deal out of it," you should find time to discuss these issues with your child. Even the occasional remark will show where you stand. Let her know that you know that schools grade only academic performance. She is a whole person with many attributes more important than her latest marks in plane geometry or French.

On a Roseanne Barr episode, her daughter's grade dropped from A to C because she refused to dissect a frog. With a smile and a hug, Roseanne said, "Schools don't give A's for holding to what you believe in, but I do."

To your child, you are the ultimate grade-giver. Let her know that your grade scale covers the whole range of her personal qualities and achievements.

When to Worry

"Worry and wait" is the best policy at the first signs of slowing down, cutting up, or cutting out at school. Heavy-handed intervention will probably be useless or even counterproductive when the only problem is that a grade has slipped from A + to A, or even from B to C.

Comment on the slide. Ask if there is something to talk about. No? Well, note casually that most students have trouble concentrating at some point in their academic careers but those times usually pass.

Then, wait to see what happens at the next marking period. Often, the lower grade will push your youngster to try harder. If not, and slippage continues for more than a semester, it's time to take stronger action.

Body Blocks for Falling Grades

What happens when you get three rabbis together to solve a point of law? According to a hoary old joke, you get four opinions.

Much the same thing happens when parents discuss ways of dealing with school problems. You get the tough approaches, like these comments from one of my Parent Tactics sessions:

"You've got to be on top of a kid's schoolwork every minute. You need to know what their assignments are, when they're due, and how the kid is doing them."

"Kids need lots of oversight and structure when it comes to schoolwork."

"My kids know they can't go out on a school night. I don't care if they get free tickets to the World Series. School comes first."

"A good parent keeps his kid working and is the teacher's partner."

Other parents take softer approaches, as mine did when I bounced on and off the honor roll in high school. They believed that children learned if a teacher was doing his job right. I was never hassled about homework or grades, unless there was something unusual in my pattern. For example, my usual D's in geometry were considered okay, but a drop to B + in English brought suspicious comments. This laid-back style worked well enough for me, but it was unfair to one of my brothers. Because of a slight learning disability, he needed structure and supervision.

David's parents were more authoritarian. That worked well with his siblings, but he could get A's without seeming to study. Forced to study in a structured way at home, he became so resentful that learning became less fun and more difficult.

The moral: You have to be flexible, learning for yourself which approach is the best for each adolescent individual.

The students who do well in school, in every sense of the phrase, regard academics as their job, not as a method of winning parental love. They aren't overwhelmed by the pressures of competition.

How did they develop? Usually, the dependable student's parents used a fairly tough approach in elementary school, when kids are eager to please grown-ups and need to learn how to study. In those early school years, it helps to insist on regular study hours and completion of homework assignments. As the child moves into adolescence, however, the parent has to start letting go. The teenager must take responsibility for his school performance.

I'm not sure you should take this advice as far as one father I know. When each of his children entered seventh grade, he backed off academic matters entirely. The kids were allowed to decide for themselves when to study, go to bed, and leave for school. He'd write a note when they were ill but do nothing if they just wanted to stay home all day. When teachers asked for a conference, he insisted that the child be present and make all decisions.

The first years of this scheme were too hard, I think. One son failed all of his courses for two semesters. He had to go to summer school and pay for it, too. But he did graduate on time, and with honors. In this family, the extreme policy worked.

Most of us, though, should adopt a less radical approach. I think the optimum goal for parents is to be able to get disengaged from constant academic oversight by about the ninth grade. Starting well before that, perhaps at the onset of the first term in the seventh grade, try defining your child's first step toward total responsibility for his schoolwork. You might say something like this:

"Going into seventh grade is going to be a big change in a lot of ways. You are old enough now to start figuring out how to handle some things entirely on your own. Why don't we see if you're ready to take full charge of your schoolwork?

"I won't interfere as long as your grades stay in the acceptable range. Last year, you had an 86 average. As long as you can maintain that, you can decide for yourself when and how much homework to do. And if, without any help from us, you can do even better, then it's your decision to do so."

Once you strike this bargain, any number of things can happen, so be prepared. If your kid's grades get better, let her know how pleased you are. She's doing better without your help! If they begin to fall, say nothing, until they breach the acceptability threshold. Before that, even if a bad trend seems to be developing, stick to the deal. Your child may get back on track by herself, and that's what you want her to learn: how to get the message from plummeting grades and respond on her own.

Even when grades do fall below the agreed limit, I'd suggest waiting a semester, if you can stand it. Falling grades will soon motivate most children, after their first heady taste of freedom. If you can't wait, tell your kid that you know how disappointed she must be with the lower grades. Ask if she needs any suggestions about structuring her study time. Does she need a special study nook? Does seventh grade offer new challenges or new teachers who require some adjusting? Why does she think her marks have gone down? If you decide that the answer has something to do with her inexperience at handling the responsibility for her studies, be tactful, but make your point:

"With so much that's new to handle in the seventh grade, it's probably too soon for you to work entirely on your own. Isn't that what these grades probably mean? Let's go back to the old way. It was working, and this new way isn't, at least for now. Maybe after Christmas, when you're settled in, or next year, we can try letting you work on your own."

Next time you try, you may have to go through the same routine, but don't give up. Periodically, you must encourage your child to take responsibility, yet be ready to intervene if he can't handle it. Some students don't get the knack until they're in college. Most, though, will find their wings by the tenth or eleventh grade.

Slippery Slopes

Occasionally, nothing you do can stop the snowball from accelerating downhill. Each report card dips lower.

First, consider the possibility that your child simply cannot do the assigned work. Has he been placed at the wrong level in a particular class or subject? Does he have the right preparation?—an important consideration, if you have just moved from another school system. Does he have one of the learning disabilities that typically do not show up until about the seventh or eighth grade? See if your school counselor would think it helpful to run some tests. More frequently than you might believe, an undiagnosed sight or hearing problem is often the culprit, even when your child has been receiving standard medical care. Your child might try to cover up a slight disability, out of embarrassment, or not even recognize it, assuming that he sees or hears what everyone else does.

If these avenues go nowhere, you have to consider the problem of weak motivation. Whatever your policy has been, shift gears into "reverse."

Suppose you've been taking the laissez-faire approach, leaving academic matters to your son and his teachers, but now you are so worried about his grades that you can't sleep at night. First, try this announcement of a sea change:

"I know I don't normally get involved in your schoolwork, but it looks like you're having a hard time. Maybe you need more help from your mother and me. We want to see you hitting the books after dinner every night. No exceptions. We'll both be around to help, if you need help. We think this is seriously out of hand, don't you?"

If the next report card doesn't show the improvement you want, set another level of consequence. Pull the plug on TV and telephone use on school nights. Or if your kid is now allowed to go out on school nights, set an earlier curfew. For "soft love" parents, these restrictions may not come easy, but they are perfectly reasonable . . . and likely to work.

On the other hand, reverse gear for "tough love" parents is just as hard. When grades are slipping despite the monitoring and control you've exercised over the years, you may have to force yourself to say something like this:

"I guess my involvement in your schoolwork isn't helping, so I quit. You're old enough now to know what to do. You know what's at stake. But right now, I seem to care more about your grades than you do, and that's just not healthy. From now on, you're on your own, unless you tell me you need help some time."

Not only will you have trouble saying this, if you're the tough love type of parent, but you will have to face a period of severe testing, believe me. Your child will probably slack off, and the grades slip even further.

Just hold on. Remember your goal: to get your child to understand that school has to be his responsibility, not yours. If he doesn't ask for your help, don't push. At grade time, say something like the following:

"Looks to me as if you're really having a hard time. I'll help any way I can, when you're ready to start working. Meanwhile, do what you have to do. I can't help until school is important to you."

These reversals usually work, if you give them enough time and do not waver. Reversals don't work overnight, because your child has to become convinced that you won't flip-flop again. Once you have reversed, steady the course.

In the unlikely event that they don't work, there may be a major problem that requires outside evaluation or guidance. Certainly, if grades slip for more than two marking periods and failure looms near, it's time to intervene.

"F" Is for Focus

First, focus on the most likely reasons for failure.

Is your kid an average student in a high-pressure school? An above-average student with other things on his mind? A very good student who has just realized that he will never be tops in his class? A hard-working student who is not college material?

Are you asking your kid to star in your movie instead of his?

Second, recognize that you have probably picked the brains of the school's staff by this point. You need to go to an outside source for an independent evaluation—a psychologist in private practice, or an advocacy program that specializes in school problems. Your school can steer you toward such programs, but to preserve your child's privacy (and avoid the risk of seeming threatening to the school), you're better off contacting the United Way or your state's Department of Education. Besides, school officials will quite naturally recommend advocacy services they know well. You want to be sure you find an advocate who will be firmly in your corner, with no vested interest in maintaining a good relationship with your kid's school.

Don't flinch if you are referred to an agency that works with the physically or developmentally disabled. Recently, a friend of mine found it impossible to find effective help for her child, who has a minor learning disability. The answer was an agency that specialized in servicing the needs of retarded and severely physically handicapped students. For them, her son's problem was a piece of cake.

Finally, flip through Chapters 12 and 13 in the search for clues to academic failure. Grades are quickly dragged down by depression or drug use.

Off the Fast Track

Face the truth, once you learn it.

Perhaps your child's academic upper limit is a C+ average in non-academic courses. Perhaps she won't be able to complete high school successfully, let alone college. Perhaps she is bright but nonetheless dead set and determined to drop out before graduation.

Suppress your previous expectations, and forget the opinions of the neighbors. Success in life, as you know, is not guaranteed by a high school diploma or college sheepskin. Who is most successful? Probably you'll agree that it's the person who's been able to devote his energies to something he really enjoys doing.

Set aside the negative—the ongoing academic failure—and look toward the positive. Use a Caring Response to discover what your child wants to do. See what you can learn from vocational and psychological testing. Encourage your child to explore any interest or option that seems attractive. If you live in New York City, you might not think it very sensible for your teenage daughter to want to move to Colorado and apprentice herself to a blacksmith to learn to shoe horses. But if the idea brings her to life, it beats another two years of F's in domestic science. (As you might suspect, I choose that example because it happened to a friend back in 1972, and her daughter Darlene now runs a very successful horseshoe-and-tackle business in Wyoming.)

If your child has a dream that strikes you as impractical or worse, just remember that now is not forever. Better for her to be cheerfully engaged in something than dully marking time in class. Look for alternative schools that answer her needs. Think about alternative paths to a viable career.

Last Resorts

"Your kid is smart enough that school will simply torture her. Let her drop out, get a job and an equivalency degree, then I'll write a letter that will help get her into a good college."

Your worst nightmare?

When a school psychologist said that to a friend of mine, she was relieved. Both of her daughters have learning disabilities; each has had a hard time in school. Neither one wanted to drop out, as it happened, but my friend could live with the idea, if the plan included study for an equivalency degree.

Many parents have seen the wisdom of this approach, although most don't talk about it, I'm afraid. Only a few professionals will advise dropping out. But a failing student begins to succeed if she eagerly takes on the double responsibility of a job and study for an equivalency degree.

Ironically, knowing that my friend and her husband would support this kind of alternative made school easier for both girls. They knew they were staying in school to please themselves, not their parents.

As David reminds me now, Sheneque is pretty much the horrible exception among our foster kids who dropped out. Others have not done well, but most are supporting themselves in well-paying jobs or with their own small businesses. Still others, having seen something of the realities of the workplace, have hied themselves back to school or adult education programs.

So, when the last resort becomes your resort, welcome the potential for positive achievement:

1. Don't add to your kid's struggles by seeing dropping out as a dead-end. Life goes on even when good kids drop out of school.
2. Don't consider him a "quitter." He's trying to find the nontraditional path to success that works best for him.
3. Don't get angry. Your child will have an even greater need for your help, support, guidance. He may be very uneasy about the reactions of his friends and their parents.
4. Above all, don't cut your child off the way Ariel's parents did. The child you can't talk to is a child you cannot help.

TO SUMMARIZE:

Each of the academic problems I've mentioned may require more than one type of approach. It is possible that you will be dealing with academic and school-related difficulties for years. Just when things calm down, a changed situation at school—new subject matter, new teacher, realignment of friends, extracurricular competition—may spark new crises.

As with other problems during the teen years, you get nowhere until you learn how to gain your child's cooperation—and that may not happen overnight. With my Caring Response, you can keep trying, trying, trying. But remember that your goal is not to make your child over into some ideal scholar or control his development: instead, you want to help him learn to take full responsibility for his studies and learn to accept the consequences of his study habits. In the long run, the kid who is motivated to earn a B is much better off than the kid forced to pull down an A.

SEVEN

"*This* Time I'm Telling the Truth"

KID: "Why don't you believe me?"

DAD: "I keep catching you in lies."

KID: "That's because you don't trust me."

DAD: "I think you've got it backward."

KID: "Anyway, this time I'm telling the truth. I swear."

DAD: "That's what you said the last time."

KID: "This time is different."

DAD: "How do I know that?"

KID: "Because I promise."

DAD: "That's not enough. I don't believe you."

KID: "Nobody believes me anymore!"

DAD: "That's the truth."

"My father owns a Cadillac; it's much nicer than your car."

"I'm getting all A's at school."

"I've finished cleaning the kitchen."

"My mother's giving me a fur coat for Christmas."

"I'm going to the mall with Jane."

These lies, and many more, had one source in our house: fourteen-year-old, freckle-faced Susanne. Her father, an unemployed alcoholic, hadn't owned any kind of car in years. Her mother never even called her, much less sent presents, even on her birthday. She was failing everything but art and gym; she always left the kitchen with piles of dirty dishes in the sink and half-empty milk bottles on the table. True, she was going to the mall with Jane, but also with John and Harry, two boys she had been forbidden to see.

Susanne lied to keep out of trouble, to make herself feel better, to avoid work. Sometimes, I swear, she lied just to keep in practice.

Actually, Susanne's habitual lying made life easy. I was never confused, never uncertain, never taken in. Whatever she said was likely to be a lie. With the other kids, it was harder. Each one lied at least once about an important matter; some lied occasionally. When could we trust them?

Like most adults, you probably regard lies as a serious breach of trust. It can be devastating when your child lies; worse when she sticks to her lie.

I don't condone lying, and it hurts me, too, but I have learned that lying is as much a part of adolescence as the growth spurt. Parents in my Parent Tactics workshop have all caught their kids lying. When I informally polled friends, students, and academic colleagues, all admitted that they lied as teenagers and have caught their own adolescents in lies. My Zach was scrupulous about telling the truth when he was a little kid, even in the smallest matter. In adolescence, he whipped out a forked tongue on more than one occasion. Dan, the soul of honesty at ten, learned to stretch and hide the truth at twelve.

A cynic might say that learning to lie is an important adult survival skill. I don't want to agree, but I do think we have to keep our kids' lies in perspective. Have they heard us tell socially useful "white lies"? Have they heard Uncle Don brag about his inflated tax deductions?

A Lie Defined

Not every untruth is a lie.

Susanne's father never owned a Cadillac, but when he once had a job as a chauffeur, he did drive Cadillac limousines. Was she just remembering things the way she wished they'd been? When we believe our own distortions, we are not lying, except to ourselves.

The fur coat from Mom and the straight-A report card were pure fantasy, but Susanne was denying reality, hoping for the best, in an act of self-delusion. Not lying.

The kitchen? Well, she did spend a good hour fussing around and it did become somewhat cleaner.

But the trip to the mall involved a lie of omission, a clear intent to deceive me about the two boys. When dealing with kids, that became my simple definition of a lie: the intent to deceive.

Lies of omission are the most common teenage lies. Many Gotcha Wars blaze up when a youngster leaves out an important fact, but she will tell herself that leaving something out is not really lying. She answers truthfully, but only what you ask. In a way, this kind of lying-by-omission is a sign of an active conscience.

When to Worry

Don't go looking for problems. If you have no solid reason to think otherwise, assume that your child is telling the truth. In slightly suspicious situations, give him the benefit of the doubt. If he has a major problem with lying, you will find out soon enough.

Before making a case, consider your family's norm for lying. Many families accept "white lies." I don't, but I understand that most of my friends and relatives find me nutty on the subject. But my reputation for punctilious honesty gave me the moral authority to call a youngster on a white lie. It's not that I was deeply worried by that kind of fibbing. I just wanted to keep our sights on the truth as an ideal goal.

If white lies are considered okay in your house, you have no reason to be concerned when your kid tells one. But if you catch him in a serious lie, it's time to worry—yes, even one serious lie is a danger signal. Why? Consider why he lied. He had to cover up a wrongdoing or a problem. Whatever, it was something so troubling he could not tell you the truth.

Don't blow up yet, though. Try to get to the bottom of the lie and the behavior it hides, then back off. Wait, with wary eye. If your kid doesn't come up with another serious lie in the next month, relax. But if there's a disturbingly serious whopper within the next thirty days or so. . . .

Lie Busting

First, be sure you understand your own behavior and expectations in regard to lying. Let's run through my preliminary checklist:

1. **Are your rules reasonable? Have you explained them adequately?** If there are too many rules or they seem unreasonable, adolescents will bend the truth a little, then more and more. David and I based all of our rules on only three basic premises: nothing illegal, nothing dangerous, nothing that seriously infringes upon the rights of someone else. (Of course, we and our foster children did not always agree on the exact definitions of these concepts, but they gave us a framework.)

What is dangerous? Some parents ban skateboarding but permit football or downhill skiing. Some forbid football but hand over the keys to the Trans-Am. These rules don't make sense to me, so I won't let my kids drive a sports car but do let them dive and ski. That is, I'm just as inconsistent as any other parent, but my children have no excuse for misunderstanding my cock-eyed rules.

The issue of rights is equally muddy. At one extreme, some parents believe that they have the right to control everything a kid does. At the other, some teenagers think that it is their right to do anything they want. You will find reasonableness somewhere between these two extremes.

2. **Are your rules consistent with the rules set down by other families in your community?** Many foster children came to us because of conflicts that arose when their foreign-born parents tried to impose the behavioral standards of more traditional societies. One Greek-American girl had run away from home because her mother insisted upon walking her to school, meeting her at lunchtime, and walking her back home at the end of the school day. She felt suffocated and ridiculous in the eyes of her classmates.

3. **Generally speaking, the fewer rules the better.** Our house rules in our foster-parenting years barely filled one typed, double-spaced page posted on the refrigerator door.

4. **Rules should be enforceable.** Cursing, obscenities, name-calling, and verbal threats were all proscribed in our house as "offensive language." The ugliness infringes on my rights to a pleasant home environment; the hostility leads to fights. Yet I well knew that this proscription was enforceable only in my presence, a fact that I incorporated into my rule.

"How your friends let you talk to them is beyond my control, but in my presence I expect you to respect these rules," I explained. The kids understood the boundaries and obeyed the rule.

5. Involve your child in making up the rules. What does she think is reasonable? Negotiate, and bend when possible, but hold firm on anything illegal. The drinking age is twenty-one by law, and that law should always be obeyed on your premises. Don't be wheedled, and don't be flummoxed by the argument that "grown-ups do it." The best approach is the one your parents probably used: "Yes, some laws don't make sense; still, they have to be obeyed." A clever kid can argue rings around this logic, but don't let that faze you.

How Strict?

Here's the motto that applies: Be hard on the behavior, soft on the person.

In fact, too much strictness almost forces a kid to lie. When you review your rules, review your punishments, too. Check with friends, a guidance counselor, or a parent educator to see what they think. If a parent tells me he grounds his kid two weeks for being five minutes late, I warn him that he's being excessively strict. He's practically terrifying his child into lying, to cover up a minor mistake.

If your rules and your punishments are not overly strict but your child still lies, find out what he's covering up—then deal with the wrongdoing.

Treat the lie itself as a separate problem.

For one thing, your child has to learn that lying produces its own consequences. Lie often enough, and no one believes a word you say.

To make the point, don't automatically brand your kid a liar after his first serious lie. Instead, issue a warning. Point out that trust is precious, trust is fragile, and a single lie can weaken it forever.

With my foster kids, I said something like this after the first lie:

"I want to believe you, Susanne. I want to know that if I have to defend you from someone else's lies you really are an honest person. But when you lie to me, you make me doubt you. Please don't lie to me again."

After the next time:

"Susanne, this is the second time you have lied to me, as far as I know. You are making it very hard for me to believe you. One more lie, and the trust I thought we had is going to be broken."

After the third lie, trust indeed was destroyed. I never believed the child again. I always asked for proof.

"You've lied to me before, so I can't believe anything you say. If you're really going to the movies, as you say you are, bring me ticket stubs when you get back."

This approach drove some of my confirmed liars absolutely crazy.

"But, Kathy," they'd wail. "I'm not lying now!"

Probably not, but I held my ground. Even when I suspected that the habitual liar was telling the truth, I insisted on proof. Eventually, they understood the seriousness of lying, and the tide turned.

When they were ready to reform, we negotiated a return to trust. They had to promise to tell the truth, the whole truth, and nothing but. When tempted to lie, they had to learn to say "I wish" or "I think."

For my part, I devised a three-point strategy. First, I took care to praise any reformed liar for telling the truth when a lie would have kept him out of trouble. Second, I reduced the consequences for wrongdoing that was honestly confessed. Finally, I agreed to become a trusting believer again, if he could go for thirty days without lying.

Despite many setbacks, this strategy eventually worked even with Susanne. She didn't become the George Washington of the Parson Weems stories, but she lied much less. With the right reinforcement, she may someday learn not to lie at all.

Tiny lies or big whoppers, a spate of lying indicates that the child you care about has emotional problems. Someone like Susanne probably needed more help than I could give her at the time; constant liars should receive professional counseling. Your child's lying, though not pathological, has to be analyzed in the context of whatever problem she's hiding.

TO SUMMARIZE:

Don't get yourself alarmed about lying unless, and until, you catch your child in a lie. (And don't go looking, Sherlock.)

Take the first serious lie as an opportunity to reinforce the value of telling the truth.

If the lying continues, concentrate on finding the underlying cause.

That is, worry about the behavior that your child is covering up with his lies.

Deal with that behavior.

Note well: Perhaps the hardest part of this chapter is the advice to explore and analyze your own attitude toward lying. Most of us don't stop to think about it. Be brutally honest with yourself before deciding how to judge your kid's tendency to rubberize the truth.

How do you handle getting caught in a lie . . . and your kid is watching? What is your justification, and is it any better than the one he used just the other day for his own fib?

Whatever your standards may be, you should define them as clearly as possible—to yourself and to your children—and then share the pain of trying to live up to them.

Now let's look at some of the problems that lying was invented to conceal.

EIGHT

Risky Business

MOM: "It must have been someone else. You couldn't have seen my kid doing sixty on a motorcycle. She's afraid of those things. And she's always so careful."

NEIGHBOR: (helpfully) "It was Kelly, all right. Besides, she wasn't driving. She was hanging on to one of those leather boys from down on the avenue."

MOM: "What? Kelly hasn't even started dating yet."

NEIGHBOR: "Yeah, my daughter said you didn't know about it. She's afraid you might find out about the boy's reputation."

MOM: "What?"

NEIGHBOR: "Anyway, Kelly only met him a couple of months ago when he was transferred back into the regular high school."

MOM: "What?"

NEIGHBOR: "He hadn't done anything really bad. It's just that the police keep catching him riding without a helmet."

MOM: "Oh."

NEIGHBOR: "And speeding, of course."

MOM: "Oh."

NEIGHBOR: "He's probably a pretty nice kid. Just a little bit accident prone, I hear."

Our children are born to take us where we fear to go. But when your child does dangerous things as a way of life, you are right to worry.

Seth, the Luger

Beanpole Seth, a thirteen-year-old neighbor kid who always wore thick, horn-rimmed glasses, seemed like the local bookworm to me—until the day I was jogging up a winding hilly road nearby and saw Seth suddenly hurtle into view, bellyflopping downhill on a skateboard beside cars and trucks that roared by, missing him by inches. His face was a mere eight inches from a hard, gravelly road.

At dinner that night, my kids explained that Seth was "luging," using his skateboard like the one-man sleds used on bobsled runs. The more daring the kid, the more congested and winding the road. And yes, both my boys had tried this "sport." (After all, I hadn't forbidden it—since I didn't know it even existed!)

Seth's mother had refused to let him have a skateboard at all, an edict he found unreasonable. He wasn't a bad kid; he just felt that she didn't know what she was talking about. He saved his money from odd jobs and his allowance, bought his own board, and kept it carefully hidden. In a sense, his mother's overprotectiveness gave him an excuse to go whole hog. Not just a casual skateboarder, Seth became the most daring "luger" in the area.

Recently, I read an article about a dangerous practice that is popular among the poor of many Central and South American countries. "Train surfing" involves riding on the tops of train cars as you would a surfboard.

Once again, my boys piped up cheerfully.

"Oh, yeah, we used to do that a lot," said Zach. "It's fun. One day Joe hopped a train planning to surf to the next town and ended up on an express that didn't stop till it like got to Grand Central. He holds the surfing record for the whole school."

Listen to dumb me: "Well, I guess that taught him a lesson."

"Yeah. He learned how to read the train schedule."

"Zach, for the record. Do you still train surf?"

"Of course not."

Thank goodness, I thought.

"I've got my driver's license now."

Oh.

Driving on the Wild Side

When my boys were kids, they enthusiastically echoed our little safety mottos when we drove. "Speed kills," they chirped with conviction. "Fifty-five, stay alive."

Then Zach got his license.

"I've driven over ninety miles an hour," he recently confessed, or boasted.

"But not in this car," I retorted. One of my feeble strategies for dealing with the speeding problem is to refuse to buy a high-powered car.

"But I have friends with more powerful cars."

Indeed, and forbidding him to ride with those friends is a rule I can't enforce.

So, like you, when the phone rings late at night and Zach isn't home yet, I'm terrified until I find out that everything is okay.

Are you feeling relieved because your kid is a girl and thinks that driving more than thirty miles an hour will muss her hair? After all, statistics show that teenage girls are much less likely to drive recklessly than boys are.

Reconsider. Girls have found their own characteristic ways of flirting with danger that can cripple, ruin, or end a life.

How Girls Take Risks

Generally speaking, your daughter will take risks of two basic sorts. She'll go where she shouldn't. She'll get involved with people you don't like.

Sweet fifteen-year-old Cherise had the bluest eyes I've ever seen outside a Paul Newman movie. Her parents recognized her dangerous blend of beauty and innocence; they declared off-limits a bowling alley next to a bar where toughs hang out. But since her friends went there, she dismissed her parents' fears as foolish.

As she was bowling one night, a handsome college student began flirting. After a game she lost badly, his offer of a walk outside in the warm summer evening sounded like a good idea. Although Cherise would never get into a car with a stranger, this young man was educated, clean-cut, and charming. The nearby park had well-lighted pathways for a stroll beneath the trees.

After a while, they moved off into the moonlight. Cherise enjoyed holding hands with this older boy and didn't object to a gentle kiss. When the kiss went farther than she wanted, though, she was unable to break away. As she struggled, the nice college student slapped her across the face a few times and knocked her to the ground. At just that point, fortunately, another couple came into view, and Cherise was able to break free and run for help. Otherwise, she probably would have been raped.

She had taken both of the typical risks for teenage girls: walking dangerous streets; befriending a potentially dangerous stranger.

And don't forget that some girls do emulate the boys. There was at least one girl in the gang that went luging with Seth. Zach claims, with convincing envy, that he knows girls who will drive faster than he dares.

Damage Control

What can you do to protect your children from taking dangerous risks? Not a heck of a lot, frankly. The state frowns on the practice of tying kids to bedposts.

Even the police can't prevent children from endangering themselves. Near our house, there's a dangerous, water-filled quarry. It's illegal to swim there, but kids sneak in rather than swim in their parents' pools or at nearby Long Island Sound. Increased police surveillance only adds to the adventure. The kids always figure out when they can swim and dive into the boulder-filled pool without being hassled by the cops.

If these urges are normal in adolescence, if you have limited control over your teenagers, how do you keep sane?

First, be neither Nervous Nelly nor Cautious Charlie. Curb your natural tendency to issue warnings on all occasions. They backfire. You lose credibility by worrying too much. When Seth discovered that skateboarding was not as life-threatening as his mother feared, he started taking her less seriously. He began to try other forbidden things.

Wise parents tone down warnings.

Second, channel your child's lust for danger into the safest possible path. Seth's mother should have permitted skateboarding while insisting on reasonable safety measures. As it happened, she would inadvertently make a bad situation even more dangerous. She heard about the luging, found the skateboard, and donated it to the Salvation Army. Her son, enraged at what he saw as a trampling of his rights, saved his money again and bought a new one. His mother's act had taught him to hide it more skillfully and to keep a low profile by luging only at night. And he did not wear reflective tape.

Third, it would help—if it's not too late—to encourage your children to participate in rough-and-tumble activities in their childhood years. A painful bellyflop at the local Y might teach a boy how to gauge the dangers of diving into a rock quarry. Hitting his head when he falls off his tricycle might (and I do say, "might") help him understand that he should wear a helmet when he takes up motorcycles. The kid who gets his ideas about physical invulnerability from action movies and TV is asking for trouble. Younger children are more likely to listen to your warnings than adolescents and perhaps internalize the basic message. Adolescents, of course, are going to live forever.

Coping with Invulnerability

If your thrill-seeker won't listen to you, she can be exposed to professional instruction. You probably can't explain precisely why oversteering is dangerous in certain situations, or exactly when speed kills, but the expert can.

Taught to drag-race, do wheelies, and shimmy-the-chassis by my first steady boyfriend, the hood on parole, I turned a deaf ear to my parents' warnings about my exuberant driving. They couldn't possibly know as much as my Hot Rod Lover. The only thing I recall about my father's instructions was his occasional gasp of fear. To this day, however, I remember three safety rules drummed into me by Mr. Flagg, the high school driver's ed teacher. I can parallel park with one hand on the wheel because I listened to him.

As a parent, you've taught your children many things. When they become adolescents, you have to let someone else teach them.

Still, you have control in other areas. I think you'd be crazy to give your teenager a car that can go from 0 to 70 in three seconds or cruise comfortably at speeds of 90, 100, or 120. Did you give him a loaded .45 when he was five years old?

If I ruled the world, no car would be built to go faster than eighty miles an hour—or perhaps fifty-five, come to think of it. This past year alone, three teenagers in our small town have been killed in automobile accidents that involved high speeds. My heart goes out to their parents, but I think they were foolish to give their kids fancy sports cars and high-powered behemoths. I'd also restrict access to motorcycles and power boats.

Sure, as I've admitted, these strategies haven't kept my sons from taking risks. But that's no reason for us to give up trying. Taking preventive steps will at least give you some peace of mind. You'll know that you've done your best.

Risk Practice

As with fast cars and risky sports, so too with dangerous places and dangerous friends: Permitting some early exploration can allow room for minor mishaps. Your kid learns for herself how to deal with each of the dangers.

When I was thirteen, my parents allowed me to walk home alone from the movies for the first time, provided I take the long, safe way to our house. Naturally, I cut through the dark alley that had been expressly forbidden. Suddenly, there were footsteps behind me. I ran out of there as fast as I could. Mugger, rapist, neighbor taking a shortcut? I don't know. I do know that that was the last time I ever walked through that or any other alley by myself.

Like mother, like son. At ten, Daniel became entranced with a gang of young toughs I didn't like. One had a well-deserved rep for bullying other kids. Despite my warnings, my son simply could not stay away. Within weeks, the bully hit a friend of Danny's. That made him feel uncomfortable, but the attraction was still strong. After about three months, the bully bullied Daniel, and that ended his walk with the wild bunch. Better that he learn from a few rough shoves then, than have a fatal attraction in the teen years for a gang armed with knives and pistols.

Conclusion: The more your child can experience while under your wing, the better for her future ability to handle risks on her own. You have to try to let go of some of your fears as soon as possible.

How to Respond

Ultimately, life teaches teenagers caution. How should you respond while this educational process is going forward?

Consider that one of three things is likely to happen when your good kid indulges in a really dangerous practice: she will get away with it; she will get hurt; or she will break the law and get caught.

In the first case, there is little you can do. You can't punish for something you don't know about. And it's not sensible, it seems to me, to jump to conclusions on the basis of rumor. Some parents do, but I try to shine off the rumor and act mildly. I point out that rumors seem to be flying thick and fast, and I hope they're powered by nothing but hot air. Don't let rumors add to your worryin' pile. Limit your worries to what you know; don't include what others think they know.

In the second case, the hurt is usually punishment enough. Don't try to add to it. The greater the hurt, the more the child needs comforting—not a lecture. It is important to learn that life is full of hurts. We learn that lesson by being hurt.

In the third case, when your child gets caught breaking the law, you must not make the serious mistake of stepping in and getting him off the hook. I may not be able to keep Zach from riding with reckless friends or breaking the speed limit himself, when I'm not around. But I can certainly refuse to pay any speeding ticket he might get. And I can keep the car keys in my own pocket for a long time after that.

Deadly Habits

A few kids don't just flirt with danger; they become addicted.

You need to worry about two possible problems: an addiction to dangerous habits; or the appearance of any dangerous habits that are emotionally based or self-destructive.

The addiction begins because dangerous practices set the adrenaline surging to new highs. Or because a kid gets to like the rush of relief that comes after surviving a dangerous activity. These addictions can become as tenacious as a drug habit. In much the same way, they require increasingly stronger doses of the addictive behavior, ever more dangerous risk-taking.

If you think your child may have this problem, turn to Chapter 12 on drug use. If you think counseling is required, begin with the drug rehabilitation people, but it may take some searching to find someone who really understands the psychological addiction of danger.

Self-Destruction

From the time they learn to walk, some kids swing from the rooftops, while others swing only in a hammock . . . very slowly.

The roof-swinger is a potential danger addict of the self-destructive stripe. He is likely to be known as "accident prone." John, a friend's son, is a charter member of the broken-bone-of-the-month club, but the emotional cause is painfully clear, in his case. An alcoholic father abandoned the family. The boy needs help, and the "accidents" are pleas for the love his father will not give.

When is your child's accident rate a sign of trouble? Well, for a rough comparison, take my son Danny, who might be characterized as a swinger from first floors. In the past two years, he's cracked an ankle in soccer practice, jammed a thumb while roughhousing, and dislocated a finger in gym. He's certainly no hammock-swinger, but these injuries don't seem excessive for an active teenager made of flesh and bone.

In the same period, John has racked up a broken wrist, broken ankle, torn knee ligament, broken rib that punctured a lung, and two concussions. He spent eight weeks in a back brace and requires stitches almost every month. I dread the thought of his driving. His mother thinks her son is just clumsy. I think she is dangerously mistaken.

Are you living with Dashing Danny, or with Jeopardy John?

Here's a kind of baseline: if your kid has three accidents that require stitches or a day or two of bed rest within a six-month period, you may need help.

Talk to your child's physician, coach, or guidance counselor. Consider getting an evaluation from a psychiatrist or psychologist. Read Chapter 16. And disregard my usual warning about overreacting: in this case, it is better to risk being Nervous Nellie or Cautious Charlie. Your fears could help save your child's life.

Hope and Pray

You cannot prevent the inevitable: at some point, almost all adolescents will try something that is foolishly dangerous. By some miracle, most will escape unscathed. With luck, most will also be chastened by the brush with injury or death.

(Do you dare confess to your child the most dangerous risk you ever took as a teenager?)

For much of the time, all you can do is pray, if you believe in the power of prayer. Or hope, if you do not. Such prayers and hopes must not go unanswered, because practically all adolescents eventually become adults, who then learn to worry about their own children.

We are right to worry about dangerous practices. But when we have done our best, we are also right to recognize that the odds are with us and our children.

NINE

Liaisons—Dangerous and Otherwise

BOY: "Why the f__k do I get the heat? She wanted to get laid, too."

GIRL: "I did it because he said he loved me."

BOY: "Right. She knew I was just talking."

GIRL: "I was in love with him. I wasn't thinking about gross things like condoms and all."

BOY: "This is the nineties, okay? She ought to know how to take care of herself. What am I supposed to do, give her the third degree about her period?"

GIRL: "Anyway, we just did it a couple of times. It's not as if we planned to. We just got carried away."

BOY: "Yeah, that's right. We just did the natural."

GIRL: "I mean, it's real weird, getting all that stuff together before you go out on a date. I don't like thinking about it."

BOY: "Yeah. And I know she's clean. I mean, you depend on nice girls to take care of themselves."

GIRL: "And he knows a way, you know, so that you don't get in trouble."

BOY: "Yeah."

GIRL: "You depend on boys to know these things."

When it comes to the earth-moving power of sex, your power as a parent is inherently fragile. Consider, if you will, selected scenes from your own adolescence.

For David and me, the foster-child years brought the virginal, the nonvirginal, and the promiscuous. Much of our vigilance was devoted to preventing sexually active teenagers from making babies or acquiring sexually transmitted diseases. After only two months of this intense worrying, however, we learned the first of many, many lessons about the limits of our control.

It Only Takes a Minute

Blond, beautiful Michelle, fourteen, was our teacher. Shoo-in for the Levine Spoiled Brat of the Year Award, she was self-centered, boring, hypercritical, and obsessed with her looks. Imagine the young Marilyn Monroe with the handicap of growing up rich and pampered. She was not easy to like.

Nevertheless, as you might expect, the boys in the house forgave her personality flaws. Though she seemed indifferent and nattered on incessantly about her mature boyfriends, they did not give up the chase.

One day, I made a surprising discovery. The house was sparkling and the kids were on their best behavior for our annual Levine Open House, attended by lots of social workers, community people, and officials. In the midst of the festivities, Michelle suddenly came over and nervously pulled me aside.

"Kathy, you have to get me an appointment with Planned Parenthood. You have to do it right now."

"Good grief, Michelle, there are fifty people crawling all over the house and garden. If you're pregnant, why didn't you tell me yesterday or the day before? Why right now? You're just going to have to wait. I'll make a doctor's appointment tomorrow."

"You don't understand, Kathy. Sammy and I just had sex. Now I feel sick, and I'm sure I'm pregnant. I want an abortion, and I want it today."

With more than a hint of exasperation, I replied, "Michelle, you and Sammy were helping in the kitchen only five minutes ago. And now you tell me you just had sex?"

"Do you think I'd lie about this? We went into the pantry and did it standing up. It never takes more than a few minutes, you know. We stood against the door so no one could come in. Now I feel sick to my stomach, and I better get a test right away, or I'll tell all these people what happened."

The blackmail didn't work. I convinced Michelle that the feeling in her stomach probably came from an overdose of chocolate cake and soda. As it turned out, she wasn't pregnant, although she was inspired to go to Planned Parenthood and get herself some birth control pills.

But the important lesson for the Levines was that scene in the pantry. Lesson One: "It" only takes a minute. Parents who think they know where their kids are and what their kids are doing should probably think again. Your watchfulness cannot ensure pregnancy prevention.

Now, more than ever, the facts of life are linked with a fact of parental life: your control is limited and is, in some areas, nonexistent. You might be able to influence your child's decisions about things sexual, but you cannot reasonably hope for more than influence.

Was life really easier, once upon a time? That's the myth, at any rate. Sex education, especially for girls, could be summed up in one word: Don't. Boys were supposed to try; girls earned respect by saying no. Then, according to the myth, everything changed, and virginity became an embarrassing burden, to be shed as soon as possible. Suddenly, the girl who said no was suspect. To some, it looked as if boys were the real winners in this reversal of values and girls were exploited, but the sexual freedom of the sixties, seventies, and eighties was not always completely copacetic for boys, either.

Fathers Don't Always Know Best

Kelvin, with his red hair, freckles, and snub nose, looked like the kind of kid who gets caught stealing apples in a Walt Disney movie—mischievous, but good as gold. When he asked to speak to me privately one night, however, I learned that he'd been tasting another kind of forbidden fruit. His thirteen-year-old girlfriend had just told him she thought she was pregnant, and I was about to learn another lesson: new meanings of the old Double Standard.

"What do I do?" he stammered, unwittingly asking a question guaranteed to irk any woman.

"You do nothing," I snapped, "except help your girlfriend decide what she wants to do."

"But she wants an abortion," he whined. "In fact, she says she's getting an abortion no matter what I want. But abortion's murder. It's a sin."

"Kelvin, not everyone would agree that an abortion is murder, but you don't have a say in this. It is up to her." His eyes widened as if I had begun to molt. "Nature set it up that way. The baby is in her body, not yours."

"It's not fair," he said finally, and he stomped out of the room.

Thus was opened the door to many heated discussions in our household. Boys and girls alike had strong and diverse opinions about boys' sexual responsibilities. Some of my foster sons would say, "It's her problem," if a girlfriend's period was late. Some would affect indifference: "It's probably not my baby." But the majority worried just as much as their partners did about the possibility of pregnancy.

Just worrying, though, was not enough, in my view. The boy ought to be willing to do something about the problem. That became one of my criteria for helping a youngster decide whether or not he was ready to become sexually active. Here's how I put it:

"Most teenagers get more pain than pleasure from sex. Don't laugh. Just look around you. But if you really think you are old enough to have sex, I think you ought to prove it—I mean, get birth control, and use it!"

Personally, I don't think the majority of teenagers are mature enough to handle sexual intimacy and its consequences. Certainly Kelvin and his girlfriend weren't, although he gradually learned to face the reality of his personal situation. For the record, he came to understand that he had to become sexually responsible if he didn't want to be partner to an abortion. He decided that obeying the dictates of his religious belief probably meant that he had to abstain from sex before marriage.

Most of my foster kids were not eager to choose that option. And I myself do not believe that sex, however immaturely handled, is bad. Having sex is not on my list of the bad things good kids do, unless it is irresponsible sex.

Double Messages

For some people, "irresponsible sex" is defined as "sex before marriage."

To me, there are other definitions:

• Just letting sex happen, rather than consciously making the choice to become sexually active.
• Not using birth control, when you cannot support and do not want a baby.
• Neglecting to protect yourself from disease.
• Exploiting someone else.

If you're a parent who believes premarital sex is wrong, some of the advice that follows will still be helpful to you. I support your right to your values. But in a society that constantly advertises the glories of sex, an excessive emphasis on chastity may create more problems than it prevents.

Here's the double message: the ads promote sexual bliss; family and authority figures promote chastity. Confused, teenagers do not make a conscious choice to have sex. Kelvin and his girl, for example, considered sex "bad," so they were not prepared. After five months of steady dating, the afternoon came when they became "carried away" in their lovemaking. Remorseful afterward, they vowed never to do "it" again. But the girl was not a virgin and a restraint had been removed. The next time was easier, and the next, and the next.

The excuse of being swept away, however legitimate, eases a teenager's guilt about wanting to do the forbidden. It does not allow time for responsible preparations for sex. Like many adolescent boys, Kelvin let desire suppress conscience. He was not purposely exploiting his girlfriend. For girls, too, getting carried away wipes out individual responsibility. Harvard's Jerome Kagan believes that this kind of thinking is part of the cultural landscape: "Americans believe that being overwhelmed by a feeling justifies whatever actions flow from that feeling."

At least Kelvin really did care about his girlfriend. He was able to learn responsibility. Far too many adolescent boys cannot see farther than the double standard that is as alive and destructive today as it was when I was growing up.

Double Standard, Double Bind

Clarissa's parents were sure they were doing the right thing. Because both had had positive sexual experiences before their marriage, they talked carefully with their daughter about responsible sex. At thirteen, she felt good about herself, comfortable with her body and its changes. She decided then that she would be like the heroine of Judy Blume's novel, *Forever:* Sure, she'd have sex before marriage, but she'd be in love, she'd be protected, she'd be smart.

At fifteen, when her gynecologist referred her to me for counseling, Clarissa was severely depressed. Three months before, she had had an abortion. The teenage father, Eric, no longer found her as desirable as when she had refused to sleep with him. When she walked into my office, every aspect of Clarissa seemed downcast: shoulders sagged, mouth drooped, eyes constantly filled with tears.

"I dream night and day about my baby, about the baby I murdered," she finally managed to say. "Mom and Dad have been super, Mom tells me over and over that I didn't really murder a baby, but I keep thinking about what might have been—and I can't get rid of that thought. I could be having a baby in another couple of months. I even dream I'm still pregnant. . . . I wish I had it to do all over again."

"What would you do differently?" I asked softly.

For a brief moment, anger flashed through the misery in her eyes. "I'd say no. No sex until I'm ready to have a baby. And if the boy can't wait, then goodbye, boy!"

Her story was not remarkable. She and Eric, seventeen, had dated for six months, gradually growing closer emotionally and physically. When he gave her his class ring, she decided to implement the plan she made at thirteen, but her gynecologist could not schedule her right away. One night, when waiting proved too much, knowledgeable Clarissa and her first serious boyfriend made love—with great passion, without protection.

They slept together three more times, using condoms. Clarissa was ecstatically happy, but Eric suddenly announced that they were getting too deeply involved. He wanted to date other people. In fact, he had been dating someone else all along. They were "going steady" when Clarissa discovered she was pregnant. She never told Eric about their baby.

Today, after dealing with her grief for the baby, her own loss of innocence, and the devastating blow to her faith in all-consuming romantic love, Clarissa is doing just fine. She has decided for herself that the abortion was not an act of murder. She was also helped by writing a letter to Eric, following my advice, that calmly and clearly held him accountable for behavior that was sexually irresponsible, emotionally abusive, and exploitative. (What effect that letter had on Eric remains unknown; Clarissa was the third girl he jilted after a few months of romance led to intercourse.)

Even the Erics of the world, of course, are being influenced today by the advent of AIDS. In most middle-class communities, teenagers agree that condoms are "in." At one suburban high school, a clique of fifteen-year-olds celebrates birthdays by giving the honoree a year's supply of condoms. But you can't rely on adolescent fear of AIDS to ensure that your child protects herself in every sexual encounter. She's immortal, remember, and passion is an excuse for almost anything.

What Parents Can Do

Define your goal.

Decide how you hope to achieve it.

For example, do you want your son to remain virginal until marriage? Despite the permissive sexual attitudes that seem prevalent in our society, you can be successful.

Look at how some fundamentalist religious sects manage to keep their children chaste. They create an environment in which all adults agree to teach their kids that intercourse is a holy act permissible only when sanctioned by marriage. Generally, they keep boys and girls segregated and busy, but also provide safe forms of physical release. Hassidic Jews practice lots of unisex dancing that is both physically fulfilling and spiritually uplifting. Such activity can redirect sex drives and encourage chastity, and children will feel a strong satisfaction in doing only what family, friends, and the group's leaders view as good and right.

Finally, by promoting early marriage, many sects help bring biological clocks and community standards of chastity into greater harmony. In most parts of the world today, as in our own recent past, marriage in the mid-teens is a fact of life. If you are determined that your child remain chaste before marriage, your goal is more easily attainable if you encourage him to marry early, perhaps immediately after high school graduation. If you and he agree on that limitation years before, he too has a definable goal for himself—a reinforcement of his resolve.

Most parents today, however, are less concerned about chastity than about delaying a child's entry into adult sexuality.

This goal is reasonable and usually obtainable, in my experience. You make certain that you keep track of your kid's comings and goings. You do not allow her to spend a lot of unchaperoned time on her own with a boy, even if you like and trust him. As a kind of preemptive strike, you discourage early dating. Instead, encourage her to develop a lot of different interests, including some strenuous physical activities. If you follow these guidelines—and talk frankly with your child about sex and sexual responsibility—you are doing about all you can to prevent her from becoming entangled too early in the demands and confusions of adult sexuality.

Sex Talk

Another invaluable lesson from my foster kids: They forced David and me to talk about sex with our sons long before we would have otherwise. They also helped me become comfortable asking and answering questions about sex. They helped me define my ideas and learn how to make my opinions known.

All of this took time to learn, despite the eagerness of my teenage teachers, so be patient with yourself. Few parents find birds-and-bees discussions easy, but open talk about sexual responsibility is the necessary prerequisite to preventing early intercourse. It's the only way you can begin to discharge your responsibility for your child's sexual education.

Teenagers, too, are uncomfortable in these discussions. Why? One reason, not generally acknowledged, is that talking about sex arouses sexual feelings. For many lovers, of course, sex talk is the beginning of foreplay. A kid just beginning to burst with all sorts of sexual feelings will be embarrassed as those feelings arise during a talk with his parents.

Another problem is the hidden suggestion, when parents bring up the subject of sex, that it is now time for the kid to become sexually active. How's this for a mixed message:

"I want you to know about birth control, son, but I expect you not to act on that knowledge."

This problem cannot be avoided. If you want your child to be sexually responsible, you have to bite the bullet and share sexual knowledge with a person who is capable of adult sexuality.

If you have been avoiding this subject, today is the day to change your ways—with due and appropriate speed. Resolve to have a heart-to-heart with your teenager before this time next week. Even if you talked to your good kid in her early teens, it won't hurt to have a review session.

Let me give you a game plan for first-time sex talks.

Casually, join your kid when he's watching an episode of a TV situation comedy that features teenagers and their problems—"Who's the Boss?," "The Cosby Show," "Roseanne," "My Two Dads." Chances are, a plot twist or some of the jokes can be used as a springboard for discussing sexual responsibility. The next day, bring up the show when your kid comes home from school, get his reaction, and initiate a discussion about the implications for his sexual behavior.

If you have a VCR, rent a teen-oriented movie like *The Sure Thing, Footloose, The Breakfast Club,* or *Risky Business.* This week, watch it on your own. Then, develop your script. What message do you want to get across? What is the single most important thing your child should know about your thoughts on sexual responsibility? (For example, the first message I tried to convey was that there is such a thing as responsible sex.) Next week, get your kid to watch with you.

You will find your own themes, but let me suggest a couple of approaches. *Footloose,* for example, is good for discussing your fears as a parent, if you hope that your kid will remain chaste until marriage. If you believe your teenager is sexually active, or if you don't object to premarital sex, *The Sure Thing* is more to the point.

Here's what I said to a foster child after we watched *Footloose* together:

"Those parents are worried about their children going too far. All parents worry about that, because we don't like to see our kids get hurt. How you decide when to have sex is your business, but I'd like you to know what I think about such things. I want you to know, most of all, that there is such a thing as sexual responsibility."

Or, after watching *The Sure Thing* with a kid:

"That movie was a lesson in sexual responsibility. I don't know if I've ever told you directly what I think responsible sex is. Give me just five minutes, and I can explain. It's a simple idea, but it may be the most important thing for you to learn right now."

With these kinds of introductions, well begun is half done, but be prepared ahead of time with the rest of your script. Here's how mine went, but yours will be the product of your own beliefs and goals:

"I hope you will always be sexually responsible. I mean, you won't ever let yourself just get swept away. . . . . You'll choose to be sexually active. You'll give the matter some thought ahead of time. And you should also use birth control and protect yourself from disease. If you can't do that, you haven't thought enough about getting ready to have sex. Finally, you'll try not to hurt or exploit your partner.

"I also think that the longer you wait to have sex, the more likely it is that you will be able to behave in a responsible manner. In the meantime, you can learn a lot about sex by exploring your body yourself, as well as by necking or petting. That way, you'll be more prepared for adult sex and a better partner in the long run."

Oh, yes. I do suggest masturbation as an intermediate step to intercourse. Girls, especially, need to hear this message. Unlike boys, they do not have a lot of peer permission to masturbate. You may be uneasy with this subject, but hear this: masturbation is neither physically nor emotionally unhealthy, in itself, and it can slow down the rush to sexual involvement.

Rehearse

Once you've got your script, practice saying it.

If you're watching one of the TV soaps and a character behaves irresponsibly, pretend you are giving your sex speech to her. It's really a useful exercise in concentration and focus. Or rehearse with a friend. You'll both have serious fun, and she'll probably have some good suggestions. Participants in my Parent Tactics groups may spend four to five weeks learning to talk comfortably about sex.

As soon as you're comfortable with the general idea, imagine having the sex conversation with your kid. For a week or so, take note of the opportunities that naturally arise in your family's daily life, and figure out how you can take advantage of them. Practice mentally, until you're ready.

Finally, just do it. You can be formal: that is, sit down with your kid to watch one of the TV shows or movies. Or you can seize the moment: wait for an opportunity to present itself in conversation.

If you stumble or turn red in the face, let your kid know why:

"My Mom and Dad didn't talk about sex very easily, and I can't, either, but I'm going to keep at it. Bear with me. I have to tell you what I think about sexual responsibility."

When you've had your say, ask gently for a response:

"Are you surprised by this? Do you have any questions you'd like to ask me? Do you have a different opinion? Do your friends feel differently?"

Now, I do not expect miracles from every initial talk about sex. My suggested script is the ideal, not the norm. Your kid may be unable to do more than stammer in embarrassment. He may race for the nearest exit. Your attempt to open the door to a prolonged discussion is still worth the try. When a foster kid couldn't handle my sex talk right away, I backed off:

"I can see you need to think about this some more. You're not comfortable right now. That's okay. Few kids like to talk about sex with their parents. But I have to let you know where I stand. It's part of my job as a parent. Just remember: if you ever do want to talk about sex, I'm always here. If you prefer to talk to some other grownup, that's fine, too. Just think about these things, okay? And talk them over with an adult you trust. The important thing is to be responsible."

I always specifically suggested getting advice about contraception and directed them to their social workers, personal physician, or Planned Parenthood. Brochures from Planned Parenthood were always scattered around the house, but even so, my foster kids, like most teenagers, rarely chose to go. They thought that such visits announced that they were sexually active. Instead, they preferred a school-based health clinic. Boys and girls alike resist sex discussions with a doctor they've known since childhood. At least boys can buy condoms on their own. Since girls at this age need a gynecologic exam anyway, set one up with a doctor your daughter doesn't know personally. In that context, a discussion of sexual responsibility should be less embarrassing.

Always, even if I could get little else across, I made certain my kids heard clearly the Levine Rule: Anyone who isn't ready to talk about birth control with a professional and with her partner isn't ready to have sex.

Furthermore, anyone who has to ask parental permission to have sex should always be told no, loud and clear. That youngster is simply not old enough, or emotionally mature enough, to have sex. You can explore his feelings a little, find out what is going on, but you can never give your kid permission. The choice has to be his. You can explain your views and share your feelings about sexual responsibility, but he must understand that you cannot decide for him. Don't let him put that on you. Ever.

By the way, I think you should encourage your child's other parent to share the pain of sex talks. Some parents even manage to handle a joint birds-and-bees conversation, but most prefer to go at it separately. Your kid deserves to know where each of you stands. You don't want him thinking, "Oh, Mom's so old-fashioned, but Dad would understand." Fill in the blanks.

And if you disagree with each other? I doubt that it will be the first time. We're in the real world, not the Oz envisioned by the self-help books that encourage parental unity on this and lots of other subjects. Do some heavy thinking about your differences. Are they minor, or do they really go to the heart of the matter? More than likely, you will agree substantially on the basics; emphasize those.

But if the gulf separating your views is wider than the one separating Florida from Mexico, just 'fess up. Tell your child that you and her other parent do not totally agree. (She's not likely to be surprised, either, at this point in the life of the family.) Tell her you understand that she should listen to her other parent's point of view with an open mind. Remind her that differing opinions are not necessarily destructive. Often, it is likely that realistic options can be discovered by considering a wide range of opinions.

In the long run, both parents must be realistic:

1. The decision about becoming sexually active belongs to your child, not to you or to her other parent.
2. Yet, you are right to make the assumption that, in making her decision, your child would like the benefit of some adult opinions.
3. Therefore, make sure your opinion is heard.
4. Recognize that you've done all you can.

Irresponsible Sex: Two Dangers

Disease, possibly fatal, and unwanted children are the disastrous results of irresponsible sex.

Protection from both is not hard to find. Information is available at school and on television. By and large, most institutions of society encourage sexually active teenagers to choose safe sex. Why, then, have the rates of teenage pregnancy and venereal disease not dropped dramatically?

One Friday evening, three of my girls teamed up to do the dishes so they could have more time to get ready for a dance at the high school. Brown-haired, blue-eyed Nancy, a pretty fifteen-year-old who acted much older, whispered, "I think we'll do it."

I overheard. Knowing she was attracted to a particular boy, I asked, "If you two are planning to do it, what are you planning to use for birth control?"

"What I always use," she smirked. "It's my safe time."

"But you just had your period last week," I countered. "Even if rhythm works, now is the time to say no. You are not safe during the middle two weeks."

With the aid of a public health pamphlet, I eventually won the long argument that ensued. Nancy recognized the danger of having "a little knowledge." She did not go to the dance that night. She made an appointment with Planned Parenthood the following week because she was clear in her own mind that she wanted sex but no baby.

Most teenagers are somewhat more conflicted about whether or not to have sex—so much so that they cannot initially make plans for protection. According to the Children's Defense Fund, less than 50 percent of teenagers use birth control when they first have sex. As they grow older, use of contraception increases.

Some girls, however, desperately want to make babies.

Riva Jones, born before her parents were married, had a bubbling personality and cute, cuddly looks that attracted boys in swarms. Her doting father, recalling his own youthful indiscretions, was so determined to keep her chaste that he followed Riva literally night and day. He drove her to school, picked her up to go home, monitored her phone calls, chose her friends, drove her to church and to choir practice . . . and to running away.

When Riva was placed with us, David and I were skeptical of her tales about her dad's sentry duties, but our eyes were soon opened. The man was disturbed. Every morning, there was Mr. Jones on watch at the bottom of our driveway as his daughter marched across our lawn, walked down the block, turned right, and safely traversed the remaining 1,500 feet to the local high school. He was waiting in the afternoon when she retraced her steps to our house. On weekends, he sat in his car outside from morning to night. At least three times a day, he called to beg me to make sure that Riva was not spending time alone with those "greaser" boys living with us. Finally, he petitioned the court to have her moved to an all-girl foster home.

Not surprisingly, with this kind of paternal encouragement, Riva conceived her first child at sixteen. Overcontrol almost always produces the opposite effect from the one you intend. For one thing, it can make the forbidden seem more attractive. For another, overcontrol creates the impression that temptation must be too strong for the child to resist by herself. So she gives in.

Perhaps also, in Riva's case, there was an aching need to have a baby of her own. For both sexes, producing a child is a passport into adulthood. Today, this once normal event—teen parenting—is disturbing for two reasons: our society does not need lots and lots of kids in order to survive; it does need citizens who are well educated. Since some kids cannot easily attain a college degree but have no trouble making a baby, becoming a parent is, in their eyes, the only way to force the world and their parents to acknowledge them as grown up.

Keep the Door Open

During your sex talk, pound in the message that you are always there to help if he gets into sexual trouble. This is not as easy as it might sound. Point out that even sexually responsible girls and grown women can become pregnant. Birth control is not yet 100 percent effective.

And don't avoid the nitty-gritty. I've known a number of girls who refused intercourse but became pregnant after heavy petting. In one case, the boy apparently used his semen as a lubricant. In another, the boy ejaculated near his partner's vagina. Since she had never had sex, this couple believed that her hymen was still a barrier. Make clear to your child that any petting that leads to ejaculation can pose a risk of pregnancy.

This means, of course, that a good kid can be sexually responsible and still end up pregnant. You want to say something like this in your discussion of sex:

"Being sexually responsible means not making a baby. That's Job One. But if you get pregnant, or father a child, the next best thing is to get the help you both need as soon as possible. I won't be happy if you make a baby, but I will be there for you. I will help."

And be ready to follow through on that promise, in the worst-case scenario.

When you discover that you might become a grandparent before your time, face squarely a related sobering truth: You may think you have control of the situation, but in fact your options are relatively limited.

Legally, you cannot force your daughter to have an abortion, place a baby for adoption, or raise the baby as her own. Nor can you throw your child out of the house, though you can refuse to let her return home with a baby in tow. You are liable for your kid's support until age eighteen; you are not at all liable for the support of your grand-child. Your rights to participate in any decisions affecting your son's child are restricted. They depend upon proof of paternity. They gen-erally are considered subordinate to the rights of the mother, father, and maternal grandparents, in that order. Seek sound, informed legal advice immediately if you want to exercise some legal ties to a son's child.

Aside from the legal concerns, your overall goal in this situation is the same for a son or a daughter: to see your child through this poten-tially traumatic situation with support and love. You will have to live with the decision he or she makes. If that troubles you greatly, because you have strong feelings about a particular option, like abortion or adoption, you must nonetheless avoid the temptation to tell a child what to do. Button your lip, no matter how highly you are regarded as an understanding parent. If necessary, get counseling for yourself and find an independent counselor for your child. (If you haven't done so yet, you might want to look ahead to Chapter 17 for help in decid-ing when outside advice is a good idea.)

Your Caring Response should begin with the question, "What do you need from me?" That keeps your focus where it legitimately belongs. You won't decide the baby's fate, but you will decide what you will or will not contribute—time, emotional attachment, room in your home, money.

Be clear about this. When gestation begins, your role in your child's life is dramatically restricted. Your child has another life to think about now. You can listen, you can provide solicited advice, you can decide how much you want to get involved in helping. Most of all, you can concentrate on giving a Caring Response.

Same-Sex Love

Gay love, or same-sex love, is a variation of love that, as you can guess by now, does not make my list of bad things.

No one understands fully why some people are sexually attracted to members of their own sex. We do know that sexual attraction is variable in uncounted ways, often determined by cultural norms as much as personal preferences. Modest women in West Africa, say, go bare-breasted, but cover every inch of their legs, which are considered highly erotic. The reverse is true in your neighborhood. Look at the chubby bathing beauties of the 1890s, the anorexic flappers of the 1920s, the pneumatic starlets of the 1950s—Nature didn't mandate an unchanging heterosexual idea. And this plasticity suits humans well; it means we all have a greater chance in the mating game.

Perhaps it also means that some of us will prefer mates of the same sex. Experts believe that, generally speaking, about 10 percent of men and women in all human populations are homosexual. In some sexually liberated societies, the rate may climb, but rarely higher than about 18 percent.

Whatever the statistics, it has always been true, and no doubt always will be, that some kids are erotically drawn to members of the same sex—no matter what society says, no matter what parents feel. You can't legislate sexual stirrings.

As everyone else is playing "Boy Meets Girl," exploring their sexuality, some teenage explorers are going to find that the script should be rewritten. And they may find that they have a tougher role to play. Adolescents don't want to be different; being gay is different in one area that they are thinking about much of the time. You can't help by giving easy assurances to a teenager who discovers that he prefers same-sex love. He knows well that, in America, such a realization is not generally considered cause for great celebration.

One thing that all parents and teenagers should learn is that sex occurs on a continuum. If some people are exclusively heterosexual and others exclusively homosexual, most are somewhere in between. Famed sex researcher Kinsey posited a seven-step gradation from heterosexual through bisexual to homosexual. Neither you nor your child should worry, for example, simply because he gets turned on during wrestling class or some other unexpected moment of same-sex physical intimacy. We're all sexual creatures—never more so than during adolescence. Certain touches, certain activities, arouse us no matter who the partner is. A girl isn't gay unless she prefers same-sex love most of the time. Bisexuality means liking heterosexual and homosexual love about the same. A heterosexual prefers opposite-sex love most of the time. Not knowing these simple distinctions causes many adolescents a lot of needless confusion. Kids can even be driven to suicide when they misunderstand their own sexual feelings.

At first, almost all gay youngsters struggle against their feelings, desperately trying not to be "different." A number of my foster children were attracted to members of their sex, but none ever could discuss her gayness with me. The attitudes of society, even in our relatively permissive era, did not encourage this kind of sharing. The spread of AIDS did not help.

Therefore, if your child has not been able to discuss his same-sex feelings, you are not necessarily to blame. If he has, you have done very well, indeed, considering all of the pressures out there in society.

Either way, you should know that many other parents have come to terms with a child's same-sex feelings. Support groups have been founded and can be reached through any agency that works with the gay community. Meeting with others, you can learn how to discuss the issue with your child, deal with siblings, handle your own feelings of guilt or shame, and in other ways accept your good kid's individuality.

If you are convinced that homosexuality is a bad thing, you are in for hard times, I'm afraid. Throughout this chapter, in regard to every manifestation of sexual feeling and practice, there has been one insistent theme, and it bears repeating here: You can make your opinions known, but you cannot control your kid's behavior.

Face it.

Teenage sex, in all shapes and forms and sizes, pulls your kid into adulthood and away from your home in profoundly basic ways. Sexual explorations are no less a part of nature than parental love. Don't make the mistake of pitting them against each other.

TEN

"And I'm *Never* Coming Home!"

"Where are you calling from? Where have you been?"

"I'm not telling, Dad. I don't feel like coming home. I just wanted you not to worry."

"Not to worry! You storm out of the house and don't come home all night and your Mom and I aren't supposed to worry?"

"I knew you'd be this way."

"Come home, and we'll discuss it."

"I don't want to."

"You're our daughter, and you belong at home. Right now!"

"Goodbye, Dad. Give my love to Mom."

"What kind of talk is that? Your mother is sick with worry."

"Bye, Dad."

"Where are you?"

"Bye."

First thing in the morning, during our foster-care years, David or I went from bedroom to bedroom counting noses. At least half of these kids had run away—from their own families, from foster homes, from group houses.

Often there was an empty bed. Some kids came back safely, but some were never heard from again. Even now, when I read about an unidentified body, I wonder if it could be one of my wandering foster children.

If your kid has run away, even for an hour or two, you need to read this chapter carefully. Chronic, long-term running away—the kind that ends in prostitution or other dangerous ventures—usually begins with short-term sprints. Learn how to deal with this behavior so that you can help your child break a potentially destructive habit.

At the same time, you must look closely at your kid's behavior before overreacting. Running away, in some cases, is just a declaration of independence. Moreover, a child who breaks a rule—for example, curfew—might be afraid to come home for a few days. Upsetting as these two types of flight can be to parents, they can often lead to growth and greater strength of character if you handle them properly.

Sara's Declaration of Independence

Sara, fourteen, and her parents locked horns one night. She wanted her usual ten-thirty curfew extended when she went with friends to the local skating rink, which closed at eleven-thirty. Her parents wanted her to leave well before closing time, when fistfights often broke out in the rink's parking lot. Sara was sure she could take care of herself. When her parents held their ground despite her impassioned pleading, Sara snatched her skates and, green eyes flashing and red hair flouncing, slammed out the front door.

"If I can't stay out until twelve with your permission," she shouted, "I'll stay out all night without it!"

Sara had a flair for drama, so her parents did not at first take this threat seriously. But eleven came, then eleven-thirty, then midnight. At five after twelve the phone rang. It was their daughter's best friend: "Sara's spending the night at my house; she wanted you to know she was okay."

Her parents called me right then. Sara's enraged father wanted to drive over and retrieve his daughter from the friend's house; her mother was uncertain. My advice: Call the friend's parents to confirm that Sara was there, explain that she was angry over a disagreement about rules, ask if she could stay until she cooled down. Sara's mother was in the better mood to make this call. I suggested she keep it short and simple, while adopting the attitude that this was a typically adolescent escapade—exasperating, but amusing.

For the next two days, prodigal Sara moved around. Each night, a different friend called. Each night, her mother, following my advice, said something like this:

"Tell Sara we love her, but this is not the way to work things out. When she calms down, she should come home and talk. But if she wants to live here, she has to abide by our rules, even when she thinks they don't make sense."

Each time, Sara's mother insisted on talking with the friend's parents to tell them what was going on. She kept calling back, if necessary, until she reached an adult and could explain just what was going on. By showing concern as well as reasonable tolerance, Sara's mother gained the support and sympathy of her daughter's friends and their parents, all of whom worked on Sara to return home.

After three days, Sara strode into the house right after school, head held high and eyes still flashing. Her mother was prepared. Without hesitation, she gave her daughter a big hug and told her that the family was going to meet that night in my office to talk things over. Following my advice, neither she nor her husband, who was still fuming, said anything about the running away.

In our meeting, we worked on an agreement that dealt with the seriousness of the problem and its potential for further harm. Beforehand, Sara's parents and I had agreed that her running away was a ploy in a Gotcha War and had to be punished. That was non-negotiable. Otherwise, she might make flight a habit in her efforts to get her own way. Her parents told her that they had decided to ground her for a month. She whined, but it became clear that she would accept this punishment as reasonable. On her side, however, she persuasively argued that her parents were overprotective—especially her strict father—and had imposed rules that were harsher than those her friends had to observe. To his credit, her father listened without causing static. He was surprised to learn that she was the only girl in her set of friends, all of whom he trusted and liked, whose ten-thirty curfew was inviolable, no matter what the event. He promised to think about how to revise his curfew rules once the month of grounding was over.

Sara's parents were not interested in just winning a battle in the Gotcha Wars; they wanted to address the problem. At my suggestion, they got together with the parents of their daughter's skating buddies to discuss their concerns. Wonder of wonders, it turned out that most of the other parents had also been worried about the fights but had given in. Together, the adults worked out a new plan. The kids could skate until closing time, but each week one of the parents would pick up the whole crowd, take them to a McDonald's for a snack, then drive them home. The kids were not 100 percent happy with this scheme, which smacked of chaperoning, but they had to agree. Their parents had forged a united front.

As for Sara, she never ran away again. Today, she thinks that her parents became more tolerant after the episode; they believe she learned a valuable lesson. Perhaps all three are right. More important, they can all look back and laugh about it.

But this situation had a lot going for it. Sara's parents were reasonable, and their rules were not all that inconsistent with those prevailing in the community. The relationship between daughter and parents was generally positive.

Later on, we'll talk about cases that require stronger action. But let's take another of the easier problems first: the youngster who does not return home as scheduled.

Joey's Week on the Town

Sexy Joey, a sixteen-year-old with heavy-lidded, sensual eyes in the Johnny Depp manner, didn't run away. He just didn't come home one night. Whatever the girls might think, on the basis of his looks, his parents knew that he was a shy kid who tried hard to do the right thing. The night in question, he had told them he was going to a party. When he didn't appear on time or call, his mother was frantic.

She waited an hour after his curfew before calling the party. Someone told her that Joey had already left. She called his friends, but no one admitted knowing where he was. She managed not to notify the police, but by noon the next day she was calling all of the local hospitals and emergency clinics. Just as she was about to try the police, Joey called and explained that he'd fallen asleep on the couch at a friend's house.

This was hardly the whole story, of course.

He hadn't fallen asleep, he had passed out. But only after earning a black eye and a split lip in a fight. Quiet, calm Joey was used to nursing a bottle of beer at parties, just to keep up appearances. He didn't really like to drink. This time, for some reason, he decided to drink his fill, became argumentative, and got decked. He had avoided going home because his wounds would provoke a lot of questions he didn't want to have to answer.

An hour after his first phone call, Joey called again and told his mother he was going to a friend's house in the country for the weekend. She told him not to, but he rang off. He was planning to stay away from home until his face healed completely, but after four days he ran out of friends who would cover for him. Meanwhile, his mother was suffering sleepless nights, not knowing where he was or what could explain this uncharacteristic behavior. His stepfather, never an easy man to live with but fond of Joey, was stretched to his limits, torn between concern for his wife and anger with her son.

When Joey finally had to face the music, he was grounded, lost his allowance, and couldn't use the phone for two months. It took six months to restore his relationship with his stepfather. Joey learned to come home when expected.

Sara and Joey typify the usual reasons good kids run away: either to prove a point to parents, or to avoid being punished for wrongdoing. This behavior is as normal as Tom Sawyer and Becky Thatcher. Essentially, your strategy is threefold: worry until the situation is resolved; react with strong consequences to the kid; wait to see if another episode follows. If your kid doesn't run away again, store the event in your stockpile of memories. You can retrieve it when your child has children of his own.

But should you try to force your wayward teenager to come home?

How to Get Them Home Again

Should the police be called? Not in cases like Joey's and Sara's.

In both situations, the parents knew that their child was safe and staying with friends. Calling the cops right away would have needlessly escalated hostilities.

Instead, if school is in session, it's better to call her guidance counselor or a respected teacher. Some schools have a social worker who should be skilled in helping you find a quick resolution. If someone at the school agrees to help and suggests that you come for a joint interview, follow through immediately. One caution: It's probably not a good idea to involve school officials if your kid has had substantive difficulties on campus and is viewed as a problem student.

Definitely, the police should have been called if Sara, say, had not convinced her friend to telephone that first night. Often, your local cops can give you good advice, if you explain the situation honestly and completely.

And they should be called if your kid stays away longer than three days, which is plenty of time to face facts and head home. Warn your child or his contact person first, though, and set a definite deadline for return before you dial your precinct.

Another factor in deciding whether or not to involve the police is your child's anger. If you had a fight and he stays out long past curfew, he could be doing something uncharacteristically dangerous or stupid out of spite. How long should you wait before calling?

Well, law officers in most communities are unlikely to become concerned until at least twenty-four hours have passed. Their experience suggests that your child will cool down and come shambling in, safe and sound and embarrassed. If you live in a small town, the police might go into action sooner, particularly if your kid is only twelve or thirteen. Even so, you probably should wait twenty-four hours in most situations, unless you have reason to suspect foul play.

Instead, I'd wait until the following morning and start spreading the word to relatives and friends. Let them know that you're worried and would appreciate a phone call. When one of our foster kids stayed out all night, this tactic was usually enough to get someone to tell me what was happening. If I didn't hear directly from the kid within twenty-four hours of the original curfew, I'd go back to the grapevine and give my ultimatum: the kid had two hours to return home, or I'd call the police. As a foster parent, of course, I was legally required to take such action, but it should work just as well for your straying child. Don't use a threatening tone. Focus on your own feelings. Explain that you're frightened, you're worried that something terrible might have happened, you are desperate and don't know what other action to take.

Usually your kid will telephone, and you must be prepared to handle the conversation carefully. Your approach is dictated by the specifics of the situation. If you don't know why your child ran away, simply tell him to come home. Explain that, although you don't know what is going on, you are sure that whatever caused his flight can be worked out together. Express your relief that he's all right.

But if your child stormed out, trying to force a change in the rules, remind him that you care deeply about him, then make clear that his running away is not going to blackmail you into relaxing your restrictions. Say something like:

"I hear that you think our rules aren't reasonable, and yet that's what you'll have to live with when you decide to come home. The choice is yours."

Perhaps you are terrified to make this kind of ultimatum, especially after the worry you've just endured. But take my word for it: If the running away is just "experimental" and not the symptom of a problem that needs professional attention, your kid will come back home, even though you are not promising a change in the irksome rules.

That doesn't mean he will give up. He may continue to try to provoke you.

Do not weaken. Stay calm. Remember our magic responses to Gotcha Wars:

Yes.

No.

Really.

Whatever.

Wow.

Um . . .

When your kid calls, you might have to try "fogging": Acknowledge her complaint, but don't change your rules. Say something like:

"Yes, I can see that from your point of view my rules don't seem entirely fair, and maybe it isn't easy to live with them, but that's the way things are. I love you and want you to be able to live at home, but I have to set the rules that I think are right, whether or not you agree with them."

If your child still won't let up, try your own variation of my gambit, "Come back when you've cooled off." I had to learn this approach, because many of our foster children were chronic runaways. Some even picked fights to have an excuse to flee, but as they stomped out, I made sure to tell them to come back when they calmed down. This helped defuse their shame or guilt and made coming back a lot easier for them.

Similarly, if your runaway is provocative when she calls, make this point:

"It sounds like you aren't ready to come home yet. I wish you were, but I can accept that you may need more time to think things through. I love you. I know things can be worked out. So, keep yourself safe, and come home when you are ready to live with our rules."

Or perhaps you'd rather take a slightly different tack:

"I can agree with you that we need to work out how to revise some of our rules, now that you are getting older. But this is certainly not the way to do it. So, for now, the choice is yours: Come home only when you're ready to look at your behavior rather than complain about our rules. When you can show us that you can handle yourself with more maturity, we'll think about revising the rules. Right now, though, your behavior has made that impossible."

Both statements put the ball squarely in your child's court, clearly indicating that coming home is a sign she will agree to follow your rules. After she makes that decision, you have the option, like Sara's parents, of reevaluating your rules. You can devise a way of revising them periodically, as your child's development warrants.

Calling the Police

If you do not get that telephone call within three hours of your deadline, you should certainly bring in the police.

Don't be embarrassed. You're not unique. In *All Grown Up and No Place to Go,* David Elkind estimates that over a million teenagers are reported as runaways every year. He believes even that figure only touches the tip of the iceberg, since official reports are not filed in many brief, "experimental" flights from home.

Don't abuse 911. This is not a police emergency, no matter how worried you may be. Call the general number at your local police station during regular hours and ask to speak with the youth officer. If your precinct does not have one, the switchboard operator will connect you with the right officer.

Be straightforward and factual. Explain what has happened and what you have done so far. Ask for advice. At this point, you may be asked to file a missing person's report, but you can choose to wait, if you prefer. When you do decide to file, you will have to provide a detailed physical description of your child and the clothing he was wearing when you last saw him, along with a recent photo. Finally, share with the police any idea you have about your kid's possible whereabouts or third parties who might be able to help with their investigation.

Don't expect an immediate sweep of the community. Reports will be filed, some phone calls will be made, and each tour of duty will be notified to be on the lookout. Unless there's an unusual factor in your case, you will have to do most of the work of finding your child yourself, for at least the first week. The police have seen it all before. They are not insensitive. It is just that experience has shown them, as it has me, that your good child will come home soon.

When she does, then what?

When the Prodigal Returns

If your child walks in the door of her own accord, I suggest following slight variations of my tactics for phone contact. The exact line of approach depends on the reason for the flight: A misdeed? Or a ploy to change the rules?

In the first case, greet the miscreant warmly and lead her off to the kitchen for a snack. Reestablish normality, heating up leftover pizza for her and making tea for yourself—or whatever is the familiar pattern of your lives. When you sit down, assure your kid you will not reject her, no matter what she's done. Explain that you assume she ran off because there is something she's afraid to admit to you and your spouse. (Perhaps you can share a time when you felt the same impulse in your adolescent years.) Urge her to spill the beans now, because you want to help, but cannot unless you know what's wrong.

You are the adult and have to appear calm and controlled, but be inwardly prepared for the worst. Your daughter may be pregnant. Your son may have impregnated his girlfriend or picked up a venereal disease. Accusations from school officials or police, bent fenders or broken headlights, lost jackets or wristwatches—any of these teenage miseries is hard to admit to parents.

Listen well, and consider the possibility that you are only getting part of the truth right now. Your kid may test your reaction to slightly upsetting news before telling you the worst. For the moment, deal with what you have.

Your first reaction should be: "What do you need me to do to help?" Do what your child asks, unless it is illegal or involves a kind of deception or evasion of responsibility that you cannot approve.

If the returning child ran off as a ploy to get his own way, you have already laid the groundwork in your last phone call, if you followed my suggestions. Greet him warmly, then note gently that you're glad he's willing to come home and abide by the rules of the family. Say something like:

"It's good to have you home again. I know our rules don't always make sense to you, but we love you and this will always be your home.

Right now, what do you need so that you can feel okay again? Are you hungry? Do you want to go up to your room and change, or take a shower, before we discuss the consequences?"

Usually, your kid will opt for a snack or shower, delaying for a bit the inevitable talk about consequences.

Consequences are essential for both types of runaway. You can go easy when the problem itself is a consequence—pregnancy, fines or jail, disease—but there still has to be a distinctly separate penalty for the act of running away. As a general rule of thumb, I take the normal consequence for a serious violation of curfew and multiply it by the number of days the kid has been gone from home. If a fight sparked the running away, add an additional punishment. If the wrongdoing does not carry its own punishment, add a consequence for the misbehavior to your punishment for the running away.

For example, Sara was usually grounded for a week for being more than thirty minutes late. For staying away three days, she was grounded twenty-one days, plus an additional week for provoking a fight.

Joey was usually grounded two days for a curfew violation. He was gone six days, which (by my rule) should bring twelve days of grounding. He hadn't fought at home, but it would be reasonable to add one week for drinking, another for getting into the fistfight at the party. By my standards, then, his parents' punishment of six months' grounding was excessive. For the record, however, Joey didn't think so, and that was crucially important. He knew his stepfather was a hard-liner, and he realized that he had caused his mother a lot of worry.

You may wonder why I suggest less punishment for failing to come home after doing something wrong than for picking a fight and then fleeing the scene. In the first case, the child's fear of returning home is already a partial admission of wrongdoing. In the second, you are faced with the larger issue of your child trying to change your rules by engaging in inappropriate behavior that must not be allowed to succeed.

When a problem carries its own sad consequences, however, be firm but fair. One of our foster kids ran off for a week when his girlfriend became pregnant. Although he ran away from us, he ran to the problem, spending the time talking with her and trying to figure out together what should be done. She decided to have an abortion, a decision he respected but found very painful. I added nothing to our standard punishment for running away. Our rule was one day's grounding for each curfew violation; doubling that for running away, we grounded him for fourteen days.

To summarize, running away for a first or second time is most often an effort to avoid punishment for wrongdoing or to change family rules. In either case, your first goal is to get your kid home safely and welcome him with warmth and concern. Next, you make clear that running away is the wrong way to handle the situation and certainly won't convince you to change any rules. Finally, you must impose consequences that are reasonable but attention-getting.

Habitual Running Away

If you follow my advice and your child runs off a third time, a serious problem may be brewing. You will have to take additional steps when running away or staying away overnight without permission becomes a habit.

Red-headed, pasty-faced Jimmy was fourteen when he came to us, deep hurt always visible in liquid brown eyes that reminded me of the country-and-western hit, "Don't It Make My Brown Eyes Blue?" His mouth was pinched, his shoulders hunched, his expression on the verge of tears. One of six children, he had run away from home for the first time at age eleven, when his mother died of cancer, and stayed away for three days. That set the pattern. Whenever something hurt the boy, he vanished for a couple of days, then returned. His beleaguered father got used to this behavior, but the courts stepped in when Jimmy began skipping school.

Living with us enhanced his habit. If something at our house disturbed him, he lit out for home. If he was on a visit home and there was a problem, he raced back to us.

Like most chronic running away, Jimmy's behavior was a flight from pain. If your child has this problem, your goal is twofold: to figure out the cause of the pain; and to help him learn to live with the hurt rather than run from it. Jimmy did not learn to face his grief until he spent a few sessions with a good therapist. He was able to understand what he was doing, and the running away stopped for good.

Another motive for running away habitually is unlikely to be the case in your house, or you would hardly be reading this book: I'm talking about physical, sexual, or emotional abuse.

Some of our foster kids had good reason to leave their home situations. A few ran away and did well, many are still living on the street, and at least three, to my knowledge, are dead.

Just in case there is 1 chance in 500 that you are an abusive parent, let me briefly sketch the most common forms.

Sexual abuse is a crossing of the incest barrier. Most blatantly, of course, this involves sexual intercourse, but it can take subtler forms. Sometimes, it is an inappropriately sexualized relationship involving fondling that you wouldn't practice in public in front of a minister or rabbi. Don't fool yourself. If any contact with your kid doesn't pass that test, halt it now.

Physical abuse comes in infinite variety. Hitting, which is most common, is not abuse when it's no more than one slap a year. (It's not the preferred disciplinary method, either.) Weekly slaps, however, are abusive, as are any slaps or hits that leave physical marks. If you have hit your child so hard you've left marks more than three times, you need professional help. Burns are the second most frequent form of parental abuse and are intolerable. You never have a legitimate reason for burning your child. Physical abuse can also include locking your kid in a room or closet, or restraining her with ropes, chain, handcuffs, or wires.

Less easy to pin down accurately is emotional abuse, but here are some good clues. If you believe your child is bad, if you are almost always angry with her, or never feel warmly toward her, or spend most of your time telling her she is no good, it is highly probable that you are being emotionally abusive. If this strikes a chord, get help now. With each day, you are damaging your kid all the more seriously.

You should consider the possibility of all of these forms of abuse if the child you love does not live with you and is a chronic runaway. As a test, have the child returned to your custody, if possible, or to a neutral environment. If the behavior stops, it's likely that the previous environment was toxic, if not actually abusive. Don't make accusations of abuse, however, until you gather specific, verifiable information. Then make your charges only with the help of a lawyer.

But if the running away continues, even in the neutral environment, it is possible that your child is seriously disturbed.

Mary Ellen and Brian

Mary Ellen, who believed she was a witch and liked to be called Vampira, had been hospitalized three times for acute psychotic episodes before she came to us. She wore pasty-white face powder and circled her eyes with black eyeliner, claimed to see ghosts, and frequently chatted with "spirit friends" invisible to others. A chronic runaway, she skipped out on us at least once a week, just as she had run from her mother's house and a group home.

Brian, another memorable runaway, looked "pure prep," as my foster kids would say. Tall, well-built, handsome in the manner of a young Sean Connery, he was one of the few kids in our care to earn his full allowance ten weeks in a row. But if you spent any time talking with all-American Brian, you realized that something was wrong. He was essentially an emotional blank. I don't remember him ever laughing, showing anger or sadness, or even smiling sincerely. One day, he just disappeared. We never saw him again. When I packed his belongings, I came across his diary. Voices had followed him from his parents' house to ours, he had written, and were now talking to him through a lamp in our living room. Like Mary Ellen, Brian was psychotic.

These extreme cases may seem far from your experience, but while Mary Ellen's problems were immediately evident, Brian's were not. If your child runs away frequently and does not want to return home, you should arrange a psychiatric evaluation. A child who runs away repeatedly is a child who needs help.

When a Child's Missing

I have no magical formula for retrieving a child who has run away and is still missing after a week or more. You have probably already tried every avenue I can suggest:

1. Maintain contact with your kid's friends. Make sure they know that (a) you want to know that he is alive and well; and (b) you want to work things out so he can come home. Ask them for suggestions.

2. In all appropriate areas, put up posters offering a reward for information leading to your kid's whereabouts.
3. Call all of the runaway hotlines. Make sure they understand that you are ready to do anything necessary to get in touch with your missing child.
4. Hire a reputable private investigator who specializes in locating missing persons.
5. Take care of yourself by finding a support group.

In addition, pay special attention to the next chapter. It's not unlikely that the child who has been missing for a long time will eventually be returned to you in police custody.

ELEVEN

Police Stories

"Hello?"

"Is this the Nelson residence?"

"Do you know what time it is? Who the hell is this?"

"Mr. Nelson?"

"What do you want?"

"This is Sergeant O'Toole of the Forty-ninth Precinct. We have your son David in custody."

"Oh, my God."

"We'd appreciate your coming down as soon as possible. We have a little problem here."

"Is he hurt? Is he all right?"

"Oh, he's fine, Mr. Nelson. But it's possible that someone else is going to press charges against him. We need to sort this out right away."

"But he's never been in trouble."

"Yes, sir. When do you think you can get here?"

Few things are more frightening to a parent than the telephone call informing you that your good kid is in police custody. During our foster-parenting years, David and I received countless calls from police— some serious, some not so troubling.

There were loss-of-control arrests: for running amok with friends; for getting into a fight; for vandalizing property in a fit of anger. There were the minor crimes, like shoplifting, but also there was drug dealing, auto theft, breaking-and-entering, and burglary. Perhaps you think your child, particularly if you live in the suburbs, doesn't have an inner-city kid's need to commit such crimes—and won't. Think again.

Early one Thanksgiving morning, our wake-up call came courtesy of our local police department: "We've just had a phone call from the Port Chester Police. They want you to move your stationwagon. It's illegally parked on the Lincoln Avenue median strip near Lyon Park."

We were baffled. David had bought the vehicle at a used car lot just the day before and left it parked in our driveway. His first thought was that the dealer or one of his employees had kept a key and stolen the wagon during the night. The truth was revealed in a note posted on the front door. Zach, then fourteen, explained all:

Dear Mom and Dad,
  I don't know how you will forgive me.
  I know I won't forgive myself. I don't know how I could have been so stupid. If you send me away forever, I will understand. It will be what I deserve.
  Last night after you were in bed, some friends and I took the car for a ride. I had a little accident, and the car is parked on Lincoln Avenue in Port Chester. Here are the keys. Please forgive me. I will never do anything so stupid again. I promise.

Love,
Zach

Thanksgiving Day was tense. Our good kid had put over fifty miles on the car during his joyride, skidded out of control in some wet leaves, and smashed into a tree, causing $1,200 worth of (uninsured) damage to the front end. We were appalled and frightened, though it helped somewhat that our son was obviously shaken and guilt-stricken— and he understood our anger. Without prompting, he promised to work to pay for the repairs. Within the week, he found an after-school job as a soda jerk. He hated it but stayed until the bill was completely paid off.

Instantly, like most parents, David and I blamed ourselves. Aside from our everyday human imperfections, we had to devote so much time to our foster kids. Had we neglected Zach? Were the foster children—as many people in the community explained—bad influences on good kids? We had a rough period of self-doubt and self-examination.

Slowly, however, we began to see the outlines of a different picture. From friends and neighbors, we learned that taking the family car for a joyride had become a rite of passage for the town's thirteen- and fourteen-year-old boys. One eighth-grade boy had been tooling his family's second car around the back country roads of northern Westchester County for weeks. He was caught only when his mother drove home unexpectedly one day as he was backing out of the drive. He panicked and collided with a tree. A fourteen-year-old had picked up the habit of cruising after midnight in his father's jeep. His parents were none the wiser until the night the cops called, having arrested the boy after clocking him at sixty-five miles per hour on Interstate 95. These stories also put in perspective the escapades of our foster kids. Before he came to us, one undersized thirteen-year-old had been caught driving a stolen school bus. (Shades of a certain Tibetan spiritual leader . . . .)

All things considered, we realized we should be relieved that Zach had come a cropper and been discovered his first time out. We found that other parents were relieved to discover their sons weren't the only good kids doing something bad. And the juvenile drivers were relieved when caught. "I couldn't stop myself," said one boy, "but I was scared the whole time, and it just didn't feel right. I was glad when the police pulled me over."

By the way, these kids did not realize that, aside from driving without a license, they were liable for arrest for grand theft, auto. Some of our foster kids had been arrested for nothing more than stealing the family car.

The suburban kids were worried more about parental anger than confrontations with the law, so they became pretty good at keeping their joyrides a secret. And girls could be tempted as much as boys. Even in my generation, a friend "borrowed" the family car one night and demolished the passenger side when she sideswiped a tree. She beat it back home and parked the car in the street, with the damaged side facing outward. When her parents discovered their smashed car the next morning, they were mildly mystified, since neither could remember parking it where it was. But they never suspected their daughter. Recently, she told me that they quarreled about the incident for years, each blaming the other. "I still feel terrible," my friend said, "but I never told them the truth, and I don't think I ever will."

Joyriding is not the only flirtation with minor crime that seduces the good teenagers in our stable, comfortable little "bedroom" community. Several drug rings have been broken up in various high schools throughout the area. Because of my foster children, I used to keep track of the daily arrest sheets, and many a drug suspect's name came from one of the "better" families. One of my teenage clients in therapy confessed that she had managed to steal nearly $200 worth of jewelry from a local store before her conscience clicked in. She was never discovered. Other clients have told me about peddling prescription drugs, picking pockets at the supermarket, and taking advantage of chance opportunities to steal. None of these good kids was caught. Eventually, on their own, they just stopped doing the bad things.

More rites of passage? I don't think so. In fact, I don't believe that most adolescents are involved in this kind of behavior, and I certainly don't think you should worry that your good kid is likely to make a habit of breaking the law. On the contrary, assume she is law-abiding until facts prove otherwise. You may be tempted to play detective. You know that the world is full of dangers lurking in the path of your good kid and that adolescents don't have the best possible judgment. It is frightening that you have so little control over their lives. Even so, err on the side of positive thinking. If your faith is misplaced, events will educate you soon enough.

David and I made the mistake of playing detective when we first began our foster parenting, but we soon found that we never uncovered anything we didn't already know. We also learned that we had no hope of preventing a determined youngster from committing illegal acts. Finally, our detecting was damaging because it eroded trust. It interfered with our caring relationship for the child, almost making us the enemy

On the other hand, you should certainly take note of how much money your child has and how it is being spent. Alarm bells should ring at sudden acquisitions of expensive clothing, jewelry, CD players, and the like. If you are putting away your kid's clothes in the closet and discover a cache of car radios, you're not guilty of intrusive detective work. You have been given an obvious signal to take action.

What to Do

The first time your child breaks the law, push the panic button only halfway in. Make your upset loud and clear, impose the appropriate consequences . . . and then watch and wait.

Consequences, by the way, should always fit the crime and the child. Zach's offer to pay for damages was appropriate. If the car had been insured for collision, however, I would have exacted a fine to cover the premium costs. Your best response is always the one that feels like a reasonable punishment to a suitably remorseful child.

Also, Zach had immediately apologized in his note, while we still slept peacefully unawares. He had promised not to be so "stupid" again. He made restitution, agreed with our "punishment," and changed his behavior. We would have worried—and rightly so—if he had broken any law and not reacted in all three ways: shown remorse, apologized, and made restitution. If your adolescent lawbreaker cannot come through on these three counts, you have serious problems ahead. Especially disturbing would be an inability to show remorse after knowingly breaking a law—not on the level of jaywalking, but the kind of illegal action that is generally tried in criminal court. Probably, this attitude indicates a need for professional counseling, and you should use a Caring Intervention (see Chapter 15) to see that it is obtained.

An important indicator of healthy remorse is your kid's reaction to "punishment." Now this word is avoided by most professionals; as you've noticed, we tend to speak of "consequences." But a petunia by any other name is still a petunia: painful consequences punish. The right form of punishment applied in the right manner can help your errant teenager shape up.

To be "right," the punishment has to make sense to the child. Don't assume that your kid feels he has done something wrong, even if he has broken a law. As part of your Caring Response, you first have to investigate his point of view about the whole incident. Ask what he thinks is wrong about the unlawful behavior. For instance, Zach didn't consider himself a car thief, although he would have been arrested if we pressed charges. He did consider it wrong to drive without a license, to do something he knew we would have forbidden, and to damage our car in an accident. These were the wrongs he felt he should be punished for.

Once you know what your kid thinks he did wrong, get him to

participate in determining the punishment. Given this opportunity, most of my foster children assigned themselves punishments that I considered too harsh. As the adult, you have to remember the purpose of punishment: to stop the wrongdoing. Severity by itself doesn't necessarily prevent a repetition or worsening of the unwanted behavior. To be effective, punishments, or consequences, should fulfill three criteria: fit the crime; fit your child; and stop your good kid's bad behavior. If three months pass after punishment and no repetition has occurred, lay all your worries to rest.

By the way, don't be afraid to act as judge and jury when the law does not provide consequences. Zach's joyride brought no charges from the police; that's why David and I had to punish him. Some of my foster children successfully eluded the authorities when they shoplifted. If I caught them, however, Levine-mandated consequences were applied. The thief had to return the contraband to the store manager and apologize. She was then banned from all stores for a month.

Dealing with Police

The first rule of dealing with law officers may startle you. No doubt you've taught your good kids these two things: respect our police, and always be cooperative and truthful. But when your kid is picked up and taken to the station, she should respectfully decline to tell her story until she has received legal advice, even if she knows herself to be completely innocent.

Innocent or guilty, adult or child, we all have the constitutional right to speak with a lawyer before answering questions. Teach your kid to exercise that right. This does not mean that she should make a scene, shrilly demanding to see an attorney. Instead, any kid under eighteen should explain that she wants to be cooperative but you have ordered her not to give out any information but her name and address until she telephones you. Take time to prepare for this eventuality. Tell your teenager that situations arise when anyone might be picked up by the police for questioning and she should learn to say something like this:

"I've been told by my parents that whether I'm innocent or guilty, I shouldn't answer any questions unless they are present. Please arrange for me to call them. I'll answer your questions when they are here and tell me to."

When you get the call, you can decide whether or not to call in your attorney. Generally speaking, however, it's always good thinking to get a lawyer's opinion when someone is being questioned about possible criminal behavior. Definitely, you contact a lawyer if your child is going to be charged with anything more serious than speeding.

How can you make sure your child follows through? For one thing, explain that an "innocent" child hanging out with a lawbreaking friend can be considered an accessory to a crime. Answering questions without you and perhaps a lawyer present can give the police enough information to bring charges against her.

Please don't read inaccurately between the lines here. I strongly support the police, respect them for their hard, dangerous work, and believe that the majority would not take advantage of your naive child. Still, it is their job to see that charges stick, not clear a suspect. Your job is to educate your child so that she will protect her rights, while behaving in a cooperative manner.

You should also be cooperative, even if you feel that the police are totally wrong, have falsely arrested your kid, or have possibly brutalized her. Cases are tried in courts of law, not police stations. Do not get involved in discussions of guilt or innocence. If the police are gravely at fault in any way, your lawyer can bring a civil suit. If, on the other hand, you believe the police have caught your child in a criminal act, you still keep mum. Your lawyer should do the talking. In all cases, I believe that the best general tactic is to assume, for the moment, that the police have acted responsibly, according to the facts as they know them. Don't make matters more complicated by making enemies in blue.

If the police tell you on the phone that no charges are pending or being made, you can pick up your child without bothering to check with a lawyer. At the station, you'll be told what happened, what (if anything) is going to happen next, and what you have to do to have your kid released into your custody. Usually they will lecture her about shaping up. Rarely they will offer you suggestions about keeping her in line. You may be asked to sign a form indicating that you have picked up your teenager. When appropriate, you will be given a summons for her court appearance.

Don't make things more confusing by trying to discuss what has happened until you complete your business with the police and leave the station. To my foster children, I usually said something like, "Well,

I'm glad you're still in one piece. . . . I'm not happy about having to come here to get you, but we'll talk about that and what happened when we get you home."

Most kids are embarrassed and just as eager as you to get on home. They'll button up. But if your child's still angry and eager to stir up more trouble, acknowledge his feelings but refuse to argue the merits of his complaints. A slightly annoyed response should get the two of you moving toward the door:

"Of course, you are upset, but now is not the time or place to talk about that. We'll talk when we get home."

If your kid keeps spouting off, forget tact:

"The car is out front. It isn't locked. Shut your mouth and go wait in the car. I'll be right out."

When he leaves, apologize for the trouble he's caused, fill out the paperwork, and make your goodbyes. Don't overdo the talking. You and your family have already made a large enough dent in the public payroll.

Whether your kid is being charged or simply released into your hands, the first thing you want to do at home is find out the facts. Insist on the truth. If the incident resulted from bad behavior, you must work on preventing a recurrence in the future. Usually, the hassle of being detained can be considered sufficient punishment for a first-time offense that does not result in charges.

If there will be charges but you believe your kid is innocent, just be supportive and help him win his case. Even if inappropriate behavior put him in the wrong place at the wrong time, the ordeal of a court appearance and related matters will be punishment enough.

In Police Custody

Remain as calm as possible if the police or your kid calls to report that she's being detained for arraignment. This means that there is evidence indicating to authorities that she has committed a crime.

If your child makes the call, remind her to cooperate but not answer questions until you and your lawyer appear on the scene. Tell her you will immediately contact the lawyer and come down as soon as possible. Tell her to try to relax and assure her that you're on her side. After you hang up, call the lawyer, tell him your story, and follow his advice.

If the police place the call, find out where your child is being held and assure them that you will be there as soon as possible. Ask to speak to her. Usually, that is possible, but not always, so don't make a fuss. If they don't bring her to the phone, just accept that and say you're on your way. Before leaving the house, however, arrange to have a lawyer meet you wherever your child is.

After the Trial

If your child is indeed guilty, you do not have to add punishments to the legal consequences. Once the fine is paid or probation endured or time served, put the whole incident in the past. Do not be on the lookout for a repetition of the behavior, for it is not likely to recur. Do not bring up the police and court episodes as a warning when your kid goes out for the evening. Case is closed.

If legal sanctions do not work, however, and the illegal activity is repeated, your kid is in trouble. Use a Caring Intervention to see that he gets the professional help he needs.

"A Bad Thing"

My notion that good kids do bad things was echoed recently in the national news—in a case involving adults. Late in 1990, three airline pilots were given prison terms and subsequent probation for flying a passenger jet while intoxicated. In determining the sentences, the judge followed federal guidelines, but he explained his decision this way:

"Gentlemen, you are good men who have done a bad thing."

As you deal with any behavior that gets your child in trouble with the law, you should remember to adopt the same attitude. The crime, whatever it is, earns appropriate consequences. Punishment addresses the bad deed; it does not become a brand on a "bad child." Like the judge, you should work hard to censure the act but not the person.

TWELVE

Substance Abuse

"Good grief, son. You take a shower every day. Why do you need to splash on all that aftershave? You don't attract pretty girls by suffocating them."

"Oh, Dad."

"You smell like . . . Wait a minute. Have you been drinking?"

"Just one beer, Dad. Everybody else was drinking, so I took one and nursed it all night."

"Right, and poured the rest of the six-pack all over yourself? You reek. You're drunk."

"Just a little high, that's all. I'm not used to it."

"Yeah? One beer all night, and a six-foot, 200-pound ballplayer can't get his sweater off without struggling?"

"It's shrunk."

"Cut the comedy. You think a father can't tell when his own son is three sheets to the wind?"

"Come on, Dad. I'm no alky."

"I didn't say you were."

"Okay."

"So . . . why did you bring it up?"

On any given Saturday night in a small suburban town like ours, many churches will have a crowd of people, young and old, milling around the parking lot, talking, joking, and then getting into their cars to drive home. These healthy, happy-looking folk look as if they've just attended a church function. In fact, they are recovering alcoholics and their families, chatting after an open meeting of Alcoholics Anonymous. I know, for I have attended many of these sessions.

Any American parent these days is sensible to worry about the possibility that a teenager is drinking or taking drugs. Perhaps you believe, as do many of my colleagues, that parents always know when a kid is using. In fact, the professional term is "denial" to describe the situation when parents don't know because they don't want to know. Denial can certainly be a problem, for normal caring includes wanting to see a teenager in the best light. But it simply isn't true that parents have to fool themselves; they can be fooled by their kids, as my experience in counseling teenagers and their parents has frequently proved to me. In my foster-parenting years as well, I was also reminded of a simple truth: Often, parents do not know until drug use turns into drug abuse.

Melinda

"I was high on pot from the seventh grade until my first year of college, and to this day my parents don't know a thing about it."

Tall, slender, with the high cheekbones and intense eyes of a brunette Glenn Close, twenty-six-year-old Melinda was a student in one of my social work classes last year. When we discussed teenage drug use, she had a very instructive story to tell.

"I'd leave for school early, smoke two joints on the way, two more during lunch, another two on the way home, and a couple in my room at night just before going to sleep. My grades were fine. I didn't get into trouble. Nothing in my behavior changed for the worse.

"In fact, I thought grass was good for me, because it made me feel less morbidly shy. I smoked mostly with my best friend Joannie, whose brother got the stuff for us. In all those years, we had it under control, but things changed when we went to different colleges. I got involved with a straight crowd and stopped smoking. Joannie's usage slipped deeper and deeper into serious abuse of hard drugs. We remained close, so we talked about her problem, but she believed that she couldn't face life without them. Eventually, she was turning tricks at $200 an hour just to feed her habit, but that didn't last. It wasn't long before she was lucky to get $10. Two years ago, the police called her parents to identify a body in a hotel room. Joannie had OD'ed on heroin.

"My parents were stunned. They told me how grateful they were that I had never done anything as stupid as try drugs. They still think smoking grass always ends in heroin addiction. Of course, I've never told them the truth about my smoking, and I never will. The fact is, lots of kids use, but if you're smart, cover your tracks, and don't get into serious abuse, your parents really won't know what's going on."

Tom and June

Professionals, too, can have the wool pulled over their eyes. Drug counselors Tom and June knew drugs inside out from both their training and their personal histories; he had been a teenager abuser, and her father was an alcoholic. But their fifteen-year-old son, Perry, used drugs for almost two years before they caught on.

"What a fool I was," June recalled recently. "When Perry was thirteen, he came home one day smelling of beer, and empties appeared every now and then on the lawn over the next few weeks. I bore down on him gently, the cans vanished, and he never came home high or reeking again. Obviously, my following the book-recommended rules of parenting had worked. My kid had experimented a little, I'd reacted firmly but reasonably, and Tom and I had nothing to worry about. Ha! What we had done, of course, was drive his drinking and drugging underground."

Light dawned when Perry was arrested during a drug sweep at his school because he was carrying twenty vials of crack. The judge ordered him into rehab, and he is clean today. Sadly, he was so addicted at the time that he barely remembers any details of his middle school years. But his drug counselor parents hadn't a clue.

The Seductive Appeal

"Not my child," you might say, but the odds are stacked against you and your teenager by at least three factors: the heavy advertising emphasis on the joys of partying; the social belief that drinking is somehow a necessary aspect of being adult at last; and the grapevine word that drugs can make you feel wonderful when you're down.

The facts are indisputable. Most kids will experiment with one or another drug. Most will start with beer or liquor, then probably try marijuana. Depending on many personal, social, environmental, and perhaps genetic factors, a significant percentage will continue their experimentation to the realm of harder drugs and risk becoming addicted.

David and I learned not to be very optimistic about totally preventing all experimentation. One group of drug dealers—the manufacturers and sellers of beer and alcohol—spend millions purveying the message that life is a party. In their ads and licensed products, the party is incomplete without the use of mood-altering substances. Government regulations, industry self-policing, and community group pressures have moderated the message somewhat, but it still assaults the senses nearly everywhere a teenager turns.

Not only in ads but also in other communications and subtle social messages, socializing with drink in hand is portrayed as an enviably adult activity. Your teenager may desperately want to be considered mature; downing half a fifth of Southern Comfort behind the gym may, in some circles, earn respect.

Finally, drugs do indeed fulfill a part of the promise. They can relax you, mask your insecurities, make you feel cheerful and competent. Life is suddenly much more fun, you are on top of the world, you even look better in the mirror. All of us humans tend to do what makes us feel good. In the short term, if only then, drugs can often give great pleasure. You will get nowhere with your child if you try to avoid or circumvent that basic fact.

Because of so many tremendous pressures and seductive lures, I think you should assume that, eventually, your kid will experiment with alcohol or drugs of some sort as part of a social situation. Obviously, such experimentation does not necessarily lead to abuse, overindulgence, or addiction, but how do you know? It's the uncertainty that drives us all crazy. I'd recommend the Nobel Prize for the chemist who could devise a Parent Comfort substance that would cause a kid's hair to turn purple for alcohol, pink for pot, green for LSD, blue for coke. . . . The deeper the hue, the more serious the use. We'd know right away that help is needed.

"With some of the new designer drugs on the market today," drug expert Peggy Lovirgne admitted to me, "I couldn't even catch my husband using, so long as he didn't want me to know and remained more or less in control. In the latter stages of addiction, loss of control becomes obvious and denial can become pathological, but in the earlier stages, you just can't figure things out easily."

I'm not trying to give you sleepless nights. Quite the contrary. You should calm yourself, despite the obvious dangers out there, and recognize that you do not, and cannot, exercise complete control over your child's decisions about drug and alcohol use.

Addiction Potential

Forget complete control, but devote some energy to damage control. For example, it may help to assess your child's "addiction potential." Typically, one of four factors helps determine whether or not a person becomes addicted: (a) genes; (b) the relative availability of drugs; (c) the prevailing cultural attitude toward usage; and (d) personal unhappiness.

By far, genetic predisposition is the most common determinant of addiction. You might be able to carouse yourself into a stupor during Mardi Gras but rarely feel the urge to touch even a drop of sherry most of the time. I might have only a martini or two before dinner yet think constantly about when I can have my next drink. My genetic trait would not be a problem, however, unless an addicting substance becomes available to me. Chronic alcoholism is a severe problem in many American Indian communities today, in large part because of genetic predisposition, but generations before them were not aware of the danger. It took the coming of Europeans to introduce them to the debilitations of alcohol.

So, (a) plus (b), genes plus availability of drugs, is bound to lead to addiction, but any of the four factors is sufficient by itself to turn some people into addicts. The more factors present in a person's life, of course, the more likely it is she will succumb.

To help them endure the horrors of the Vietnam conflict, many soldiers turned to drugs, including heroin. Those who continued their addiction at home fell into two major categories: those with a genetic predisposition; and those who lived in the inner-city environments that are popularly called war zones. The latter group were caught in a combination of factors (b) and (d), the unceasing availability of drugs and the deep unhappiness of their ghetto existence.

Finally, there is the stream in which we all swim: the cultural attitude that happens to prevail at the moment. Patterns of living and socializing in both Italy and France, for example, tend to promote heavy drinking, but Italians have contempt for the drunkard, whereas the French are tolerant. After a three-hour, wine-soaked dinner in a public place, an Italian man will not stand up and leave unless he can walk steadily to the door. If not, he waits until he has sobered a bit. Not surprisingly, alcoholism is a graver social problem in France than in Italy. In America, however, heavy drinking is not only tolerated; in some places—high schools, colleges, male-bonding fishing trips are good examples—getting smashed is promoted. Wild abandon is mandatory. Drink will get you there.

Consider the first of the four determining factors in relationship to your own kid. He is probably at genetic risk if any of his blood relations has or has had problems with drinking or drugs. The closer the blood bond, the greater the likelihood of his own predisposition to addiction. If you or his other parent is an alcoholic, for example, he stands a 50 percent chance of becoming a problem drinker. You should worry also if aunts, uncles, cousins, or grandparents are or have been abusers. Sometimes, the problems seem to skip a generation. In my family, each generation of drunks is succeeded by a generation of teetotaling compulsive caretakers, and then the cycle is repeated.

To get a picture of your child's genetic vulnerability, draw a family tree that includes all known relatives. Circle the known or suspected alcoholics in red. Underline the names of those who, in your opinion, drink too much. Now, circle the fervent teetotalers in another color. Often, someone forswears drink entirely because a mate or family member is a heavy drinker at home. If more than two of your teenager's close relatives cannot control drug or alcohol usage, she has a higher-than-average risk of becoming an alcoholic or addict.

When this is the case, the first course is to educate yourself. To learn the truth about drug and alcohol abuse, go to an AA or Al-Anon meeting. You'll learn more than you could from reading a thousand books about the subject. Because these meetings can vary a lot, however, depending upon the problems and experiences of the people in each group, get a list of several from your local AA hotline. Shop around until you find the one that seems to offer most aid and comfort for your own situation, then attend at least six sessions. If you are asked to speak, don't be embarrassed. Sharing your personal story is considered a part of each of the twelve "step experiences" in AA. Just say, "I am here to listen and learn. Thank you all for your sharing."

If you are sure that participating in such a meeting would make you uncomfortable, then go to a local mental health agency that specializes in alcohol or drug counseling. Set up a meeting with a counselor and discuss your concerns about your kid's genetic history. She will help you put things in proper perspective and suggest what to do next.

In either case, you should sit down with your child once you feel that you have grasped the basic facts that apply. Explain her risks of becoming an addict just as you would explain the dangers involved in driving a car. Make clear that you aren't voicing a suspicion of her behavior or revealing a lack of trust in her judgment and good sense. At first, like many adults who should know better, she may not understand that you are talking about a problem that has to do with physical makeup, not mental or moral weakness. Use pamphlets and brochures to back up what you have learned. Don't assume that she has a firm grasp of genetic theory. Make a comparison to the pattern baldness that always strikes the males in your side of the family in their early thirties, no matter what they do, or the oddly shaped bosoms of that group of cousins in Rochester.

Even if your child is not genetically at risk, a little education can be, despite the old saw, a very helpful thing. It may be enough to read a good book about alcoholism and addiction (see "Suggested Reading", page 248), or attend one of the public service informational meetings that abound these days.

Afterward, talk with your kid about the likelihood that he will someday "experiment" with alcohol. Many first drinks and first episodes of drunkenness result in nothing more than a funny story, and you should recognize that. But your child has to recognize that a first drink can sometimes be deadly. Telling the following true story might make a lifesaving impression.

A Deadly Tale

On a quiet night in a small Pennsylvania town near Philadelphia, a boy almost died because of drink. He wasn't a teenager who plowed into a telephone pole. He was only twelve, and no car was involved—just the boy and a bottle.

His name was Matt, but his friends called him "Dillon" because he looked so much like brat-pack movie star Matt Dillon. When his mother dropped him off at a friend's house for a pool party celebrating the end of the school term, she checked to see that it was properly chaperoned, and so it was. Both parents of the host were present, a lifeguard was on duty, and three college kids were there to serve and clean up.

The party went well. After the refreshments had been demolished, the kids asked permission to play a contemporary version of hide-and-seek, "Blackout." The parents saw no reason not to agree. They relaxed by the pool, and the lifeguard joined the catering help in the kitchen.

None of the adults knew that the game was an excuse, planned in detail days before, to get out of sight and "party." Some couples wanted to neck. Other kids, including Matt, wanted to welcome the freedom of summer by getting pasted. Vodka was the drink of choice because it lacks a tell-tale smell. A month before, Matt had swiped a fifth from the supply his parents had set out for a party.

As bartender, he would pour a drink for a friend, then take a swig himself directly from the bottle. Soon, he was feeling no pain, and his pulls were getting longer. There was at least a quarter of a bottle left when his friends decided they'd had enough. With a great show of bravado, Matt chugged it all, tossed the dead soldier into a trash can, took three steps, and collapsed. He did not come to until late the next day in a hospital. Neither Matt nor any of the other kids had known a simple truth: too much liquor consumed too fast can kill.

Matt was lucky. On a dare, a fifteen-year-old boy in our area chugged a whole fifth of Scotch. There were no adults around when he passed out, and his friends were too scared to get help. He died.

Usually, the stomach spontaneously rejects an overdose of alcohol, but in both these cases, the kids downed the stuff so fast that they stopped breathing before their stomachs could respond. The same thing can happen when a youngster mixes marijuana and too much alcohol. Every year, teenagers die from alcohol overdose because the pot has suppressed their stomach nausea. In your chat with your kid, make sure she understands these facts.

Drug Watch

If you have been looking for signs of drug abuse, you've probably already encountered one or more of the lists designed to help you. They can help, sometimes, but most of the items can be confusing because they are exaggerations of teenage behavior that is typical. For example, most lists cite moodiness or irritability, yet mood swings and peckishness are common in normal adolescence. Drug use might be indicated by loss of motivation, shifting friendships, increased sleeping, changing interests, withdrawal from family, or rejection of religious affiliations. On the other hand, these may be perfectly normal for a teenager. As you surely have noticed already, not all irritable, unmotivated, sleepyheaded kids who change friends, shift interests, become secretive about their comings or goings, don't want to be seen at church, and avoid their families are addicted to drugs.

The lists are not really useful unless they signal when it's time to take action. During our foster-parenting period, I developed a checklist so that I could immediately institute a drug or alcohol watch when I saw a combination of those behaviors:

LEVINE ALARM LIST

1. Personal involvement with drug-oriented identities, as indicated by posters, clothing, jewelry, patches, and similar signs. Fanatic adherence to a drug-oriented rock group like the Grateful Dead or some of the psychedelic groups who play drug-associated "house music." A fondness for T-shirts advertising liquor or a drug-oriented musical group, tie-dyed shirts, jewelry shaped like marijuana leaves.
2. Friends who obviously use drugs or are known to party every weekend.
3. Unusually intense mood swings.
4. Coming in the door "high" more than once. One time is "experimental"; twice is using.
5. Drug paraphernalia on her person or in her room.
6. Rumors about drug usage or expressions of concern from school officials or others in contact with the child.
7. Stealing from others, or credible accusations of such behavior.
8. Using at home.
9. Getting picked up by the police during a drug sweep or for public drunkenness, DWI, or using in a public place.

How do you perform a drug watch? Just share your concern with your kid and warn him that you intend to watch his behavior carefully from now on. Remind him that you are the same responsible adult who wouldn't let him play with matches ten years ago. Now, in the same vein, you are not going to let him play with drugs or alcohol. Furthermore, the evidence seems to suggest that he is doing so.

In one instance, with David backing me up, I said something like this to a foster kid I was concerned about:

"I get worried when I hear all of your friends talk about nothing but getting high and partying. Because you insist on hanging out with that kind of kid, I'm going to do lots more checking up on you. I'll check you over the minute you come home, and if I get worried enough, I might even go through your bureau drawers. Neither of us will feel good about that, but I have to do what I have to do, to protect you. Stay straight, and there won't be any problems."

Now, we harbored few illusions about the effectiveness of this approach, and so should you. Sometimes it just guaranteed that the drug use would be more effectively hidden; at least that result indicated that the usage was being controlled. It never made me happy that a foster child or one of my sons might be secretly using, but I believe there was nothing further I could do but follow the AA slogan, "Let go, and let God."

On the other hand, if your drug watch uncovers more evidence of drug use, you have to do more. David and I developed a strong no-use statement for this eventuality:

"We didn't want to believe that you are actually doing this to yourself. Now that we know, we are telling you right now, in no uncertain terms, to stop. You are not to use any drugs or alcohol. That's it. Stop. If you need help in order to stop, tell us, and we'll get it for you. Now, we both know enough about kids to know that you may not be able to tell us if you keep using, but if you don't stop and we do find out, we have to assume that you cannot stop without help. That means we'll do whatever we have to do to get you the help you need. We care about you and don't want to see you hurting yourself with this stuff."

Don't be idle while you are waiting to see whether or not your warning is heeded. I suggest you begin a three-point program immediately.

First, read a book like Dick Shaefer's *Choices and Consequences,* a very accessible survey of drug behavior in the teenage years. Other titles are listed in my reading suggestions at the back of this book.

Second, form an alliance with the parents of your kid's closest friends. Invite them over for coffee so that you can all share your mutual concerns about drug use. Some parents won't show up; others may come once but not see the need for continuing meetings. Don't flinch if a parent says that her kid's problems are caused by your kid's influence. Don't argue if a parent claims that his child is perfectly clean when you know otherwise. Despite the obstacles, you should be able to develop a core group of parents willing to share information and keep tabs on all of the children.

Third, start going to a twelve-step group like AA or Al-Anon. Believe me, if it turns out that your child is going to keep on using, you'll need more help than I can give you in this book.

Twelve-Step Programs

Twelve-step programs offer two essentials for dealing with a dependency: a community of caring; and a plan for handling any area of life that has become unmanageable. Recovering addicts and alcoholics who participate in an AA session, for example, form the community of caring. Each is likely to include people at various stages of dealing with their problem. The plan is based upon twelve specific steps that constitute a spiritual or moral retraining program.

The first step is recognizing that you cannot control your particular problem, or, as the AA version puts it: "We admitted we were powerless over alcohol and that our lives had become unmanageable." In the first three steps, you learn to accept what you can control and to let go of what is beyond your capacity to control. Taking personal inventory is step 4; admitting the exact nature of your wrong is step 5. These and all subsequent steps build to the twelfth and final step: "Having had a spiritual awakening as the result of these steps, we tried to carry this message to others and to practice these principles in all our affairs."

Many different twelve-step programs are available, they are free, and—for many, many people—they have proved to be lifelines. When your child's drug use indicates that you should become involved in a program, you will learn to do three important things: read the twelve-step literature every day; go regularly to meetings without fail; and find someone to talk to who is also involved in a twelve-step program.

For the program nearest you, look in the White Pages of the phone directory for AA or Alcoholics Anonymous, even if you are more concerned about drug use than alcohol abuse. You'll be helped to find the meeting that is most appropriate to your personal situation. For a wide range of personal problems, AA is one of the best examples of what humans caring for one another can achieve.

When you go to your first session, you'll find free literature and a daily meditation book that costs under $10. You can also obtain a list of people who are at different levels of recovery. As you attend subsequent meetings, seek out someone you can identify with and ask if you can call to discuss your concerns. If they aren't yet ready to help, don't take this as personal rejection. People have lots of reasons for saying no, and none have anything to do with you. Just keep asking until you find someone you can call. That person can help you figure out what to do on a regular basis.

A Word of Caution

Why don't I recommend counseling or psychiatric help the minute you discover a child's drug abuse?

Often, family and individual therapists alike believe that substance abuse can be solved through insight therapy for the individual and family therapy for the entire family. Their professional bias leads them to believe that drug problems fade away when other problems are dealt with. That's incorrect. For a potential drug abuse problem, you begin with the drug experts. Psychotherapy, psychiatric help, and family counseling are simply not enough for battling substance abuse. A twelve-step program combined with a drug rehab program as well as individual or group counseling is the treatment of choice; perhaps family therapy may be useful, too. But the addiction or abuse must be controlled before the other forms of therapy can even begin to work.

Let me show you what I mean:

Shane Jones, a tall, burly, swaggering kid with a learning disability, began to experience problems when he entered high school in Scarsdale, a community so academically competitive that A's aren't considered special unless they're earned in honors courses. He was bright and tried hard, but his marks rose barely above the pass line. Nevertheless, all during football season, Shane's prowess on the playing field kept him happy with himself. It was only after the last game of the season that the gentle giant became a frustrated, roaring bear.

"I never knew what to expect in the mornings," his mother told me. She was a nursery school teacher who had had no problems with her two older children, both girls. Her accountant husband had always had a close, caring relationship with his son. "School mornings were hell. His father would call him, I would call him, Shane would curse us both and sleep on. Lots of days he didn't make it to school until third or fourth period. On weekends, he'd sleep until five in the afternoon, clean out the fridge, and leave the house until midnight or even one or two in the morning. Our lives revolved around getting Shane to school. I discovered that if I took him breakfast in bed his moods were better and he made it to school easier. It seems crazy now, giving a healthy seventeen-year-old breakfast in bed, but that's what our lives had become. It worked, it got him up, and it kept his father and me from fighting about what was wrong with him.

"I wondered about drinking or drugs. Some nights he came home smelling of beer, but he claimed that all of the football players drank during the off-season. For years my daughters had said the same, so I accepted his drinking as normal. I assumed it was occasional and part of the usual socializing in his group. Besides, I never saw him drunk, and he never tried to hide the fact that he'd had a beer or two. Then, in his senior year, Shane was arrested for selling drugs to another kid. That's when I learned he'd been a crack addict for nearly eight months."

Here's my point. For six months before this addicted kid's arrest, the Joneses had been involved in family therapy, at the suggestion of the high school's social worker. Shane, taking a tack typical of drug abusers, had magnified parental problems and complained to her that his mother and father fought too much. The social worker, who was not experienced with drug abusers, fell into the trap of parent bashing. Shane successfully put her off the scent of his very real abuse problem.

The family therapist fared no better, suggesting that Shane's mood problems were a metaphor for their marital problems. Develop greater intimacy in marriage, he advised, and the boy's problems would vanish as the morning mist. Certainly, severe problems can drive a kid to drug use, but the therapist had it backwards, in this case. The addicted Shane was creating problems in a family that was otherwise okay.

"Family therapy wasn't helping Shane at all," Sally recalls. "All it did was push Peter and me apart. I blamed my husband, and he blamed me. Our quarrels, which had never strained our marriage before, suddenly became a 'problem.' Then Shane was arrested and my mother insisted I start going to a local Al-Anon meeting. She'd gone when my brother became involved with drugs. Well, the stories I heard there upset me and helped me both. Some part of every tale reminded me of Shane, and that was scary. But the stories also helped me stop blaming myself and Peter. Ultimately, we switched therapists and went to one who had experience with drug addicts. That has made it possible for me to go on with my life, even though our son is still not sober."

The twelve-step program began to achieve what the other therapies could not even recognize as the actual problem. Without such help, you cannot emotionally survive life with a child who abuses drugs or alcohol. For heaven's sake, don't let pride, shame, shyness, or any other feeling prevent you from going to a meeting. And don't wait until your kid's other parent agrees to go. Just go, even if you have to go alone. Shane may never be rehabilitated. He has been in and out of rehab programs for the past two years. But he would have had a much better chance if his parents had been able to discover his problem earlier and taken action with the help of the knowledgeable people you meet at AA or Al-Anon.

Of course, one valuable lesson you will learn—and it is frustrating for some parents—is that you can control only yourself and your environment. What do you do about the child you have on drug watch?

In the Meantime . . .

While you are going to your twelve-step meetings, the first task is to hope for the best. There may not be any more evidence of drug use. In that case, you keep "working the program" (attending meetings regularly) for at least six months. If things are still going well with your kid, congratulate yourself and him. You can assume that the problem is solved. At that point you may want to keep on attending meetings, or not. Whichever you choose is fine.

But if you do find signs of continued drug use, it's time to plan a Caring Intervention. And don't delay. You may have heard that addicts will not accept help until they "hit bottom," but that bit of folklore has been disproved. My Caring Intervention is a carefully orchestrated, all-purpose effort by which people who love the addict and have witnessed the ravages of his abuse can intervene long before he reaches bottom. (For more information and advice, turn to Chapter 15, "The Caring Intervention.")

If possible, seek professional help in planning an intervention. With luck, you can succeed on your own, but you aren't likely to treat breast cancer by yourself, and the deadly disease of addiction also requires professional care. I give advice on finding the right expert in Chapter 16, "Getting Professional Help," and the Appendix lists many sources of potential help for this situation.

TO SUMMARIZE:

Any experimentation with drugs should set in motion the following chain of events:

1. Issue a drug watch on the spot.
2. If there's further evidence of drug use, issue your no-use warning, form a support group of concerned parents, and attend at least one Al-Anon meeting a week.
3. If your kid keeps using drugs, plan a Caring Intervention in order to move him toward acceptance of his problem.

Never forget this chilling little motto, which you can chant like a kind of diabolical mantra if it helps you keep focused on the problem: Addiction Kills. If your child's use of any chemical substance or alcohol is worrisome, trust your instincts. Every moment of delay could be the destruction of a few more brain cells or liver tissue, the further hardening of an artery or warping of a personality, or the moment when the accident of overdose or overcorrecting a wheel destroys the child you love.

THIRTEEN

The
More-Than-Moody Blues

MOM: "Sweetheart, did you hear what I said?"

KID: "Sure."

MOM: "Well, you usually get so excited when Sara calls and you always phone her back right away."

KID: "Yeah."

MOM: "Is something wrong?"

KID: "Wrong?"

MOM: "Did you two have a fight?"

KID: "Of course not."

MOM: "Well, what is it?"

KID: "Just leave me alone. Okay?"

MOM: "But you haven't talked to any of your friends all weekend."

KID: "I'm tired."

MOM: "From what? You've been sleeping late every day. You napped all afternoon today."

KID: "Mom, please. I'm going to my room now."

MOM: "But I'm getting worried about you."

KID: "Don't worry, Mom. There's nothing you can do. There's nothing anyone can do."

Feeling mad, bad, and sad are teenage facts of life. For all of us, learning to survive the blues is one of life's most important lessons. Depression happens. According to Dr. Daniel Offer, who spent a decade studying adolescent feelings, about one in five teenagers is depressed. Other estimates go as high as 30 percent. Viewing life as empty, painful, hopeless—this is a normal phase even good kids go through, but a few may choose the very bad solution of self-murder. Suicide and other forms of self-destruction are the acts of good kids whose depression has plummeted out of control.

You may not see overt signs of a dangerous level of depression because teenagers mask it expertly, even from themselves. Your child may not recognize that he is depressed; he thinks he is bored, hassled, nervous, exhausted, ticked off. In fact, depression underlies much of the acting-out misbehavior I've talked about in the previous chapters. Unacknowledged teenage blues can cause many a good kid to do bad things. Time after time, David and I discovered that when a foster kid stopped his drug abuse, risk taking, running away, or Gotcha Warring he suddenly realized the depth of his depression. Consider Judith:

She was angelic in appearance—petite, blond, radiant—but she put us through five weeks of hell. The first time she walked into our house, she looked us over for a couple of minutes, dropped her bags without comment, and strode out the back door. She came back the next day to play Gotcha War for three days, then ran off for five. Something like this pattern continued week after miserable week—and suddenly stopped.

No longer fighting or running, Judith stayed in bed all day and cried herself to sleep every night. When she began to talk about hurting herself, we called in a psychiatrist, who hospitalized her briefly. As it happens, she would recover from this serious depression and handles life well today. The alarm signals for her self-destructive feelings, though, had been rung long before she took to her bed. Her anger, like her desire to run away, should have alerted us to the depths of her pain.

Fred, another chronic runaway, was always joking and teasing, but his eyes conveyed a profound sadness that frightened me. He lasted with us three weeks, then ran. After running away from five or six other places, he stole a car and wrecked it. At the juvenile detention center, he had to be prevented from hanging himself.

Odd-looking Gary, whose face was too narrow for his lemur-like eyes, was hyperactive and into everything. We never saw him look sad or seem lonely. One day, after his regular appointment with his probation officer, he came home and tried to hang himself.

Both boys survived. Both suicide attempts apparently surprised everyone who knew them. In fact, Gary's probation officer had thought he was in a very good mood that afternoon.

Blues in Varying Hues

We usually link depression with despair and hopelessness, but boredom, guilt, and excessive irritability also play roles. Depressed kids often lose all interest in old friends and former pleasures. How can you know when your child's depression is verging on the suicidal?

Many sleep-related symptoms could be clues: too many hours spent in sleep, difficulty in sleeping, early morning awakening. Extreme changes in eating habits, either complete loss of interest in food or gorging, can also be indicators. But always remember that any of these behaviors can be sparked by the normal ups and downs of adolescence.

The waters are very muddy, as I was reminded when the mother of a sixteen-year-old suicide victim told me the following:

"It's been three years since Melody killed herself. I've spent those years trying to understand what I could have missed, why I didn't know she was so unhappy. I've talked with every one of her friends, with family, with teachers . . . and we all came to the same conclusion: Melody hid the extent of her unhappiness. Not one of us knew, or even suspected. She was the last person in the world you'd expect to do away with herself."

Scary? You bet—and not an isolated incident. Last year, at a private school near us, three kids tried to commit suicide in the space of one week. One of them, Suzy, was an honor student, top athlete, and BWOC, loved by her classmates.

According to John Meeks, a psychiatrist nationally known for his work with children and adolescents, Melody and Suzy can be classed as type-A kids, driven to succeed. Since their drive often disguises poor self-esteem and major fears of personal inadequacy, such teenagers live in a prison of their own making. They think in all-or-nothing terms: if they drop down from A+, they're failures—failures, too, if they don't make varsity football or get the best-looking date to the prom. Larry, the president of my ninth-grade class, killed himself with a shotgun in college. A minor injury sustained in a championship football game was likely to keep him from becoming an Air Force jet pilot. All or nothing.

Suzy slit her wrists because a boy rejected her, as she was eventually able to reveal in therapy. To this day, no one knows what slight, what perceived failure, what hurt drove Melody into the suicidal depression that ended her life.

Fortunately, the completely unexpected type-A suicide is not the most common. The copycat suicide attempts of Suzy's two classmates did not come as a surprise: one was an overprotected child; the other a learning-disabled loner. Both had worried their parents and school officials for a long time.

Overprotected, overindulged Ellen was the victim of too much love. Born when her parents were well into their forties, she was the miracle baby, the light unto their world, the joy of their existence. Because her least effort earned high praise and she was buffered from the normal pains of daily life, Ellen grew up expecting adoration from the outside world. It was not forthcoming.

She managed elementary school, but junior high was wrenching. In the insular world of other fourteen-year-olds, family praise counted for nothing. She tried to talk with her parents about her loneliness, but they couldn't understand. Only when she took an overdose of sleeping pills did they learn the painful lesson that too much love can harm as much as not enough love. They heard the cry for help in her suicide attempt, and she got the help, both professional and familial, that she needed.

Her learning-disabled classmate was friendless, too. Because his handicap was moderate, hard work had served him well enough in elementary school, but in junior high he stopped studying. Alone, achieving nothing, he felt life was bleak. Even his looks changed, as his inner pain caused him to droop. Then, for a brief period in the tenth grade, he pulled himself together. He even talked about getting into college, but he soon saw that he was going to fail the term, despite his new efforts. In the same week as Suzy and Ellen, he made his suicide attempt.

Two other kinds of adolescent suicide involve teenagers who are overly fascinated with death, and those who threaten suicide to manipulate.

Typical of the first case, fifteen-year-old Aurora was a sensitive, shy youngster who wrote poetry and idolized Sylvia Plath, the internationally famous poet who became a cult figure after killing herself. Aurora seriously contemplated suicide for two years before carrying out her plan. During a visit to her father's apartment, she put her head in the oven and turned on the gas, just like Plath. Like Plath, too, she was successful.

Love affairs with death are not uncommon in adolescence, although they do not often end in suicide. A junior high or high school literary magazine is usually suffused with death and despair, unless the faculty advisor has exercised a heavy editorial hand. The growing awareness of sexuality is linked to a growing awareness that death is inevitable. But Aurora's obsession was unusually intense, and her idealization of someone famous for committing suicide should have been a warning to those who cared about her.

In our fifth type of suicide, repeated suicidal gestures are eventually dismissed by everyone else as mere manipulation. The attempts start out as cries for help; if they don't work, the child has to escalate. And a misfired manipulative suicidal gesture kills as effectively as any other suicide attempt.

Marcie-Ann's four suicide attempts exhausted the patience of her parents and her therapist, and they were quite right to characterize her continuing threats as attempts at manipulating them. Indeed, in yet another manipulative gesture, she took a fatal overdose of pills one afternoon at five o'clock, well aware that her father was due home at five-thirty. Unfortunately, he was detained, and manipulative Marcie-Ann died. The moral is that even the most annoyingly obvious manipulative gestures have to be taken seriously. They threaten your kid's life. They indicate that she has a serious problem that has to be addressed—not that she is merely overdramatizing her feelings or "crying wolf."

When to Worry

When your kid has one sad day, or even three to four, I wouldn't worry too much. That's normal enough for people of all ages. There is a better way to stay on the lookout for serious depression, a so-called SAD PERSONS scale developed by four specialists in suicide assessment, which I've modified slightly for our purposes.

First, you score your kid according to the scale, then use his score to decide what action should be taken:

SAD PERSONS SCALE

Sex . . . males get 1 point.

Age . . . all teenagers (and people over 45) get 1 point.

Depressed . . . 1 point for acknowledging depression.

Previous suicide attempt . . . 1 point.

Ethanol abuse . . . 1 point for drinking or using drugs.

Rational thinking loss . . . excessive guilts, feelings of persecution, hearing voices, and other irrational thoughts earn 1 point.

Social supports lacking . . . loners get 1 point.

Organized plan . . . 1 point if he can tell you how he would kill himself.

No spouse . . . 1 point if he has no best friend or romantic interest.

Sickness . . . 1 point

RATING SCALE FOR ACTION

0–2 points	Keep a watchful eye on your child for a week or two, and then reevaluate his score.
3–4 points	You may need to consult a professional.
5–10 points	Your child must be tested for depression by a professional.

Caution: You must seek a professional evaluation for any child who can tell you how he would kill himself, no matter how poorly considered the plan is, or who admits to hearing voices that suggest he hurt himself.

Such scales are meant to provoke serious consideration of possible problems. They are not hard-and-fast diagnoses by themselves. For example, the four-point case of a teenage boy who says he's depressed when he's suffering from a bad head cold is probably not a candidate for professional evaluation. I would worry, though, about a teenaged son of mine who's just had mono and talks sadly about the moody blues. I'd keep a watchful eye on him, and if he still seemed despondent after a week or two, I would then arrange to have him tested for depression by a professional.

I'm serious. Because depression tests can help assess whether your kid is suffering from a normal case of teenage blues or from a depression grave enough to warrant psychiatric help, your worries will be either allayed or confirmed. The right assessment is important for both of you.

Professionals employ many different tests to evaluate depression levels. As a trained social worker, I was qualified to administer such tests. The one I used was the Beck Depression Inventory. While you can't give this test to your kid yourself, you can ask his school's guidance counselor about having the Beck or another depression test administered by the school psychologist.

Why not just bring your teenager in for psychiatric evaluation? Because it's something most teens would resist, whereas test-taking is something they are used to. Most of my obviously sad children were eager to see just how depressed they were with the Beck Depression Inventory. In fact, as with even the silliest pop-psych personality tests that kids find in magazines, my other youngsters were eager to investigate their feelings with this test, too. Sometimes, the Beck picked up a youngster who had been successfully masking his feelings.

Terry, whose mother was a heroin addict, had never known his father and had endured a chaotic, impoverished life. Quiet, unassuming, he seemed to think our house a haven. Pamela, however, was sleeping half the day, crying frequently, and constantly talking about her depression. When I suggested she take the Beck test, Terry happened to be in the room. To my surprise, he asked to take it, too.

I was floored by the results. Pamela's score indicated a kid suffering life's normal ups and downs. Terry's score indicated serious depression. You may be surprised to learn that both kids were pleased with their scores. Pamela was relieved, of course, but so was Terry.

"Now I know I'm not crazy," he said to me. "I'm just depressed. I really thought there was something terribly wrong with me."

If your kid is depressed, she, too, will feel better if she can put a label on her feelings. She will recognize that something has to be— and can be—done about the problem. Terry sought psychiatric help and seems fine today. Without the test, he may never have had the right impetus to address and deal with his serious depression.

Don't make a big deal of suggesting the test to your kid. Just say,

"You've seemed 'down' for a fairly long time; I've just read about a
test that measures depression, and I wonder if you would mind taking
it." If she agrees, arrange for her to be tested. If she doesn't, let it go
for now. Usually, her curiosity will be piqued and she'll change her
mind. If not, there are other ways to assess her feelings.

Other Gauges of Depression

At least three factors can help you.

First, consider the extent of depression or addiction in your family
history. The two often go together, since many addicts are using drugs
or alcohol in a doomed effort to "cure" depression. Look for clues in
more than two family members across three generations. For example,
if Great Aunt Hildegarde committed suicide, Uncle Tabios was a sot,
and your nephew Jude has just come out of rehab for drug addiction,
your family is probably at genetic risk for depression.

Second, how many losses did your kid suffer in childhood? Early
loss of loved ones through death or divorce often sets the stage for later
depression, especially if accompanied by related losses: a drop in living
standards, a move away from good friends and social supports.

Third, take a close look at more recent losses, even if your kid has
not said much about them. Friends might have moved away or chosen
to go off with another crowd. Perhaps some long-held dream has died,
or he's not able to handle the inevitable teenage recognition that you
and his other parent are fallible, or some childhood comfort has paled
and not been replaced. Don't use your own adult values in judging the
significance of a loss to your child. The death of a pet, the loss of a
school election, a low grade from a favorite teacher—these kinds of
events can trigger dangerous periods of depression.

Any of these factors can signal that it's time to talk things over with
your kid. You might start with an observation: "You seem sadder than

usual." If she agrees, let the discussion flow naturally. Resist offering the quick fix, the easy assurance, or your child will think you don't really understand. You want to listen carefully in order to find out just how blue is blue. You can open the door to greater sharing by saying something like, "You really are hurting about this."

If, on the other hand, your child does not immediately respond to your first question, keep plugging: "Are you feeling especially down or blue?" If he says no, accept his answer, but close the conversation with an observation like this: "Life is hard, and it's always hardest when you're a teenager, so if you ever get really down, let me know what you need from me to help."

Then back off and wait. If the moody blues keep playing, reopen the issue again. Let your child know that you are more than curious; you are concerned. Here's the message to try for:

"I don't mean to pry, but I do want you to know I love you and want you to have a happier life. It looks to me as if you've been down for a long time, and I don't think that's necessary. If you don't want to talk to me, I can help you find someone you can talk to. Would you like that?"

Facing the Worst

Finally, you may have to ask the questions you most dread asking. If your child is willing to talk and admits that she is very blue, brace yourself and put the worst in words: "So blue that life is no longer worth living?" Listen very carefully to her answer. Anything short of "Things aren't that bad" or "Of course not" should lead to further questioning.

Here are three questions that can help you probe the depths of your child's despair. Progressively, each digs more deeply than the one before:

1. "You seem really unhappy. When people are as blue as you seem, they often think of hurting themselves. Do you ever have thoughts like that?"
2. "You've thought of hurting yourself. How seriously did you think about that? A lot of people think about such things, but they know, down deep, that they would never follow through. How about you?"

3. "You do think seriously about hurting yourself, I see. What does that mean to you exactly? What would you do to yourself? How?"

Once your child admits thinking seriously of committing suicide, it's time to get professional help for both of you. The more detailed his plan, the more immediate the crisis. With my foster kids, it was off to see the psychiatrist at our local hospital's emergency room. You will probably want to speak first to your kid's physician and get her help and advice in arranging a psychiatric consultation.

Meanwhile, institute a suicide watch. While you are waiting for his evaluation, your kid must always be in the company of someone who knows that he's seriously depressed and that suicide is a distinct possibility. After the psychiatric evaluation, and after your kid has entered a treatment program (if recommended), you can lift the watch.

What if your child refuses to see the psychiatrist?

Well, what would you do if she were bleeding to death and refused to go to the hospital?

You don't need your troubled child's permission to get him to the lifesaving treatment he needs. If he is hemorrhaging emotionally, you have the parental responsibility of finding skilled help in staunching those wounds, too.

Reality Check: As in so many teen problems, you have to find the proper balance between denial and excessive worry. Don't let news stories about teenage suicide knock you off balance. Don't let the apparent comfort, serenity, or normalcy of your family life fool you, either. In this chapter I've discussed the five types of adolescent suicide. Your first step: See if any of them matches your own kid's behavior or personal situation. Your second step: Make use of the various assessment tools I've given you. Third: Take the appropriate action, in a calm, controlled, caring manner.

FOURTEEN

The Caring Response

COUNSELOR: "Daryl says you don't give a damn."

FATHER: "That little s____t!"

MOTHER: "We work hard. We give him everything. What does he expect from us?"

FATHER: "He's the one who doesn't give a damn. He's ruining his life, but will he listen to us? No way!"

MOTHER: "That's right. We're just his parents. We don't count."

COUNSELOR: "Well, there is a way to get his attention. . . ."

FATHER: "Sure, but I don't think we can afford a nuclear warhead."

COUNSELOR: "No, but if you've got the time, and the patience, there's a method that does work—"

MOTHER: "To get that kid's attention? We're ready to try anything!"

COUNSELOR: "Okay . . ."

FATHER: "I appreciate what you're trying to do, but this time, I think you've met your match. That boy's hopeless."

COUNSELOR: "We'll see."

Tough Love vs. Soft Love

In skimming the how-to-parent books at your local bookstore or library, you undoubtedly have encountered plenty of examples of both sides of the what-to-do see-saw. Or, in other words, conflicting advice from professionals. When I first began parenting, the books drove me crazy. I'd been student, graduate student, teacher, and practitioner in my field; my academic texts agreed with each other, by and large. But now I picked up the book that advised parents to get a hell of a lot tougher, then the book that warned us to become softer, next, the book that accused us of being too weak, followed by the best-seller that attacked us for being insensitively rigid.

Basically, there are two extremes out there in Adviceland: "tough love" and "soft love," and never the twain shall meet. Well, David and I stopped riding this particular see-saw when we realized that each approach is in touch with one, and only one, side of the truth. Tough love works in some families; only soft love works in others. Occasionally, the best remedy is a switch in positions, from soft to tough, or vice versa. But switching at the wrong time can throw you hopelessly off balance. To help you decide which approach to take, and when to switch, I'm going to teach you the strategy I developed through trial and error: the Caring Response.

A Caring Protocol

I developed my Caring Response as a step-by-step protocol, or plan, to help parents do the following:

1. Care and confront an unwanted behavior.
2. Ally with the child so that the caring can go on.
3. Review all factors involved in the behavior.
4. Investigate possibilities of change.
5. Negotiate a change.
6. Go on caring.

Caring = Confronting Unacceptable Behavior

No caring parent ignores unacceptable behavior. For me, as you know by now, that includes hurting other people or animals, destroying property, or breaking the law. I'd add that you have a parental right to control of your home environment and peace of mind. If you have been able to stop behavior that crosses these general lines, good for you. If you haven't, you need to try the Caring Response, which requires that you keep caring and responding until you find a solution.

Communication = Response

If you respond negatively to unacceptable behavior and your child reforms, your message has been successfully communicated. If she doesn't? The message was not received.

The Caring Response helps you evaluate the message she received and then decide how to get across the message you originally intended. Why isn't she hearing you? Are you sending the wrong message? Is it swamped by other unintended messages? Here's what I mean:

You say, "Clean the kitchen."

But you mean, "Clean the kitchen now."

Your son hears, "Clean the kitchen when you feel like it." (Oh, yes, that's a legitimate interpretation.)

When you walk into the kitchen an hour later, penicillin is still growing in the breakfast dishes.

You say, not without snappishness, "I said to clean the kitchen."

"Don't freak out. I'll get to it."

"Now! Not later."

Your son groans but moves toward the grungy sink. The job gets done. You congratulate yourself on finally getting him to act.

Let's try another example:

Just making conversation, you ask, "How's school?"

"Why are you always on my back about school?" your daughter snaps. "Can't you leave me alone? Doesn't anything I do ever please you?"

Startled, you realize that the message you sent was not the message your daughter received. You now have a number of options:

You might say, "Is there something going on at school I should know about?"

Or, "I was just making idle conversation, for heaven's sake. School is your business. You know I think you handle it well."

Or, "What's going on? I ask an innocent question, and you have to dump all over me?"

Or, "Sorry, I didn't mean to sound pushy."

You can't be certain what to say because you aren't certain what your daughter is trying to communicate. You don't know how to respond, and communication is response. My Caring Response can help you maintain a caring stance while you try to get the response you want from your teenager.

Caring Communication

Remember, you use the Caring Response when your normal strategies fail. Take the example of schoolwork. Suppose you normally monitor your child's studying. Suddenly, her grades begin to slide, so you monitor more closely. It doesn't work anymore. The grades continue to fall. It's time for the Caring Response.

STEP 1: CONFRONT

You say, "Your grades are still falling. Something isn't working."

Your kid responds, "I'm satisfied with my grades."

STEP 2: ALLY

You say, "Well, I certainly don't think your grades are bad, and you know that I think many things are more important than marks. Still, I can't believe you're entirely happy with this situation. Grades that slip from an A average to a B average must bother you a little. I'm on your side. And I do feel we need to talk about this."

Your child says nothing.

STEP 3: REVIEW

You say, "Tell me what you think the problem is. What do you need from me to help?"

Your kid replies, "I want you to bug out of my life. I can handle this."

You say, "So you want me to let you decide how much you need to study. You think my monitoring isn't helpful anymore. It makes you angry. Is that accurate? Do you know what worries me and how I'm feeling?"

"You're scared I won't get into the college you want me to go to."

"No, I'm afraid you'll disappoint yourself, but I also hear that you think I'm pressuring you to go to the college of my choice, not yours.

If I've given you reason to feel that way, I'm sorry. I want you to have a choice, and to have a wide choice you need a B + average."

Your child smirks. "Right. You'll be real happy if I end up at Podunk Community College."

You say, "You want to go to law school, and that's going to be hard if you graduate from a community college instead of a state university or private college. But maybe you have another career in mind. That choice is yours, entirely. I can bug out if you really think that you don't want my help."

"When I feel you are always looking over my shoulder, I feel I'm being pressured."

"Okay, I hear that. What about my worries that you need to keep the door open on some future choices? Can you understand that?"

Your child says, "Yes, I can."

STEP 4: INVESTIGATE

You ask, "Then what do you want to do from here on?"

Your teenager answers, "I want you to stop telling me how to do my work, calling my teachers, checking up on me all the time."

STEP 5: NEGOTIATE

You say, "I think I can go along with butting out entirely, but I need something to calm my anxieties. I know this is your business, but I am a worrier. What can you do to help me worry less about you and your grades?"

Your child replies, "I'll go to Resource three times a week. They're good at helping people get organized."

"Great. I'll try very hard not to interfere. You remind me if I do. You know I have faith in your ability to work things out, and I think using the Resource Room is a good idea. Good luck. I love you."

STEP 6: GOING ON

Either you stay out of the problem, the grades go up, and you do nothing . .

Or you stay out of the problem, the grades stay the same, and you do nothing . . .

Or you stay out of the problem, the grades go down, and you use the Caring Response again to confront and care.

Essentially, this brief parent–child interchange contains all of the elements of the Caring Response. Your aim is to join with your child's view of the problem and work from that basis. Joining is the essence of caring and allying. Each step of the Caring Response must be taken as an alliance—confront and ally, review and ally, investigate and ally, negotiate and ally, go on and ally.

The first step, confrontation, should be followed as quickly as possible with an allying statement. If tempers flare in the initial confrontation, take time out for a cooling-off period before moving on to the next four steps of the Caring Response.

Permission to Blow

Some parent education books, like *Parent Effectiveness Training,* urge you to keep your parenting conflict-free. Not me. As I discussed in the Gotcha Wars, a good kid doing bad things sometimes needs an angry parent. Also, there are times when you simply cannot help getting so fed up and frustrated that you blow like Moby Dick. That's life. You're human.

Yes, blowing signals a failure to communicate, but it also signals the start of an unplanned Caring Response . . . as long as it is followed by an effort to ally. A blowup can mean that you care enough to sound your angriest. It won't damage your child unless you neglect to ally right away, showing that you want to understand her needs and point of view. Repeat: Confronting (with or without blowing up) and allying must always be linked. Like the old saw that you should never go to bed angry with your spouse, you should never let your child walk away from a confrontation convinced you don't care about her. Never.

This is hard to do, I grant you, when your child is determined to play a heavy Gotcha War game. Making sure you ally in that situation requires practice. Worse, a kid can sometimes resist your peacemaking efforts because she wants to create a blowup that will give her an excuse to break your rules.

When pretty little Coralee followed me around one afternoon trying to pick a fight, I was magnificently serene. From other kids I had learned that she wanted to party that night. Her conscience would not let her be bad unless I was bad. For a grueling five hours the contest wore on—and finally she won. I blew. Even now, I can conjure up the Gotcha War victory smile she flashed when she shouted that she was leaving "this shit-hole." While she was packing upstairs, I had just enough time to calm myself down. She stormed down the staircase, still spouting obscenities, but I was ready with an allying statement:

"I'm really pissed right now, but when you come back, we'll talk about this. I do care."

No, she did not melt. In fact, she got angrier and flew out the front door. But she did hear me, and that is what mattered in the long run. Soon she was back with us, ready to look at what had happened and why.

Sometimes, when a confrontation with a kid was rapidly deteriorating from bad to worse, the best allying I could do was to say loudly:

"I want this settled, but right now I'm just getting more and more upset. We'll have to talk later. I care enough to work this out . . . but not now!"

When a youngster became familiar with this message, I could shorten it: "Time out. I'm pissed. I care."

The most bloodthirsty of Gotcha Warriors might continue, despite my call for a recess. Some kids have followed me to the bathroom and stood outside pounding on the door. Sometimes I could only escape by leaving the house. It took time, but eventually I learned, even in those hellish situations, that the child needed my anger but I had to remain detached. I practiced until I could say, "I still care. I need to get away for a while. We'll talk later."

Planned Caring

When you can plan your Caring Response ahead of time, the first step in confronting is to make an appointment with your kid. This initiative, like every other aspect of the process, must be accompanied by allying. Let's look at some examples I worked out with worried parents in my Parent Tactics group.

"Joan, you've missed three curfews in the past week. You told me that you feel there was a good reason each time, and you argued about punishment. I think you're playing games and want to change your curfew time. Maybe we should consider changing your curfew, but I want to talk about it together, not just have it happen. Is now a good time, or do you want to set up a date later in the week? I feel we can come to a solution to this problem that will satisfy us both—if we talk together."

As you recognize, this confrontational statement is suffused with alliance-building signals and behavior. Here's a slightly angrier one that was more appropriate to the needs and feelings of another parent:

"Todd, I've told you not to bring friends home when I'm at work. It is my biggest no-no. Just this week you've had someone in almost every day. You say they just stop by for a few minutes, but that's not the point. My rule is that no one is to be in my home except my children when I can't be here. I'm really angry, but I'm sure we can settle this. When do you want to talk?"

Often, your child will meet your initiative by trying to prevent further discussion. If she is reasonable and promises that the offending behavior will stop, you should go no farther at this point. Let's say that Joan claims she isn't trying to change her curfew and promises not to be late again. Her parent should accept that in the spirit of alliance, but should also set the stage for another step in the Caring Response, in case it becomes necessary in the future, by saying something like this:

"Great. You'll be on time from now on. If not, then we can talk about what's happening. But for now, I'll be happy just to hear you coming through the front door on time, as you say you will. Thanks for being reasonable."

Or perhaps Todd tells his parent that he doesn't want the other kids in the house either and has learned this week that letting someone in just for a minute can mean that he'll have a hard time getting rid of them.

"Great. You can tell them I really got angry. That should help. If you need any more help from me, just holler. We can close the subject unless I find out that someone has been here again. Thanks for listening."

These are best-case scenarios, of course. Generally speaking, you will turn to the Caring Response after several promises of reform have not been fulfilled. Let's say that you have confronted your son three times in a row about making long-distance phone calls without permission. Begrudgingly, he's paid you back, long after you've paid the bill. Each time, he's promised not to do it again, but now a bill comes with $60 of his charges. You're operating on a tight budget; you can't afford to float him $50 or $60 each month until he coughs up for his calls to his long-distance friendship or romance.

It's time to explain that you can't accept his promises any more:

"Sorry, kid. I've heard this too many times. You make promises, but I'm still left having to pay a humongous telephone bill every month. I can't afford it. We have to settle this, and I know we can. Right now, I want this worked out. If now is not a good time, let's set up a date when we can talk. That's my bottom line. You have a choice—now, or Monday night after dinner."

More About Allying

Giving your kid a choice is a form of allying. In the example above, it implies that you understand he has feelings and respect his need to think a bit before the battle begins. In any situation, it says that you respect his desire to be involved in decisions that are important to him.

Another good allying tactic is to admit your own foibles, flaws, and faults. If you're hard on yourself, your kid may ally with you. He doesn't think you are really "that bad." If he brings up the criticism, you have a similar opportunity to ally, even if you disagree with the criticism. Remember: The way your child sees you is the way you are to him. It isn't necessarily the way you are. But when you accept your teenager's view as potentially valid, the two of you are allied. Here are some examples:

A foster kid calls me crazy. I consider the crazy things I've done recently, particularly to that kid, and say, "You're right. I've done some really crazy things. But right now, the problem isn't my craziness; it's your behavior."

A kid calls me stupid. Bright as I think I am, I know that I often do some very stupid things, so I have no problem saying, "Yes, I do some stupid things, but right now we are talking about a specific problem you have, not how stupid I am."

Even if I can't find a small grain of truth in a child's accusation, I can always agree that her point of view is real:

"I see that you feel I am always out to get you. I'm sorry about that, because I don't want you to feel that way. First, let's see what we can do to solve the problem I have with your behavior. When that is solved, we can talk about how I can behave differently."

You might have occasion to use one of these allying statements:

"We can work it out."

"You have choices."

"Tell me more about what you are feeling."

"I can hear that you [paraphrase her complaint or criticism]. Did I get that right?"

"You have a good point there."

"We may have a problem, but our relationship is much bigger than our problem. We can work things out. If not today, there's always tomorrow."

Allying does not have to be verbal. A sympathetic smile can prove to a child that you're on his side. You can also ally symbolically. Feeding is a form of symbolic caring, so I often call time-out for cocoa and cookies when a Caring Response becomes hot and heavy. Sometimes I suggest a walk as we continue talking, and I interrupt myself to point out something of beauty or human interest along the way. Not only do strategies like these help forge an alliance; they also help you and your child remember that, even in bad times, life goes on . . . and so does caring.

Allying has to continue throughout the process of the Caring Response. When anger makes a time-out necessary, you have to let go of the anger during the recess. When I've had to confront a child and we've called a time-out, I make sure to give her a hug later on in the day or leave a little note of encouragement on her pillow. Sometimes I cook a special treat for dinner. These mini-acts of alliance reinforce your basic theme: You are being hard on the bad behavior, not on the good kid who keeps perpetrating it.

Review

In step 3 of the Caring Response, you need to ask whether or not the problem is really yours, not your child's, particularly if the process began with an angry outburst on your part. Is your anger justified?

We all have our limitations, as human beings and as parents. When we're upset with a boss, feeling dog-tired or otherwise primed to go on a tear, it's likely that the kid who does something mildly annoying is going to get a double blast of anger. So double-check your angry response. Exactly what did your child do wrong? How frequent has the behavior been? How do you generally respond to this particular behavior? What was different this time? Your mood? When you calm down, do you feel twinges of guilt suggesting that you overreacted? What does your spouse think?

When Jane came home ten minutes after curfew, her mother was waiting. When Jane tried to explain, her mother uncharacteristically exploded. The girl tried sensibly to take a time-out, but her mom wouldn't let her leave the room. What Jane didn't know was that her mother had had a hard day at the office; worse, her boss had just called to bawl her out about some mistake or other. Eventually, Jane knocked down a chair in anger, something she had never done before. Her mother's need to get rid of frustrations had fueled an overreaction to the curfew violation, and this unreasonable response had incited an untypically violent response in her daughter. In this case, the adult was deeply in the wrong.

Whenever you realize that you have overreacted, or suspect that you have more of a problem than your child, forswear immediately all efforts to deal with his behavior. For the moment, cancel the Caring Response. Say, "I think the problem in this situation right now is me. Please accept my apology."

If you find yourself having to apologize for overreacting more than once a month or so, you have a problem that needs to be worked out in counseling or in a support group. Read Chapters 16 and 17 with some care.

Sorting Out Feelings

On the other hand, even when you know that you are not scapegoating your kid, you still need to review your feelings. Long before you sit down with your teenager to discuss a problem, make sure you know exactly what makes you angry or worried. Be clear on what you want changed, why it should be changed, and how you will know that it has indeed been changed. Consider these issues well before you let your kid know that you're initiating a Caring Response.

For example, let's suppose that you agree with Todd's mother: no friends in the house when you're not there. That's how you were brought up, most of your friends agree with you, and so does your spouse. To you, the rule just makes good sense. But the purpose of the third step in the Caring Response is to explain "why" as well as "what."

To your teenager, the rule may seem like an indication that you don't trust him. You don't agree. You think that you trust him but don't trust groups of kids alone together in a house unblessed with adult supervision. You have to get your kid to hear what you're trying to say.

And you must continually ask yourself what really worries you. Usually parents fear that the best of teenagers, when unsupervised, will engage in such bad behaviors as drinking, drug abuse, furniture-threatening rowdiness, or irresponsible sex. Which one or more is worrying you?

Where my two sons are concerned, David and I would not be happy about any of those behaviors, but our principal worry is sex. All of the others, if they happened at our house, would eventually get back to us, and we would deal with them. Kids are more careful to hide sexual behavior, however. We do not want to find out about orgies in the attic from an announcement that we are to be grandparents before our time. Although I wrote earlier that parents have limited control over their kids' decisions about having sex, remember that I also believe in doing what I can to say no. Allowing boys and girls unchaperoned afternoons in our house is not my idea of discouraging premature sexual activity.

And there is a moral issue here. If you have a daughter, you want the parents of her friends to be on your side, when it comes to things sexual. If I had a daughter, I wouldn't let her bring her boyfriend home when I was absent; by the same token, I won't let my sons bring teenage girlfriends home when I'm not there.

Moreover, the parent of boys has to consider possible legal problems in unsupervised activities. If your twenty-one-year-old son brings home a sixteen-year-old girl for intercourse, he's guilty of statutory rape. If you knew about or sanctioned the rendezvous, you're legally liable as an accessory. And what if the girl claims that she was molested or raped during a party at your house? Your absence, or your ignorance, is no excuse. I believe you take my point.

Now, back to the Caring Response. Let's say that you've reviewed your thoughts about the problem of friends in the house and have decided what you really want and why. Once you know that you can put your ideas in words, hold the thought. Before explaining your point of view, you should ask your kid's opinion. The other way around, you risk cutting off what he thinks, and his thoughts are necessary for a successful alliance.

Say something like this:

"I know you've heard me tell you that I don't want your friends in the house when I'm not here. But I'm not really sure what you think

THE CARING RESPONSE 185

about that rule, or why you think I made it. Why don't you tell me what you think is going on?"

Parents I know have reported a wide range of responses, including the following:

"You think I'll have a party."

"You think I'll let my friends run up the phone bill."

"You think my friends make too big a mess."

"You're afraid my friends will eat you out of house and home."

"You're prejudiced. You don't like my friends because some of them are black."

"You think the neighbors will talk."

"You just don't trust me."

"You think we'll bring girls over and have sex with them."

Whatever your kid's response, take it seriously, but let him know if he's off the mark: "Wrong. Try thinking of another reason." If he can't come up with the right reason by the third try, just tell him.

"You know, everything you've said makes sense from your point of view. I understand that. But my worry is something you haven't mentioned yet. Frankly, I'm afraid that you'll bring friends here who are dating each other and it will be hard to keep things in bounds sexually. I remember when I was younger how hard it was to say no, and I don't want to be part of someone else's kids getting involved this way."

Remember: Communication is response. Some kids will be understanding of your point of view. Most will protest that you have nothing to worry about, or you're just being old-fashioned. In the latter case, you will have to review some more:

"You think I'm old-fashioned. I can understand that. I thought the same thing about my parents. But can you understand that, given how old-fashioned I am, I don't want you bringing friends home from school while I'm at work?"

Your goal here is twofold: ally with your child's perspective, but hold firmly to your own. You want him to agree that, given who you are and how you feel, your viewpoint is reasonable. Each side has to accept the other's feelings as legitimate. You have to be open; you have to allow your kid to rebut and let off steam. Once he seems to understand how you feel, you need to review his attitude once again:

"I am curious how you feel now about all this. You've heard my side, and responded. Now tell me yours."

You should listen until you really do understand his feelings about the situation, but that doesn't mean you have to give in or change your rules. Not at all. In this example, all you have to say is something like,

"I hear how strongly you feel you can handle this and that you feel you need to keep having friends over, but I just can't say yes. I gather you feel that your ability to keep friends is at risk, am I right?"

You can end the reviewing when each of you can see the other's point of view as having some legitimacy and the emotional intensity surrounding the issue has been lowered. Take heart. These two aims may not be accomplished until after several sessions with your child. Along the way, don't forget that you can always call time-out—and may need to often.

But if the issue is still hotly joined after the third session or so, something else must be going on. Perhaps you and your teenager are involved in some sort of power struggle that transcends the specific problem at hand. Such conflicts are more likely if you're a tough love parent, I believe, but they can happen with soft love parents as well. How can you tell?

In a power struggle, the issue is not how to solve the problem, but who's boss. You may not think you are excessively controlling, but what matters is what your child feels. If she feels you're too bossy, every rule is potentially the backbreaking straw. After the third unproductive session, ask this question:

"You know, we don't seem to be able to reach an agreement on this problem. Is it the main issue, really, or do you think something else is going on? Maybe you think I'm too strict about everything. Maybe this rule is the one you've decided to take a stand on. Does that make any sense? Let's talk about that."

Now, be prepared for something you may not want to hear. Quite a few teenagers think their parents are too tightly controlling. If your kid is one of them, just listen and learn what you can. As in any situation, accept the problem she describes as a real one. In other words, now there are two problems that need work: the original rule-breaking, plus your kid's feeling of being bossed around. She will probably be more than willing to agree with this assessment.

This is a good time to use a technique developed by Penelope Russianoff, as she explains in *When Am I Going to Be Happy?* It's called "from you-ness to me-ness." The idea is to begin with the other person's point of view, the you-ness, and move toward your own point of view, the me-ness. Realities vary. Your child's reality may include you as a bossy parent, despite the truth. If you recognize her reality, her anger will be defused and there's a greater chance that she can try to accept your reality, at least in part.

Here are some "you-ness to me-ness" chats worked out by parents in my group:

"Now I understand that you think I'm bossy. And I can understand why you feel that way, even though it doesn't look that way to me. I thought that I was only trying to figure out how we can solve this particular rules problem. It's not that I enjoy telling you what to do. Please try to imagine what I feel when you break curfew. I don't want to lie awake every night worried about whether you are dead or alive."

"Okay, I understand now that you don't think I trust you. I guess that must hurt. For my part, I'm worried here about what others will think if I let you bring your boyfriend home when I'm still at work. I can understand that that seems silly to you, but to me it is important. The criticism of my friends would hurt me. That has nothing to do with whether or not I trust you."

"You think I want to control you. In my view, I was just trying to get the dishes done."

Make clear that you are willing to deal with their criticism of you, but not right now. Keep the cart in front of the horse:

"You want to talk about your feelings that I am too bossy. I want to talk about the problem on the table first, because that's where we started, and then I'll be ready to talk as long as you want about my bossiness."

Most kids will agree to this order of priorities. At this point, you should call a time-out before step 4 of the Caring Response, especially if the reviewing has been lengthy, loud, and lurid:

"Why don't we sleep on this? In fact, let's let it all rest for three days, then we can get together and do some brainstorming. We understand each other's feelings now. The rest is just a mopping-up exercise."

Investigate

Caution: Step 4, to be frank, sometimes leads you into compromising on a rule that you intended to remain as firm as Gibraltar. Just as often, it can lead to a concession in some other area that will help your kid decide to honor the rule in dispute.

This is brainstorming time. Get pencil and paper, clear your mind for wide-ranging creativity, and follow this dictum: during investigation, anything goes.

One tactic is to devise lists. Todd, the kid who kept bringing friends home, was able to come up with ten things that might solve his problem:

1. Get married.
2. Bring home married friends only.
3. Become a monk.
4. Change Mom's views about teenagers and sex.
5. Get permission slips from his friends' parents.
6. Hire a chaperone.
7. Hire two chaperones.
8. Get an allowance increase so that he can take his friends to the movies or skating instead of having to bring them home.
9. Convince Mom to quit her job and go on welfare.
10. Hope that Mom wins the lottery and quits work.

It seems to me that Todd's list shows a lively blend of creative thinking and sly humor; he's having fun and he's really looking at the problem. As it turned out, item 6 was also on his mother's list and became the chief negotiating point for solving their problem. More about that later . . .

Another brainstorming technique that works well with families is "mind-mapping," developed by Michael Gelb and explained in detail in his *Present Yourself: Captivate Your Audience with Great Presentative Skills.* Mind-mapping allows you to diagram your wide-ranging thoughts while you brainstorm. You begin your mind map by drawing a picture of what you want or writing down a description of your goal in the middle of a page. For the next ten to fifteen minutes, you jot down all possible related words that come to mind, without editing them. Once your stream of consciousness is exhausted, you rank and connect the ideas. With differently colored pencils, you devise your own diagrams, arrows, or pathways for illustrating the connections between ideas. You can see what I mean in the sample mind maps reproduced on the following pages.

When you sit down with your child for this exercise, each of you will make his own mind map. Give yourselves time to draw a picture or symbol that represents your respective goals, set a timer for ten minutes and start slapping down the key words. At the buzz, exchange maps and look them over. Five minutes later, each of you takes his own map back, the timer is set for an additional five minutes, and you both add new ideas to your own maps. If your kid's other parent or other family members want to join in, be sure that every participant looks at all of the other mind maps before the last five minutes of scribbling.

The next step is for each of you to start linking ideas on your own map. First, find the themes. Usually there will be a theme of the use of rewards and punishments. Connect all of the related words with one color. Often a theme focuses on what the other person can do. You can reverse this theme to connect ideas that show what you can do. You can clean up the picture further by connecting the various flights of fancy that will not be followed.

You can rank ideas by underscoring the most useful in blue, the least helpful in yellow, and the rest in colors that clarify their ranking to you. Now, exchange the mind maps again. Everybody participating will choose a color and circle the three most important ideas on everybody else's maps.

These ideas are then set down for the potential negotiating list. Remember, each of you has chosen the three ideas from the other person's list; therefore, each item on the negotiating list shares the input of at least two participants in the mind-mapping exercise.

Study the mind maps on the following pages. In this family, a mother and father made maps with their two sons: a twelve-year-old and a sixteen-year-old who had both the wake-up problem and the school tardiness problem. The mother's map records the thinking of a soft love parent. Bent on being accommodating, she had been known to deliver breakfast in bed on rainy mornings. By contrast, the father was tough love incarnate; his map leans heavily on punishments. The kids, as their maps indicate, wanted their parents to bug out, in terms of criticism, but they also wanted to have breakfast hot and steaming at a certain time. Ingeniously, I think, they came up with the idea of having two alarm clocks apiece—one that would let them snooze, one that would clang away as the last resort. In negotiating based upon these mind maps, the whole family agreed that if Dad's butting out, Mom's concentrating only on getting breakfast ready, and the purchase of four alarm clocks didn't solve the two problems, then Dad could come down hard. Clearly, mind-mapping can generate enough

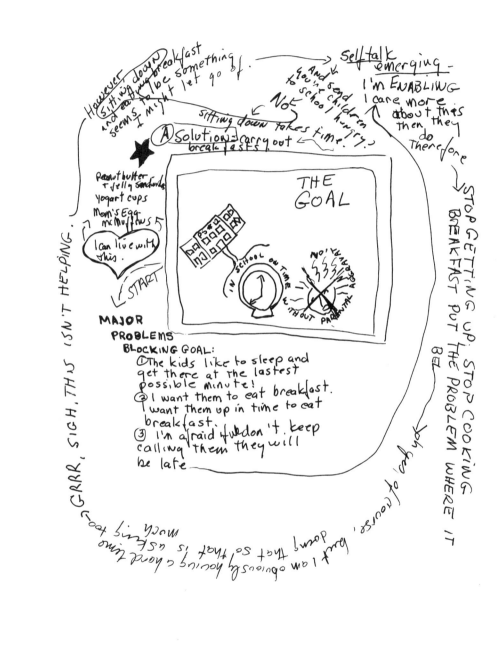

However, sitting down and eating breakfast seems to be something I might let go of.

And send your children to school hungry? NOT

Self talk emerging — I'm ENABLING I care more about this then they do Therefore

A Solution = carry out breakfasts

sitting down takes time.

Peanut butter + Jelly sandwiches
yogurt cups
Mom's Egg-McMuffins
I can live with this.
START

THE GOAL

IN SCHOOL ON TIME WITHOUT PARENTAL AGG

NO! I'LL be late!!!

MAJOR PROBLEMS BLOCKING GOAL:
① The kids like to sleep and get there at the lastest possible minute!
② I want them to eat breakfast. I want them up in time to eat breakfast.
③ I'm afraid if I don't keep calling them they will be late

GRRR, SIGH, THIS ISN'T HELPING.

STOP GETTING UP. STOP COOKING BREAKFAST. PUT THE PROBLEM WHERE IT BE-

mom being too much of course, but I am obviously having a hard time doing that so that is useful too.

MOTHER'S MIND MAP

I HATED GETTING UP IN THE A.M.
I STILL HATE GETTING UP.

PUNISHMENTS   NATURAL CONSEQUENCES
> LET THE SCHOOL HANDLE ITE

(MINE) LOSS OF CAR
LOSS OF PHONE
LOSS OF ALLOWANCE
CAN'T PLAY SPORTS

LET THEM BUY
BREAKFAST AT SCHOOL

Smiles and peace
in the morning

REWARDS
WHY REWARD
BEHAVIOR THAT
SHOULD BE ITS
OWN REWARD

TIE MARY TO
HER BED GAG HER

BOARDING
SCHOOL

PUT ROOSTERS
IN EACH BOY'S ROOM

CONCUBINES TO TICKLE
THEM AWAKE

INSTALL AN ELECTRIC SHOCK SYSTEM

I FEEL DEFEATED - WHY IS
THIS SUCH A BIG PROBLEM →

FATHER'S MIND MAP

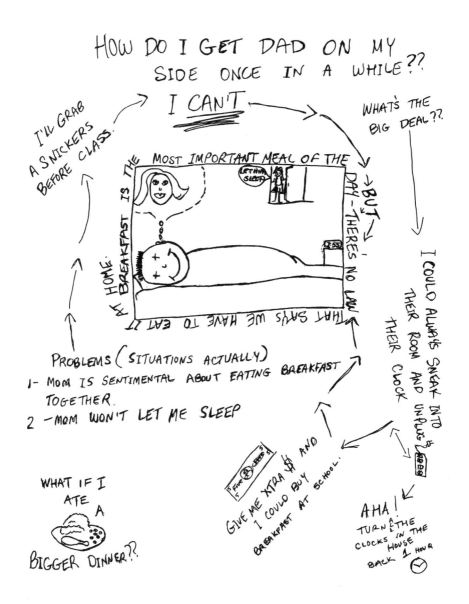

SIXTEEN-YEAR-OLD'S MIND MAP

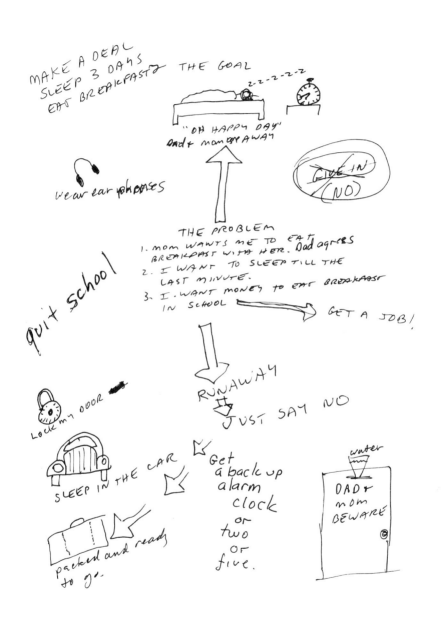

TWELVE-YEAR-OLD'S MIND MAP

potential solutions to give red meat to negotiations, the next step of the Caring Response.

Negotiate

All successful negotiating depends upon following specific rules. For parent–child negotiations, I always suggest four rules that were developed by the Harvard Negotiating Project and are explained in detail, along with others, in *Getting to Yes* by Roger Fisher and William Ury. Some aspects of my four rules have already appeared in these pages, but they bear repeating in highlighted form.

RULE 1: SEPARATE THE PERSON FROM THE PROBLEM.

The essence of the Caring Response, as I hope you've seen, is to be hard on the behavior, not the perpetrator. Your kid can not easily make this separation—you may be punishing the behavior, but she feels the punishment!—but you can. In fact, you should keep the distinction firmly in mind always. Help your kid see the difference by making comments like the following:

"I love you, and it really makes me angry when you lie. Lying is unacceptable behavior. Help me trust you, don't deal in lies. I know you want to do what's right."

"I know you are generally a responsible kid, but this is the third time you've left me waiting for you. Please be more responsible about being where you say you are going to be when you are supposed to be. I know you aren't really an inconsiderate person."

"I love you. That's why I worry when you hang out with tough kids."

"You're no pig. Why live in this pig sty?"

RULE 2: LOOK FOR MUTUAL INTERESTS.

Often, mutual interests emerge in mind-mapping—what each side wants, needs, desires, cares about, fears. By focusing on these things, you and your kid have a better chance of discovering a mutual need or interest that can become the path to compromise or agreement.

RULE 3: INVENT OPTIONS FOR MUTUAL GAIN.

If you've spent a good half-hour brainstorming with your kid, you should have come across ideas that will help you develop options that both of you can live with. If not, a third party can help, someone who can evaluate your two opposed points of view from the outside.

RULE 4: FORGET BOTTOM LINES, CONSIDER ALTERNATIVES.

Using brainstorming yet again, you should look for the best alternatives. This is key to dealing with an adolescent, especially if she has become determined not to give in. You have to move creatively from your bottom line to a workable alternative. In other words, you have to consider what you can accept as a solution if you can't reach a satisfactory agreement.

For example, Todd's mother thought of several alternatives: changing the locks and not giving her son a key; making him take an after-school job; making him come to her office after school and do his homework there; having her widowed mother move in; sending Todd to live with his father. She decided that the first idea, changing the locks, was her best alternative. Having such a fall-back alternative can keep you from pressing the panic button when your teenager continues to resist a negotiated agreement.

To these rules from the Harvard project, I add two of my own that apply particularly to adolescents.

RULE 5: CONCEDE SOMETHING.

Because your kid, like any other teenager, needs to win something from you, start your bargaining position high so that you can comfortably make a concession or two. She wants a 1 A.M. curfew, but you think midnight is acceptable. Start with 11 P.M., then concede the hour.

RULE 6: GIVE A CHOICE.

Whenever it is possible, give your child a choice. Even if the choice is between two things she would prefer to avoid, it helps her growth and self-esteem to make the choice for herself.

Once you have followed these rules and achieved a successful negotiation, it might help to put your treaty in writing to forestall future arguments about the exact terms and conditions. On the other hand, this is a choice you can give to your child. If he prefers to settle for a hug or a handshake, let that be fine with you.

Going On

Once the agreement has been concluded, just press forward. Consider the problem solved. Don't ask questions. Don't check up. I realize that this policy can be difficult, especially if the problem at issue is a longstanding one. Have I noted that life is hard? Develop some strategies like the following:

Instead of asking a question, call a friend and gossip.

Instead of checking up, reread this chapter.

Instead of worrying, plan a family outing or clean out a closet.

If you expect your kid to keep his part of the negotiated bargain, you have to keep yours.

But what if, despite your most sincere intentions and strongest efforts, you break your part of the deal? Then confess, apologize, and try, once again, to go on. If you violate your agreement with your kid a second time, you need a professional ear. Something is keeping you from letting go—your number one task after you have managed a Caring Response to a good conclusion.

Hold your child to the same standards. One violation of the agreement can be considered a slip. Twice is a relapse, and a third violation means that it is time to go back and redo the Caring Response. Worry if this round, too, seems to have little effect. Especially if the problem behavior is antisocial or harmful—someone is getting hurt physically, property is being damaged, the law is being flouted—I would recommend professional help whenever a second Caring Response fails to achieve your goals.

In the next chapter we'll cover an essential technique for convincing your child to go along with your decision to take him to a professional.

FIFTEEN

The Caring Intervention

DAD: "She's finally crossed the line, and I've had it."

MOM: "But she's out of control. She doesn't know what she's doing. She needs to see a professional."

DAD: "I agree, but you know that she won't take our advice anymore."

MOM: "Maybe she'll listen to her brother."

DAD: "When? She's never around anymore!"

MOM: "She's always respected Aunt Jean's opinions."

DAD: "I understand what you're saying, honey. But I don't think our daughter is listening to anyone. All of her friends want her to stop this behavior, but she just closes her ears."

MOM: "But we know she needs professional help."

DAD: "Yes, but we can't just handcuff her and haul her off to a psychiatrist's office."

MOM: "There's got to be a way to get through to her."

DAD: "Time is running out."

If the Caring Response fails, no matter how hard you have tried, it is time to plan a Caring Intervention. This technique is a planned confrontation of your kid's unacceptable behavior. It is carried out by the people who are most affected by that behavior. Although it involves a larger group than just you and the child you love, the Caring Intervention is a process involving steps similar to those you've learned to use with the Caring Response:

Caring enough to confront.
Accepting the person, rejecting the behavior.
Reviewing everyone's feelings and thoughts about the unaccept-
   able behavior.
Investigating possibilities for change.
Negotiating your differences.
Going on.

I'll give you models, but the Caring Intervention is inherently flex-ible, easily adjusted to your needs. It can involve as few as three people or as many as twenty. You may solve your problem within a few minutes or require as long as several months to complete the process.

A Quick Intervention

John and Sue came to me because they were worried about their daughter, Jessica. For six months her depression over breaking up with her boyfriend had been growing deeper. We had tried several strategies, but none worked. In my opinion, it was time for her to see a therapist, but she refused. We planned a Caring Intervention to convince her to agree to seek professional help.

In addition to her parents and me, those involved included her eight-year-old brother, Damon, three of her good friends, and the coach of her swim team—all of whom had expressed concern about Jessica and her state of mind in recent days. Before the intervention, I met with these participants and laid down some ground rules. Jessica was told that some friends were coming over specifically because they were worried about her and wanted to talk about it. As I warned her parents, she tried to duck out.

"No one needs to worry about me," she said. "I'm all right."

Her mother was prepared. "Okay, but you surely don't want your friends to worry," she countered. "That's why we invited them and why you really ought to talk to them." Jessica could hardly disagree.

When we all gathered in the family living room, I started the ball rolling:

"Jessica, you know that we all asked to meet with you because we are worried about you. I haven't met you before, but you know I've been meeting with your parents. They came to me because they're worried that you seem very unhappy and nothing they do has seemed to help. You tell them they shouldn't worry, but they can't stop. From their description of what goes on here, I can't help but worry, too. As a mental health expert, I have to worry when I hear that someone comes home from school and goes directly to bed, pulls the covers over her head, surfaces only for a twenty-minute dinner, and then goes back to bed. You seem to be sleeping most of your life away, and that is not healthy. Your parents and I aren't the only ones who worry. Everyone else in this room has expressed concern to your mom and dad about how sad you seem all the time."

Jessica interrupted testily. "I'm all right, I swear. I'm just handling things in my own way. No one has to worry about me."

"Jessica, people are worried, whether you want them to be or not. Let them tell you what worries them, and then you can tell us what you think and feel about their worries. If you'll let us have our say, we'll listen to everything you have to respond. We all want only one thing—to help you. We know that means listening closely to whatever you have to say."

With obvious reluctance, Jessica agreed to this plan. Her coach went first.

"Jess, lots of kids drop out of swimming. It's a hard grind, and I know that sometimes it just doesn't seem worth the effort. You know my saying: If coming here drags on you, you'll drag on the team. So it's not just that you dropped out . . . it's that you suddenly dropped out midseason, and didn't even tell me. And that's not like the Jessica I know and respect. It hurt, but I didn't worry much about it. Then I saw you two weeks ago in town and tried to talk with you, but you just turned away. What's worse, you didn't walk, you dragged. Since then, I've made a point of looking for you at school. I know from watching you that you are really depressed. You can't even fake a smile and that's bad. I know, because I've been there. One morning, when my husband and I were going through our divorce, I simply could not get up. Thank goodness, my mom was visiting. I got therapy, and I think you need therapy. I was so worried about you that I called your parents. They told me about tonight, and I knew I had to be here. You need help. Life can be better. You can be better, Jess."

Next, her friends talked about their concerns: how she seemed a completely different person, had stopped returning their calls, refused to sit with them at lunch anymore.

"You've become so mired in sadness," said one of the girls, "it oozes out of your pores. If I didn't care for you so much, I would have given up, but I do love you and I want you to get the help you need."

Her parents then spoke eloquently about their worries. By this time, her eyes welled with tears. Chances looked good to me that, by the time Damon had spoken, Jessica would agree to go for the help we all felt she needed so badly.

Though a child, Damon had a lot to say. "Jessy, I love you. Remember when Mom went to work and I didn't want her to be away when I got home from school? You helped me get used to that. You and Tom would walk me home, and you'd both tell jokes and make me laugh all the way. Then you'd spend the afternoon with me. You made a game out of homework, and you taught me to cook dinner. I was really happy. Then you and Tom didn't see each other anymore, and everything changed. Now I'm all worried and I'm scared that I made you and Tom break up. Maybe if you didn't have to take care of me after school, you'd still be friends. So I guess I don't blame you for not liking me anymore, but I wish you were happy again. I hate hearing you cry every night when you're trying to go to sleep." At that, Damon burst into tears.

Jessica, weeping softly now, gathered her brother into her arms. "I didn't mean to hurt you, baby brother. I promise, I'll do whatever everyone wants me to. Stop crying, okay?"

She kept her promise. After several months of psychiatric treatment, she was back to her old self. This was a successful Caring Intervention that worked very quickly. It's a good model, but it's not typical of real life, as the next story shows.

A Longer Intervention

Until quite recently, one of my hats was director of a group home program for some of New York City's hardest-to-place adolescents. In each home I supervised, Caring Interventions were regularly planned by the treatment team as a method of helping youngsters consider the impact of their behavior on others and on their own personal wants and needs. Our theory: In order to change, you have to want to change; in order to want to change, you have to recognize that you are doing something wrong.

I particularly recall an intervention that took four different sessions and a number of months to achieve those goals. Strong, adult-looking Charles D., fifteen, had an explosive temper, jackhammer fists, and a two-by-four on his shoulder. In his first six weeks with us, he had punched out three windows, kicked in two doors, pulverized kids in four fistfights, and assaulted the director of child care twice. We planned a Caring Intervention aimed at getting him to agree to attend the home's anger retraining program.

Our first attempt included his mother, twelve-year-old sister, Josie, Terry and Bob (two other kids in the home), five staff members, and his advocate, a member of the child care staff designated to help him plead his case. I led him into a conference room where they all sat in a semicircle. As he sat down in the chair facing them, Charles squirmed, but his advocate smiled reassuringly.

"Relax, Charles," she said. "We're all here because we care about you. This may hurt a little, but in the long run, it will help you gain control of your behavior."

"Shit, I don't need no help," Charles blurted out, still squirming.

His advocate smiled ruefully. "Charles, you and I both know how upset you got last week, after you threw a punch at Mr. Franks. Yet the very next day, you were ready to go after him again. Part of you must be scared you can't stop this behavior. All of us think that this meeting is the way to begin. We all care about you, and we've put a lot of time and effort into figuring out how to help you. Please let us try."

Charles heaved a sigh and settled down into his chair. "Okay, let's get the bullshit over. You're not going to change my mind. I'm not going to those stupid meetings about anger. But I'll listen."

That was my cue. Glancing at my notes, I began:

"Charles, you've lived here for about six weeks. During that time, we've gotten to know you fairly well. We've also spent time getting to know your mother and sister. Except for handling your anger, you've done well here. Mr. Franks tells me that most of the time you are a real gentleman. You don't seem to have trouble with our rules, you abide by curfew, you do your chores well and on time, you get yourself to school almost every day. You're smart, and you're savvy. But when you get angry you blow all that away. Today every person in this room has seen or been part of the hurt you create for yourself and for others when you lose control. We planned this intervention carefully. We want you to really understand what happens when you go off, but more importantly, we want you to recognize that with help and support from all of us, you can learn to handle your temper in less destructive ways. Do you understand that?"

Charles didn't look at me, but he nodded curtly.

I went on. "Gaining control of your temper is important, but first you have to realize how important it is for you to let us help. You won't be able to do it alone. You need the anger retraining program. That's what this meeting is about. By the end of it, we hope, you will agree to go. Now, in this home, most of your anger has been directed against three people—Mr. Franks, Terry, and Bob. That's why they're all here.

"Your mother is very worried about your temper. She wants you home, but she's afraid of what happens when you get angry. Frequently you turn your anger on your little sister, and that's why she's here. The rest of us are negotiators and planners. The rules for this session are simple. You listen to everyone else, then you tell us what you're feeling. We're all hoping that you'll be able to let us know as much as you can about what happens in you that sets off these explosions.

"Finally, we'll talk about what has to change and what you need from us in order to change. I want you to think while the others are talking. Mostly, I want you to think about this: Anger is what experts call a 'covering' emotion. That means it covers other, more painful feelings. As you listen to your family and friends, try to figure out what feelings are being covered by your blowups."

Beforehand, everyone in the room had been trained and rehearsed to make their points with Charles. They knew that the Caring Intervention involved confronting behavior that he wanted to ignore or to justify. They also understood that the confrontation had to be handled in a spirit of acceptance and alliance.

Mr. Franks began. "Charles, twice just this week, you've gotten so angry at me, you've thrown punches. The bruise still shows where you managed to connect with one punch. Being hit hurts physically, but it also hurts emotionally. If I didn't like kids, I wouldn't be doing this job. You know that. Part of me can forgive you when you hit me, but another part gets angry.

"What bothers me most, however, is what your own anger is doing to you. You want very much to go to an outside school, but we can't permit that as long as you keep punching people out. Striking out may make you feel better in the short run, but I think you really want to get yourself under control. I know that you can do it. You know how I ask you to leave a room sometimes and cool off? You've said it's because I don't like you, but that isn't the reason. I do it because I know that part of getting your anger under control is to take a time-out. Let things cool down. Trying to talk reasonably with an angry person is like asking a drunk to do a tightrope walk. Look at what happened last week. You came storming into my office, red-hot and ready to blow. I asked you to wait outside and cool off. You wouldn't. Instead, you socked me."

Charles, looking ever more uncomfortable, tried to speak, but the director of child care put up his hand and kept right on with his intervention.

"The sad part about last week, Charles, is that, before you lost your temper, you were in the right. I had made a mistake." He paused dramatically and looked directly into the kid's eyes. "Do you hear me, Charles? I was wrong. I didn't know your restrictions had been lifted and you could make phone calls. It hadn't been posted on the restriction board, but I should have asked about that and I was so busy at the moment, I just said no. Because you thought I was being unfair, you hit me. If you'd been more in control, we could have worked something out. You'd have gotten what you wanted without having to lose control. Staying in control means not hitting people or things. Staying in control also means getting more freedom."

The rest of the staff and the two residents presented Charles with similar tales of lost control and lost privileges, along with assurances that they believed he could change whenever he decided he was ready to work with them. The object of this Caring Intervention had become quiet and thoughtful, generally a good sign. But when his mother's turn came, Charles became restless again.

"I love you," she began. "I want you at home, but I'm also afraid. I'm afraid you'll hurt me, your sister, even yourself. When you're in the house, I have to walk on eggs. I know you learned some of this punching from your father, but that doesn't make it right, son. It's hard for me to keep saying you can't come home, but if you don't learn the right way to behave, you might end up in jail, and I don't want that."

Charles's eyes had narrowed to slits when his mother began speaking. Suddenly staring angrily at her, with his head held high, he blurted out, "You don't want me home. You were glad when Dad got arrested. You're glad I'm here."

Mrs. D. started to defend herself, but I motioned her quiet and spoke instead:

"Charles, part of an intervention is giving you a chance to have your say. But not until everyone else has spoken. Let your sister speak, and then you can tell us your side of the story. Right now, I want you to think for a minute about what other feeling your current anger is covering. Myself, I think you're hurting, but what you think is what counts. Meanwhile, let Josie have her turn."

Just entering her teens, Charles's sister was very shy. Like her mother, she had been severely abused by her father and then by her brother. She couldn't look him in the face. As she talked in a hesitant, soft monotone, she kept staring at the floor near his feet.

"When I was a little girl, there were times when you kept Daddy from hitting me. Sometimes, you even got hit trying to look out for me. I loved you so much, and I thought, if only Daddy would go away, we'd all be happy together. Then he did go away, and you started hitting me, just like he used to. I'd be lying if I said I wanted you to come home. I don't. Because I don't like getting hit. But Mom, she misses you just like she missed Daddy. She wants you home, so if you'll try to learn how not to hit, I might learn to like you again. I don't understand why you won't go to those anger classes. Don't you want to come home?"

Ignoring Josie, Charles turned on his mother again. "So you've managed to turn my sister against me," he snapped vehemently.

Once again, I motioned his mother to keep quiet.

"It seems to me, Charles," I said, "that it was your anger and your fists that turned her against you. But we're here to listen to what you think is going on. Now is the time to tell us your side of things."

He unleashed a torrent. "I want to go home, and I can control my temper. I only hit people when they deserve it. I can stop any time I want. I don't have to have lessons in anger management, and you can't make me. This is all a bunch of shit, like I said it would be. I want to call my lawyer and my social worker. I want to get out of this home. You're not helping me at all."

"You can call," I replied, "just as soon as this meeting is over, but the best way to get home is to control your temper, and from what you've just said, you believe you can do that. Can you?"

"Yes, I can. When I hit, it is because I want to hit."

"Good. So you want to go home, and your Mom wants you home, but only if you can control your behavior. You've never told us you could do that, so let me ask your Mom something. Mrs. D., how many weeks would Charles have to go without hitting someone or breaking something for you to believe he was in control of his temper? Would a month be long enough?"

She nodded.

I ended this intervention when Charles and I came to an agreement. For a month, he would control his temper. He wouldn't hit anyone, even in self-defense, or break anything. If he kept his side of the bargain, he could go home for an extended visit at the end of the month. As a normal part of the Caring Intervention, I asked Charles what help we could give him. "I don't need anyone's help with this," he sneered.

I accepted that. Jotting down the basics, I produced a contract that was signed by Charles, his mother, and the treatment team.

Naturally, there was one obvious sticking point that had to be further defined. Since many boys in the home would enjoy goading Charles, once the word got out, how could he keep from hitting back in self-defense? Our solution was to assign another resident and two child-care workers as his bodyguards.

Of course, our plan failed. After ten days, Charles broke two windows. Three days later, he splintered a door. On day 20 of his trial month, he punched his advocate in the stomach.

At our second Caring Intervention, Charles still refused to go to anger retraining, but he did learn something valuable. Several staff members explained that they could tell when he was about to lose it: just beforehand, he would withdraw into a meditative stance. Charles was intrigued with this observation. He agreed to let staff call a time-out whenever they spotted him about to blow. In other words, he was beginning to learn how to monitor his own anger. The new strategy helped him control his temper for about three weeks, and then he took out a door.

On the other hand, he did not attack another human being for the entire month. Perhaps he began to realize that therapeutic strategies can work. For whatever reason, he agreed at our third Caring Intervention to attend four sessions of anger retraining.

These three separate interventions required a lot of planning, cooperation, and emotional involvement from all participants, including Charles, but they were well worth it in the end. Today, he is successfully living at home. The only fighting he does is in a boxing ring at a nearby gym. He is training to box professionally.

Caring Intervention: The Guiding Principles

My Caring Interventions have been developed from the intervention system used in AA's twelve-step program, as described by Vernon

Johnson in *I'll Quit Tomorrow.* With an alcoholic, the goal of an intervention is to break down denial of the alcoholism.

Dr. Johnson's interventions are based upon seven guiding principles:

1. The facts about the individual's drinking should be presented by people who are significant in her life.
2. All facts should be specific.
3. The prevailing tone should be nonjudgmental, showing warmth and concern for the alcoholic.
4. All objectionable behavior discussed should be specifically linked to drinking.
5. The evidence should be given in detail.
6. Everyone should realize that the overriding purpose is to help the alcoholic recognize that help is needed.
7. Plans for treatment should be included in the intervention. When possible, the individual should be given a choice between viable treatment options.

Slightly translated, these principles hold true for any Caring Intervention with your kid. Everyone participating should know and care about him. They should offer their stories in a caring fashion, be specific and detailed about each event, and be willing to work together to develop a specific plan for changing the unwanted behavior. It's usually best to develop a workable plan before the intervention, but remain flexible enough to modify it during the session.

Laying the groundwork for your Caring Intervention requires reflection and imagination. It begins the fact-gathering process. It will clarify several matters for you: what your concerns really are, what changes you want, and whether or not an intervention is really necessary. Sometimes, good groundwork renders it moot.

When to Intervene

As a good general rule, Caring Interventions are necessary when any problem is life threatening or life damaging—and all of your less powerful interventions have so far failed. Typically, you will have decided that professional help is needed but cannot convince your teenager to go along with the idea. Some families have turned to Caring Interventions in less troubling situations that are nonetheless extremely distressing or disruptive to them. If your situation is life threatening, however, you should ask a professional to help you with your planning.

You should not attempt an intervention in a half-hearted fashion. Be certain that your family is motivated to solve the problem at hand, that they clearly understand the problem and agree to the same characterization of it, and that they forge a united front on what needs to be done to encourage change.

Finally, do not involve anyone who is hostile or excessively judgmental. Only people who genuinely care for your child and can make their concern clear should help you carry out a Caring Intervention.

Remembering these provisos, let's look at the situation of Joanna and Tom Jones. A tall, burly man with an incessantly worried cast to his face, Tom was convinced that their daughter, fifteen-year-old Karen, was using drugs. Joanna disagreed. At this point, then, the idea of a Caring Intervention did not even occur to me. The main actors in a child's life have to agree about the nature of a problem.

Despite Tom's conviction and Karen's moody behavior, there was little hard-core evidence. Once she had come home drunk after a party. She had apparently kept sober in the following months. A school official raised concern about possible drug use. The Joneses followed my suggestion to arrange a routine physical that included drug testing, but the results were negative.

What, then, was going on? And why was Mr. Jones so certain that Karen was on drugs? In a very short time, his daughter had undergone a transformation in behavior and conscience that was almost a complete personality change. She had given up her preppy friends for the local "Deadheads," the ardent fans of the Grateful Dead. At this group's concerts, you can get high just by walking down the aisles. While the group's leader is a recovering alcoholic and recovery groups meet at each performance, the majority of people at Dead concerts, as Tom knew, are enthusiastic users of mood-altering substances.

Also, Tom himself was a recovering alcoholic. He knew all too well that loss of conscience is a major sign of problem drinking. Karen had been lying without cause, stealing small amounts of money from Joanna's purse, and shoplifting. Whenever her parents tried to discipline her, she'd pack a few clothes and vanish for a few days, only to return surly and uncommunicative.

As this behavior continued, I agreed with Tom that Karen was probably using, even though no one had found the smoking joint. Besides, her running away, stealing, and shoplifting were life damaging and possibly life threatening, whatever the cause. An intervention was certainly warranted.

Our first Caring Intervention, held in my office, involved only the four of us. Both parents shared their concerns and fears and assured Karen that they loved her still. But they also agreed that their patience had reached its limits. If she wanted to continue living at home, she had to put an end to the lying, stealing, and running away. Otherwise, she needed to think of some other place to live. Beforehand, I had armed Joanna and Tom with a few suggestions for alternative living arrangements, but they didn't seem necessary. Karen agreed to change; Tom agreed that, if she did, he would lay aside his worries about drug use.

Only two weeks later, Karen ran off with her boyfriend to Florida, following the Grateful Dead's spring tour. Although she called home every week, she made it clear that she had decided to live her own life. Three months later, she was back home. The romance had soured, and Karen blamed her previous behavior on the boy. Indeed, for about two months she broke no rules, but then she began regularly walking in the door drunk or high. Alerted, I arranged a second Caring Intervention. This time, Tom and Joanna agreed with me beforehand that the aim was to get Karen to agree to accept admission to a drug rehab. She was convinced. Today, she is a gratefully recovering addict.

These examples do not quite cover the gamut, but they should help you remember that a Caring Intervention can either work instantly, take months of concerned involvement or, as in Karen's case, fall somewhere in between. It is also true, of course, that some never work at all, but successful interventions can save lives.

Ten Steps to Your Caring Intervention

As I stated earlier, a Caring Intervention requires fact-gathering, soul-searching, and imagination. To develop a workable plan, follow these ten steps.

1. Specify why you think an intervention is necessary. What is the unacceptable behavior?

2. Explore the need for an intervention. Have you already tried other strategies?
3. Tell your child that you have planned an intervention.
4. Explore potential participants' willingness to take part.
5. Plan how to ask others to participate.
6. Plan the desired outcome of the intervention. Set goals.
7. Prepare your statements. What are you and the other participants going to say to your child during the intervention?
8. Get your presentation ready and rehearse.
9. Carry out the intervention.
10. Debrief your group. Discuss your reactions.

STEP 1: SPECIFY WHY.

In my Parent Tactics groups, where Caring Interventions are often planned, I ask parents to explain in one hundred words or less why they think one might be necessary. Here are a couple of statements that made sense to me:

"Sara is in love with Roy, who has a rep for being violent. Twice, I've seen bruises on her neck. They look like choke marks to me, but she insists they're hickeys. Last week, she came home from a party with a black eye. She claimed she got it in a fall, but her best friend said Roy hit her. I've suggested counseling, but she thinks I'm just looking for an excuse to break up her romance—which is not that far from the truth. I definitely don't like the kid, but I am also worried for my daughter's safety."

"Shawn has come home bloodied and depressed three times after fights with friends. He seems angry all the time and talks constantly about getting revenge on somebody or another. Last week, he kicked in his bedroom door. The week before that, he smashed the mirror over his dresser. I've tried several times to talk about it, but he refuses to discuss anything with me. His school has suggested counseling, but Shawn is adamant. He is not going to see a shrink."

These two statements strongly indicate that a Caring Intervention should be attempted. In each situation, the problem is life damaging and perhaps potentially life threatening.

Consider how they differ from the following statement, which I rejected:

"Bobby is failing honors English and got only a C+ in honors French. His other marks are okay, but I tell him he's wrecking his future by not applying himself more diligently in the tenth grade. These are the years colleges look at, and he's risking his chance of getting into a good school. We've tried rewards, punishments, tutoring, straight talking. Nothing has worked. Now Bobby wants to transfer out of honors courses and we just can't accept that."

Here's another I couldn't go along with:

"Jill's relationship with Mark has got to end. He's her intellectual inferior, has to take special ed, plans to join the Marines this summer, and literally has no outside interests except our daughter. He's a leech, and I'm terrified he'll keep her so dependent on him that she won't be able to pay attention to her grades. She already spends more time on the telephone with him than doing her homework."

Sorry, but falling grades and unwanted relationships don't merit the heavy artillery of a Caring Intervention. Neither is life threatening. They may seem life damaging to some parents, but I think that's stretching the point.

STEP 2: EXPLORE THE NEED.

You don't reach for penicillin when a couple of aspirin will do the job. Similarly, you don't mount a Caring Intervention until you've made other kinds of efforts to solve a problem. Before I agree to help parents plan an intervention, I ask them to list what they've already tried. Sara's mom wrote down the following:

"First, I was monumentally patient. I hoped that this was just a passing fancy.

"Second, I tried to limit the relationship by planning family trips Sara had to join. Somehow, Romeo always wound up in the vicinity. Even when we went skiing out of state one weekend, Roy found a friend with a cabin nearby.

"Third, I took a firmer stand after the bruises. I confronted Sara with what must have happened, reminded her how much I love her, confessed how frightened I was for her, and warned her that next time I'd call the police. And so I did, next time I saw bruises, only to learn that the police wouldn't do anything on my say-so alone. Back to square one.

"Fourth, I involved her father. We're divorced, but he came over and raged and stormed, forbidding her to see the boy ever again. She kept right on.

"Fifth, I grounded her and took away the telephone. She ran away.

"Sixth, when the police found her, they suggested counseling. I agreed and told Sara I'd let her keep seeing Roy if she'd go to a counselor. She refused.

"Seventh, I gave in. I said she could see him as much as she wanted. I told her again that I loved her, but I realized I couldn't control her life. I thought that if I stopped fighting she'd see for herself what was what.

"Well, that was three months ago. Things are just as bad, and I'm at my wit's end. I am sure the boy is a threat to her life."

Few lists are as exhaustive as this one, nor do they have to be. Ordinarily, I think it may be time for an intervention if parents can set down at least three strategies that they have come up with to deal specifically with the bad behavior of their good kid. If you are considering your own situation, think about whether or not you have already followed my earlier suggestions for Caring Responses to unacceptable behavior. If you have, and the behavior continues, move on to the third step of the Caring Intervention.

STEP 3: TELL YOUR CHILD WHAT YOU PLAN.

Shawn agreed to see a psychiatrist for at least six months as soon as his parents announced that they planned an intervention. Apparently the prospect of facing his friends turned the trick. He stayed in therapy for two years, by the way, and is now in college, temper under control.

STEP 4: EXPLORE OTHERS' WILLINGNESS TO PARTICIPATE.

List potential participants in your child's Caring Intervention. Each must care about the child, know about the problem firsthand, and be able to remain supportive while discussing the unacceptable behavior. First consider your kid's other parent and siblings, then close relatives, then teachers, and, finally, friends. Sara's mother came up with a final list that included her father, brother, best friend, and another friend who had previously dated Roy.

STEP 5: PLAN THE INVITATION.

Before inviting anyone to participate, know exactly what you're going to say. Sara's mother was very explicit about the problem, her goals, and the responsibilities of anyone who agreed to help:

"I'm really worried about Sara's relationship with her boyfriend. She keeps coming home bruised. I've never seen him hit her, but I'm sure he does. I'm afraid for her, and I know you are, too. I want her to see a counselor. I've promised I won't interfere with her relationship as long as she is talking to a professional about her feelings, but she refuses to see anyone. I'd like you to meet with some of the other people in Sara's life who are worried about her and see if together we can convince her to see a counselor. We'd need to meet twice, once to plan what we want to say and the second time to sit down with Sara and say it. Do you feel that you can help?"

STEP 6: PLAN THE OUTCOME.

Because Sara was blind to the destructiveness of her relationship, the Caring Intervention had to be sufficiently detailed and specific to strike the scales from her eyes. In essence, any intervention is aimed at breaking through someone's denial of a problem.

At the planning meeting, Sara's mother explained that everyone should work together on the secondary goal—convincing Sara to go into counseling—not the primary goal—ending the relationship. The participants decided to focus on their own fears of Roy's violence. They didn't question his love for Sara; they stressed their concern that he might really hurt her someday.

Protecting a loved one from serious harm is usually the main reason for any Caring Intervention. Your kid and everyone helping him must understand this aim. Then you have a primary goal, like getting Sara to break up with her boyfriend, but probably will focus on the secondary goal, like getting her to see a counselor. You and your fellow participants should plan other fallback positions as well. If Sara had refused the professional counseling that would help improve her self-esteem to the point where she would not tolerate physical abuse from anyone, the group intended to ask her to attend at least three meetings of a self-help group for battered women.

STEP 7: PREPARE THE STATEMENTS.

Once you've decided on your group's goals, each participant should draft their statements: (a) a confrontational statement followed by (b) an allying statement leading to (c) a review of some of the specific events that produced concern. In other words, each participant should concentrate on carrying out the first three steps of a Caring Response.

Here are some of the statements prepared for Sara's intervention:

Her mother: "Sara, I'm really scared every time Roy takes you out. I love you, and I don't want you hurt. I worry every time you two are together. I know you've heard me say that over and over again, but I still need to tell you I don't want my daughter hurt. Last week, you said you got that black eye from bumping into a door. I wanted to believe you, but I couldn't. Your eyes widen whenever you lie. They shot open then. I'm not asking you to break up with Roy. I am asking you to consider getting help for both of you or for yourself alone. You don't deserve to be beaten."

Her brother: "Sara, I've talked to you lots about what you should do if anyone tries to hurt you. Remember when I taught you how to knee a guy? I never thought I'd have to teach you how to keep someone who loves you from hurting you. I thought you'd know that somebody who hits you isn't worth your time. Well, I know that Roy really loves you. I also know he likes to rough up the people he cares about. He bragged to me about hitting his mother and his sister. He thinks women should be put in their place every now and then. But I've told you that before. What I haven't told you is that he told me last week those bruises on your neck aren't love bites. I socked him, and he laughed. I love you, and I really can't understand why you let someone knock you around. That's not what love's about. Please think about what we're saying to you. If you don't want to break up with Roy for good, please go and get some counseling. Please."

Roy's former girlfriend: "Sara, maybe you think this is just sour grapes. I bet Roy said he broke up with me. That's what he told me about all the other girls he went with. The truth is, I broke up with him after he punched me so hard he knocked a tooth out. Like you, I told everybody I'd fallen down. I'm the only one here, besides you, who knows how sweet and contrite Roy is when he hurts you. I'll bet he bought you flowers the day after he blacked your eye. Did he send that cute little poem, the one about how his love for you drives him crazy, makes him do things he shouldn't do? Sara, if he really was sorry, he'd go to a psychiatrist. But that other Roy, the one that calls you names and slams you in the face, isn't going to stop hurting you. You need to take charge and get help. You don't deserve these beatings."

Finally, Sara's best friend: "Sara, I know what you mean when you say that love conquers all. I've done my share of dating weirdos, but

Roy pushes even my limits. I know you'll get mad at me for saying this here, but I can't cover for Roy anymore. Roy hits you. You've told me so. Everyone who loves you knows what's going on, but you don't want to admit it. Please admit the truth. Stop seeing Roy and go to a counselor. I can't say much more than, 'Please get help before it's too late.' "

STEP 8: GET READY.

After everyone has written down a statement, the group should elect a leader, preferably not you or your child's other parent. The leader, someone your teenager respects as an ally, will explain to her the steps to be followed during the intervention, win her cooperation in not interrupting, and help her maintain her composure during the exercise.

Next, agree on the line-up. Usually it's best to begin with the least impactful statement and build toward the most impactful. As you've no doubt noticed, my examples have typically begun with the parent, whose statement is likely to have the least impact on a child. Treasured friends probably have the most effect, as in Sara's case, and should come last.

Finally, stage a rehearsal. Each of you can offer suggestions to other participants in the interests of clarity and effectiveness. You can help each other anticipate the youngster's protests or excuses and figure out strategies for pertinent rebuttal.

STEP 9: THE CARING INTERVENTION.

At her Caring Intervention, Sara listened quietly, thanked everyone for their concern, but refused to go for treatment. She claimed that Roy had been so upset about the black eye that he had promised to get professional help himself. She did, however, accept the group's fallback position: If Roy did hit her again, she would go to three meetings of the self-help group for battered women and meet afterward with the participants in her Caring Intervention.

What happened? Roy stopped seeing his counselor after a month; a month later, he slugged Sara again. She went to the self-help meetings, as she had promised, and came to realize that she needed private counseling. During therapy, she broke off with Roy for good. Today, she is happily married to someone else. It is difficult to believe that her renewed self-esteem would ever allow anyone to abuse her again.

STEP 10: DEBRIEFING.

Whether or not the Caring Intervention is an immediate success, the group should get together sometime afterward at least once. Any intervention is emotionally draining for everyone involved, and closure is important. Just having a meal together may do the trick, though some groups prefer a more structured, formalized meeting. Let your group decide for themselves.

Sara's family and friends went out to dinner. Even though she had not agreed to go to a counselor right away, they felt pleased that a seed had been planted. She had listened; she had acknowledged a problem. They all felt that she would eventually seek help, and their instincts proved sound.

A Final Word

Some Caring Interventions may not work as you plan. Even in those cases, however, I believe that the intervention helps by reminding all involved parties of the need to care and to keep on caring.

Therefore, even when change does not immediately result, at least you and all of the other participants have done everything you can to try to remedy a painful situation. As I've had occasion to note often in these pages, control over an adolescent's behavior is not possible. Accept that limitation. With a Caring Intervention, however, you can rest assured that you have gone to the limits in inviting change.

SIXTEEN

Getting
Professional Help

"Mom, I don't want to go see Dr. Sauer anymore."

"But, sweetheart, I thought you liked her. And you do seem much happier these days."

"You can't make me go!"

"I don't want to "make" you go. I know many parents who think that Dr. Sauer was really good for their kids. I want you to get the help you need."

"Well, she isn't it. She's two-faced."

"But your school counselor thinks she's wonderful—"

"And another thing. She tries to tell me I'm wrong all the time."

"But I can't believe she would do that. She tells me that she doesn't give judgments in therapy."

"See? You always take her side. Now she's your friend, not mine. I don't trust her! I don't want you two ganging up on me. She hates me!"

Frequently I've mentioned situations that, at some point, seem likely to require professional help. Lest you think I live in some mist, blithely unaware of the realities in the world of men and women with degrees on their office walls, let me get down with you on the subject of getting the right professional help.

In life-or-death situations, your kid might need therapy or a rehabilitation program. When the problem is less drastic, you may need to find the appropriate counselor. Not all professionals can help. Finding the right person is critically important, as the following tale should indicate.

The Opening Riot

Our first week as foster parents was harried, hectic, and happy. Six children had been placed with us, but we forgot our initial misgivings and self-doubts as a household routine was established. By the end of the second week, however, things began to deteriorate. Increasingly difficult to control, the kids bitched constantly about David and me, eighteen-month-old Zach, our kitten and two dogs, and even our quiet little town. The simplest activity, like a group outing to the movies, spawned a thousand complaints.

The complaints were backed up by defiant behavior as each child chose to break a different rule. Margaret defied curfew, while Peter refused to do his assigned chores. Dennis and Dexter became confederates in mischief, keeping us up nights by giggling, laughing, sneaking out of their rooms. Joyce and Marion, not to be outdone, specialized in picking physical fights with the other four teenagers. Marion's swift kick never missed the target that hurts boys most. Joyce had a flair for the dramatic. At unexpected moments, after she'd enraged her opponent, she'd whisk a keen-edged kitchen knife out of her shirt.

Things couldn't get worse, we thought. But Murphy's Law was to be upheld. We spent a hot, humid July 3 at the beach nearby, one of the most beautiful on the East Coast. Back home for dinner, all the kids could talk about was how great their parents had been, how wonderful their homes, and how dreadful their lives now with these awful people, the Levines. David and I were grateful when the meal ended and we could retreat to the den to watch the evening news.

Suddenly, the TV weatherman's happy-talk was drowned out by music blasting above us. Next to the den, the screen porch shook in rhythm with stomping sounds. Evidently, our three girls had climbed out their bedroom window onto the roof of the porch—a definite class-A no-no.

David walked outside to find all three girls stripped down to their panties and bras, arms linked, zestily dancing a well-practiced can-can. No Khrushchev, he just laughed, shook his head, and told them to cut it out. They giggled and waved. He came back inside.

Mostly because we didn't want any trouble from our neighbors, who were already wary of our household, we decided to go upstairs to the girls' room. The door was barricaded from inside. That left us no choice but to follow the behaviorists' standard advice about unwanted behavior: ignore it. We sat in the hall and waited. Five minutes passed. Then ten . . . and quiet suddenly descended. After another five minutes, David and I breathed a sigh of relief. We decided to wait a bit before inviting the entertainers down to the den to discuss their performance.

Wrong, again. We had scarcely finished congratulating ourselves for our patience when a litany of curses reached our ears, accompanied by the sounds of furniture cracking and glass breaking. We could do little but stare nervously at each other. On the other side of their door, the girls were in charge of the moment.

The noise went on unabated for half an hour. Meanwhile, David called the social worker charged with supervising our group home. She phoned her boss for advice and called back: "Keep ignoring them."

Within minutes, the girls were shrieking about "getting them" and laying waste the rest of the house. When threats focused on Zach, David secured their door shut with a rope, sent me into our son's room, and called the social worker again. This time, she agreed to send reinforcements.

The girls were still breaking up furniture, banging the walls, and loudly threatening to kill us when the local juvenile center's van pulled up in our drive a half-hour later. The two counselors came upstairs and announced through the door that they had come to take the girls back to detention. David untied the rope, and we heard furniture being pulled back from the door. Almost instantly, Marion and Joyce appeared, astounding us all by their appearance. Each was neatly dressed in her Sunday best and carrying a packed suitcase. They strolled downstairs to the waiting van. Margaret, meanwhile, was nowhere to be seen. Finally, we found her on the roof just outside Zach's room. She had to be carried bodily from the house in shackles and handcuffs.

During this mêlée, Dexter and Dennis had honored our request that they stay in their room. "Those girls are crazy," Dexter had commented, and his confederate had solemnly nodded his head in agreement.

Not so, Peter. As if moved by powerful empathy with the rampaging girls, he had kicked a hole in his closet door, dashed his TV set to the floor, packed up his clothes, and run away. At three in the morning he was back, but went off again the following day. When he returned, he asked to be transferred back to the detention center. As Peter left our house, he shook David's hand, kissed me on the cheek, and thanked us for being so kind to him.

David and I were devastated by all of this. Just after Peter walked out the door, I sat down in our living room and wept sad, bitter tears. Drained and frightened that summer day, I didn't know what had gone wrong, what we could do differently, or how to prevent the same thing from happening all over again. Yet I was the social worker, the "professional" on our parenting team. I was supposed to know the answers.

Our despair and confusion only doubled when Joyce and Marion phoned, virtually begging to be taken back. We were tempted, but we refused. We couldn't risk a repeat performance until we understood what had happened or how to prevent it.

Eight days after the can-can "riot," a group of experts came to our house to talk about "riot prevention"—a psychiatrist, a psychologist, two social workers. It was the psychiatrist, who had interviewed all three girls and Peter, who did most of the talking.

"You are white," he began. "Joyce and Margaret are black. You live in a fancy house in a fancy neighborhood; most of your foster children are inner-city kids, and they don't like the peace and quiet of a small town. You have dogs, and Marion and Peter don't feel at all comfortable with dogs. Joyce can't make sense of some of your rules. You have a small son, and Margaret can't stand little kids."

He paused, and David and I glanced uncomfortably at each other. Aside from sending our dogs to the pound, nothing he said could be changed.

Looking directly at me, the doctor continued: "I understand you serve skim milk, Mrs. Levine. Don't you know, with your background and training, how deprived that would make these children feel? You kept them from their mothers' breasts. You gave them thin watery milk when they craved rich golden mother's milk."

Academically, this interpretation had a certain elegance—poetic, classically Freudian, skillfully analytic. Was the metaphor flawed because mother's milk is actually thin and watery? David had no trouble dismissing the psychiatrist's suggestion as so much psycho-babble, but I was sensitive to the implied charge hidden within, that I had not been giving enough, not been sensitive enough to my foster children's underlying needs for loving care.

Fortunately, I stumbled onto a much more valid interpretation of our experience a few days later. As told in their book, *Children Who Hate,* Fritz Redl and David Wineman lived and worked in a small residential treatment setting that served children who were disturbed or acting out. And, yes, they had endured baptism by riot, just as we had. David and I had not been severely lacking in understanding nor stingy with our emotions; we had simply encountered a classic case of the phenomenon known as "treatment shock."

Treatment shock is the crisis children undergo when they are moved from a hostile, abusing home situation to a more benign environment. In a perverse trick of psychology, every indication of nurturing is yet another item of proof that their own parents were abusive. Facing that recognition hurts, and pain creates anger. Beforehand, the abused child felt guilt, not anger; he believed he was bad and deserved his parents' harsh treatment. In the new environment, however, his guilt is transformed into anger. Kind, caring treatment, in this ironic twist, produces an anger that should be directed toward the abusive parents, but a kid doesn't understand that right away. He doesn't recognize that the pain caused by a nurturing gesture is really a remembrance of past abuse. All he knows is that being in the new situation causes pain, and pain justifies expressions and acts of anger.

Since my lucky revelation, I've noticed that treatment shock occurs frequently in a number of situations, including adoptive families and group homes. Yet Dr. Skim Milk had apparently never heard of it. Here, then, is the moral: When you look for professional help, make sure that your "expert" has the experience or education to understand the situation you face. Good intentions and classy degrees are not enough, and may not be to the point.

For the rest of this chapter, I'm going to be sharing advice that can help you choose the right professional, but be warned that there is no magic formula. The therapist whose perception and human warmth you admire may be a dud as far as your teenager is concerned.

Still, there are ways to tilt the odds. Let's look at four things you should decide before you search: what you want help with; what kind of person can best provide help for that specific problem; how to find that source of help; what you should be looking for when you interview potential sources of help.

When to Get Help

To expand on my earlier advice that you seek help when your kid's behavior is life damaging or life threatening, I've listed the problems that always require professional attention:

1. Threatening or trying to commit suicide.
2. Regularly drinking or using drugs.
3. Engaging in such self-destructive behavior as excessive dieting or vomiting after each meal.
4. Frequently getting hurt in accidents or fights with friends.
5. Maintaining a physically violent relationship, regardless of whether he is the battered or the batterer.
6. Repeatedly running away overnight.
7. Involving herself in a cult group or Satanic practices.
8. Repeatedly breaking major laws.

In the case of suicide threats, as I've explained earlier, you should act immediately. Put this book down and call your family physician or your local mental health center. Or, if you're near a large hospital, you can probably arrange an emergency evaluation with a staff psychiatrist. In the other seven situations listed above, try to arrange a preliminary appointment with a specialist within the upcoming two weeks. These situations are potentially life threatening, too.

In addition to my list, there are other situations that might benefit from professional help, although they may not require that you act right this minute: irresponsible sexual relationships; inability to do schoolwork; and Gotcha Warring so tumultuous that family life is being disrupted.

In all cases, tell your child when you decide to seek professional help. She may object, but giving her warning will increase the chances that she'll eventually agree to go. Tell her why you've made the decision. At the very least, you'll avoid provoking the anger you could cause with a last-minute announcement. In this situation as in others we have as parents, leveling is always best.

Which Professional Will Be Best?

By "professional help" I mean a psychotherapist, but that is a generic term. They come in many different flavors. If your child is an alcoholic, he may not receive the best help from a professional who specializes in eating disorders.

Psychotherapists include counselors, clinical psychologists, social workers, family therapists, educational counselors, religious advisors, psychiatric nurses, hypnotherapists, and, of course, psychiatrists. Each has something to offer, but some can offer more in certain specific situations than in others.

In the following situations, you can choose the type of psychotherapist your child needs according to the nature of his problem:

1. If suicidal or seriously depressed, your youngster needs to see a psychiatrist, preferably one experienced in working with adolescents.
2. If anorexic or bulimic, your kid probably needs hospitalization in a unit that specializes in treating eating disorders.
3. If your child abuses drugs or alcohol, he needs a specialist in drug treatment. **Warning:** Not all mental health professionals have had such training.
4. A child involved in a physically dangerous relationship needs help from a mental health specialist who understands battering and abusive relationships.
5. If your youngster is having considerable difficulty in school, he needs a psychologist with special understanding of learning disabilities and educational problems.
6. Any child involved in cults or Satanic activities can be helped only by a specialist in such activities, most probably a minister or rabbi with special mental health training and experience working with cult-related emotional problems.

For all other types of problems, a competent psychotherapist will suffice, but what does "competent" mean? Unfortunately, your state might allow anyone to seek out clients, just because of a desire to do counseling or psychotherapy; no questions asked. The unqualified counselor could do damage; on the other hand, some self-appointed psychotherapists are more helpful than some of their academically qualified, state-approved brethren. I never discount the value of gifted personal insight and common sense in psychotherapy.

If this sounds confusing and contradictory, it is. That's why I've developed "Levine's Five Rules for Getting Good Help." They can guide you as you do your research and experimenting in order to find the person who can provide the right help to your child.

Levine's Five Rules for Getting Good Help

1. The Rule of Shared Experiences: The most effective helpers have had experience with the problem being addressed. That's why self-help groups are so successful. Don't seek parenting advice, for example, from nonparents or even from parents who have not yet raised several kids through the teen years.

David Treadway, a well-known family therapist and expert on addiction, is the kind of professional I would trust, because of what he said in his book, *Before It's Too Late:*

"Before I had children, the answers came easily. But this year my son turns eleven. When he is angry, his face now takes on a cold, hard look that makes him look like a stranger to me. Sometimes, he tells me he can't stand our home and wants to be free and live on his own. He says that, and a cold fear stirs inside me. I imagine driving the streets late at night, looking for my son. I imagine the round of phone calls and the sitting around, waiting. Sometimes, I find myself watching him while he is sleeping. The answers don't come so easily anymore. I used to think that parents just needed to get tougher, but now I realize that parents really do not have much power when kids are out of control. Because when it comes to confrontation over control, many kids are willing to die in order to win. That terrifies adults, and it should. Any therapist who thinks that parents can easily control adolescents hasn't parented one."

Yes, this kind of therapist knows the score. The Rule of Shared Experiences works partly because the helper has an increased understanding of the specific problem. Sympathy will predominate over blame, as is even more evident when the professional fits rule 2.

2. The Rule of Caring: Your child needs to feel that her therapist really cares about her. The greater the communication of a caring feeling, the more likely the therapy will be helpful. Even professionals who believe in maintaining technical neutrality, like most psychodynamically oriented therapists, can let your teenager know they care. Listen to your kid's personal reactions to her prospective therapist. And don't force the issue.

"We saw three family therapists before we found one whom we all believed to be caring," a friend told me recently. "The first was a woman who was so standoffish and cold that none of us felt comfortable around her. When she talked to our two kids, she seemed to relax. Maybe she could have helped them, but our family needed someone we all felt good about. The second was a man my husband and both children liked, but John also noticed that, no matter what I said, this guy put me down. He didn't much like women, it turned out. The third therapist, thank goodness, was someone we all liked right away, and she's given us the help we needed."

You're not home safe even when you find the right therapist, however. You will have to keep monitoring the relationship. Occasionally, for example, treatment can be flawed by a "transference reaction." In "transference," a patient assigns to her therapist certain feelings, or ideas, or beliefs that really belong to someone else. Be on the alert. If your kid's feelings toward her therapist begin to change, she may be transferring. If she begins to think that the therapist is angry with her, say, she may be transferring her own anger onto him. Mary, a quiet and thoughtful fifteen-year-old, came to see me because she felt her therapist no longer cared about her.

"I thought he understood me," she recalled. "From the very beginning, I was sure that he really wanted to know my side of things. But recently it seems to me that he has changed. He never seems to take my side anymore. I think he believes I'm doing things I shouldn't be doing. I think he hates me."

As she talked, it became clear to me that Mary's suspicions that her counselor disliked her were associated with any discussion of the difficulties she was having with a boyfriend. Because she felt that she was doing bad things, she became convinced that her therapist felt the same way and judged her accordingly. She was transferring her own feelings of blame and guilt onto him. I insisted she go back to her therapist and tell him how she feared that he no longer cared about her.

"You were right," she told me later. "He actually laughed at me—not in a nasty way, but sweetly—and told me he knew that I was doing things I didn't feel good about . . . and so do most people. He said it's his job to help me understand what's happening. That I should stop doing certain things, and other things are okay, but mostly I should stop feeling guilt."

And, of course, stop transferring the guilt to him, turning him into the image of her own hypercritical mother. Maybe, if things start going badly in your kid's therapy, she is having a "transference reaction." Explain the concept to her and encourage her to discuss her feelings with the counselor. If talking doesn't help, arrange a consultation with another professional.

3. The Rule of Shared Explanations: The sharing of experiences usually leads to shared explanations of why a problem arises and what is necessary to solve it. Shared explanations, in their turn, help therapy move along faster.

For example, if you believe that astrology explains your problems, you would be best served by a psychotherapist who shares your view that we are playthings of the stars and planets. If you believe nothing can be solved without involving the rest of your family, you should find a family therapist. If organized religion is important to you, you need a counselor who feels the same way. If you believe that behavior is dictated by the experiences of early childhood, so should the therapist you select.

As teenaged Peter put it, "Dad believes in psychoanalysis. When he had a lot of problems with his mom and dad, an analysis helped straighten him out. So when I started having trouble in school, he wanted to send me to his shrink. I went along, but I just couldn't agree that my problems came from the feelings I had for my parents when I was a kid. I needed to talk with someone about what's going on in my life right now. Like dealing with my friends. The youth leader at school was the person I finally talked to, and she really helped me."

This kid's mother had other reasons for rejecting the analyst. "I have a deep-seated philosophical bias against Freudian analysis. I'm glad it helped my husband, but for myself, as a feminist, I needed a different type of therapy. I found a radical feminist therapist in a center that specialized in helping women. She helped me in a way no Freudian analyst ever could."

The moral: Each of these three people needed to match a personal point of view with a therapist's philosophical or theoretical framework. Your child may not have a sophisticated vocabulary to cover technical issues in treatment, but she will soon understand whether or not she and her counselor share explanations. If they do not, that might be the source of any dissatisfaction with her treatment.

4. The Rule of Many Eyes: Reality exists. Whether or not I hear it, the fall of a tree in the forest is an actual event. You can't see the chair I'm sitting in as I write, but it's real. If it ceased to exist because you can't see it, I'd be smarting soon. Unlike Tinker Bell, I don't have to ask you to believe in order to save my dignity.

But if I did ask each and every reader to envision my chair, you'd conjure up a wide range of images—an ergonomic contraption, a comfy overstuffed armchair, a severe attention-inducing ladderback, a Danish modern slingback. But if there are thousands of readers—nay, hundreds of thousands!—some of you will accurately conjure up my actual chair. As philosopher Gregory Bateson has put it, the more views there are of any object, the more likely it is that the correct view will be found.

The Rule of Many Eyes explains why I like group approaches to helping figure out problems that arise between people. My Caring Intervention, for example, provides multiple views to a teenager whose understanding of his problem has been limited to what he can see by himself.

This rule does not invalidate the importance of individual or family therapy, but it does suggest to me that your kid's treatment with a professional should be strengthened by the addition of some form of group experience. (Don't fear for your life's savings; groups are less expensive than individual work, and any twelve-step program is free.)

5. The Rule of Who Goes First: Let me tell you about my three good friends who should know better.

One, a mental health professional whom I love very much, is deeply troubled because her husband's flagrant infidelities not only hurt her but also upset their children. The Gotcha Wars are continuous in their household. She desperately wants him to go with her to a marriage counselor. Since he refuses, she does nothing herself.

Another dear friend's sixteen-year-old son is an alcoholic who won't take her advice to seek treatment. In fact, neither he nor his father will admit there's a problem. I urge her to go alone to Al-Anon or a Family's Anonymous meeting. She won't.

Yet a third close friend worries about his rebellious, defiant daughter, who has run away several times. She and her mother refuse to see a professional. My friend called a well-known family therapist for help, but she said she would only work with the entire family. (She was wrong; she should have seen him for at least a few sessions to help him explore ways of convincing the whole family to come or else find help for himself.) After this conversation, he decided there was no point in trying to get treatment.

Each of these people should have gone for individual help. And so should you if you are worried enough to want a child you love to see a professional. The "I-won't-go-if-they-don't-go" game is a power play, not a caring stance. Go in place of your troubled child. Go for him, but also go for yourself. It's self-defeating to wait stubbornly for someone else to do the right thing. At least one member of the family will be getting a clearer hold on sanity. And you won't be punishing yourself with further needless suffering just because your teenager isn't ready to accept treatment yet.

How to Start Looking

Now that you have Levine's five rules for evaluating therapists under your belt, you need to start the search.

When my friend Jane picked her child's therapist out of the Yellow Pages, she was lucky; the treatment was a success. When my client Gerry did the same thing, she found herself talking to a male counselor who specialized in the problems of gay women; she was looking for a psychologist to help her deal with her daughter's learning disability. When Joyce went to her best friend's therapist for help with her son, the therapy failed, and so did the friendship. Xavier took his son to a friend's counselor and the therapy worked out.

There's no simple formula for finding the right psychotherapist, but you have to start somewhere and keep looking until you make the match that will benefit your child.

First, ask your teenager if she has any ideas. You may get an angry "No one!"—but at least you tried. It's at least as likely that your kid does know someone whom she feels can be helpful. You might be surprised. From friends in therapy, from scuttlebutt at school about a counselor on staff, or from casual talk at church, she could have heard about a professional who is liked and respected by kids. If she does know of someone, set up an appointment for her and skip ahead to page 229. If not, consider four sources that can help you come up with a list of potential counselors: relatives and friends; the telephone book; self-help groups; and your kid's school.

A friend or relative knows you and your child well. If she also knows a counselor, she probably can guess whether or not the match would work for you.

Most phone books list community service numbers somewhere in the front matter: alcohol and drug abuse counseling, domestic violence, runaway hotlines, mental health services, suicide prevention hotlines. These listings will also appear in the Yellow Pages, along with many others that can be helpful: e.g., counselors, family service agencies, hospitals, psychiatrists, psychologists, social service agencies, self-help groups, training institutes, university clinics.

In addition, the White Pages will give you the numbers of your local chapters of such professional organizations as the American Psychological Association, the American Psychiatric Association, and the National Association of Social Workers. Each can give you the names of specialists who practice in your area. (A more complete list of professional organizations is included in the Appendix.)

Hotlines and self-help groups can help you compile a list of potential counselors. Listen to people who have made the rounds; they can tell you which therapists in your community are most knowledgeable about your kid's specific problem.

If your teenager's school has a psychologist or social worker on staff, seek his advice in making your list. If not, the guidance counselor can sometimes be helpful. Be specific when you contact school officials, as in these examples:

"I'm worried that my fourteen-year-old daughter might be so depressed that she's going to hurt herself. She can barely drag herself to school. When she comes home, she goes straight to bed. Often, she won't get up even for dinner. She claims she's just fine, but this is not like her. Recently, she broke up with her boyfriend, and maybe this is a reaction, but I think it's going on too long. I think she needs to be seeing a therapist."

"Three of my fifteen-year-old son's friends were just arrested for burglary. I think he was with them, but got away. I need to talk with someone who can help me decide how to handle this situation. I think he needs help, but he tells me to let him live his own life. His father says I'm worrying about nothing."

"My sixteen-year-old daughter is seeing a nineteen-year-old boy who is known to bash girls around. She came home last night with a mouser. She says she fell, but I don't believe her. I need to talk with someone, and I think my daughter does, too."

"My thirteen-year-old seems fascinated with the occult. I know this could be just a passing phase, but it seems to be all-consuming right now. I need to talk with someone about whether or not he needs help. If he does, I need to know how to persuade him to get it."

What You Should Look For

When you have at least three names of potential counselors on your list, interview them by telephone. If you are still undecided and your finances permit, you should also set up an appointment to meet with each of them. In general, you are looking for someone who is sincerely interested in adolescents, appears to be genuine, has good listening skills, and can explain herself clearly and unaffectedly to you.

Consider these basic questions:

1. What does she think causes the problem you face?
2. How does she work to solve this particular problem?
3. How long will it take to help your child?
4. How will your kid's therapy involve the rest of your family, if at all?
5. What feedback will she give you about your child?
6. Does she believe that the problem can be solved? You want someone who communicates hope. Beware of pessimists. (On the other hand, be wary of someone who promises miracles.)
7. What is her fee scale? How will payment be handled? (You will have to find out on your own whether or not your insurance coverage applies to her treatment program for your teenager.)

Don't be shy in your interviews. You are the buyer. You are shopping around for the optimum product, if you will. Many parents simply take the above list and go down it item by item. The psychotherapist's answers may lead to the discussion of other issues that are relevant to your specific situation.

At this point in the book, you have a pretty clear idea of my views on many issues. Given that context, let me answer the above seven questions as if you were interviewing me. This should help you know what to expect when you go comparison shopping.

1. "Your kid's problem, like most problems facing this generation of adolescents, is probably caused by a blend of her genetic make-up with what she's experienced in your family, the neighborhood, her school and country, added to the meanings she has drawn from combining and contrasting her genetic traits and experience. I use this equation: "Genetics combined with life experiences creates beliefs that produce behavior."

2. "I work with the most changeable aspect of the above equation— the beliefs of your child and the rest of your family. In order to understand everyone's point of view, I spend a lot of time seeing parents alone, a kid alone, then everyone together. Our goal is to modify any beliefs that are creating your kid's problem. Once I think I understand a family, I prefer to work in groups, perhaps sending each family member to a different group. In groups, I tend to educate, give advice, signal directions. This approach will solve some problems quickly— perhaps all of them. If not, we all learn a lot and have a better chance of figuring out different ways of dealing with the problem."

3. "My length of treatment varies. Generally, I like to gather background information by meeting with parents at least twice. After that, if your kid is cooperative and talkative, two or three sessions may be enough to get us going. Next, we have one family session, followed by groups. After six weekly meetings of the groups, we have a second family session. Often, your teenager's problem will be solved by this point. If not, we discuss what additional action can be taken. The cycle keeps repeating until all of us agree that we've done all we can to move things forward. Rarely, a family or troubled adolescent will see me for a year, but two or three cycles are enough for most problems.

"Studies have shown that most therapy takes as long as the therapist thinks it will take, so beware counselors who predict that it will require years and years to solve a problem. Very deep-seated emotional problems can take two to three years to resolve, but I've helped lots of kids and their parents turn things around to everyone's satisfaction in six months or less. I give progress reports every three months. I also agree that we should get together and consider an alternative plan of action if there has been no productive change after six months of treatment with me."

4. "As is clear from my answer above, I believe that involvement of the whole family is valuable to a kid's treatment. If some members do not feel they can become involved, however, I am happy to work with whoever does come. If only one family member sees the problem and wants to do something about it, I work with her."

5. "My feedback to you, the parent, comes in our family sessions. I give progress reports but rarely report what your child has said to me, unless life-threatening or life-damaging issues are involved. With that exception, I promise confidentiality to your child. If I have to make another exception—say, therapy is being blocked because of something that the parents should know about—I tell your kid that I'm going to have to share the information. I do so only in his presence at a family session.

"By the way, I have to warn you that I play by the same rules where parents are concerned. If you have a secret that is retarding our progress, I reserve the right to bring it out of the closet, in the interests of solving your kid's problem."

6. "I can't always tell you that your teenager's problem can be solved, but I do believe that all problems can be eased, provided everyone involved wants to cooperate. Unfortunately, some problems can be eased only by reaching the understanding that they cannot be changed.

"Early on, I try to assess whether your kid's problem is related to any of the major mental illnesses. Manic depression or schizophrenia is likely to afflict your teenager for the rest of his life. I'm not qualified to treat such diseases, but I can help you find the right treatment. Moreover, I can help you, your kid, and the rest of your family face the consequences of living with chronic illness and connect you to sources of support and help.

"I also can't promise that I can successfully treat drug or alcohol abuse, although I can help plan a Caring Intervention and provide follow-up care. Chemical abuse requires specific treatment, and recovery is often possible."

7. "My lowest fee is ten dollars more than the rate at the local clinics; my highest is twenty dollars less than the full fee charged by psychiatrists in our community. Occasionally, when the problem and the financial need are severe enough, I offer full scholarships. Most professionals offer a similar sliding scale.

"Because I am a social worker with an 'R license,' many medical insurance policies will cover my fees. Read your policy to see how much coverage you have and what type of therapeutic help it covers. Some policies pay only for psychiatrists; others apply to a variety of properly licensed therapists.

"As to methods of payment, I don't involve myself in the slow torture of billing insurance companies. I expect to be paid before the beginning of each session, and I cancel treatment if a client misses payments twice in a row. I do not charge, however, for sessions canceled at least a week in advance or if a client brings a physician's note for illness. Most therapists have similar rules. They reflect a need to make a living as well as the conviction that financial responsibility for treatment underscores a commitment to the emotional work.

"If your financial resources and insurance will not provide much help, don't despair. Clinics are a good alternative to private counseling, as are facilities operated by the county and state. Self-help groups like AA, Al-Anon, and Families Anonymous are essentially free, although most participants donate at least a dollar a session. Lack of money should never prevent you from getting your child the help he needs."

Getting Your Kid to Go

Your choice of a therapist is just the first step. Next your child has to be convinced, as I've discussed throughout this book. You've already broached the issue, of course. Now, just say that, after looking around and interviewing candidates, you think that you've found someone she would like to talk with, someone who seems likely to listen carefully and caringly to her side of the problem.

As always, it will help if you give your child some choices at this point. Does she prefer to see the therapist alone or with you? Should the first appointment be scheduled immediately or within a few weeks? Does he prefer Friday afternoon over Tuesday evening? Does he want you or his other parent to drive him to the appointment, or would he rather get there on his own?

By making these choices, your child is signaling his agreement to the treatment program, however grudgingly. Your battle is half over. If he resists, you need to follow the program I've outlined before: first, a Caring Response, and if that doesn't work, a Caring Intervention. Turn back for review, if necessary. If not, let's move on. It's time to learn how to care for the person you've been seriously neglecting while you've been worrying about your good kid's bad behavior.

SEVENTEEN

Caring for Yourself

DAD: "Holy cow! That's an Absolut martini, not Evian water. You're supposed to sip it, not slug it back like a sailor."

MOM: "Don't even start! Just fix me another before I disintegrate."

DAD: "Hey, I'm serious. You've had two already."

MOM: "I've earned that—and more! Do you know what it's like to deal with our sixteen-year-old lout all day, when he's in one of his moods? Let me answer that. No, you don't. And you don't know what hell it is to go over to that school and have to hear the damned counselor go on and on about how little Sarah really should stop cutting math, as if I'm an idiot or worse."

DAD: "Honey, I know you have a lot to deal with—"

MOM: "Don't give me that. Have you had a "discussion" with either of our kids lately? You want to get screamed at? You want tears, curses, whining from our two little darlings?"

DAD: "What am I supposed to do?"

MOM: "Lord give me strength. . . ."

Realize this one crucial point: You can't care for your kid unless you take good care of yourself. Trust me. For the good of your teenager, you have to expend as much energy on your own happiness as you do on worrying about his.

Do you think you can't handle both assignments at once? You are about to learn how. I sum it up in three steps:

1. Do something every day just for your own pleasure—and for no other reason.
2. Accept responsibility only for what you can control—and detach yourself from all other worries.
3. Get yourself adequate support and help.

First Things First

First, close this book and spend half an hour doing something just for yourself.

Did you do that, or are you still reading without pause?

Do it!

Go walk in a beautiful garden and, depending upon the season, drink in the fragrance of the lilacs or the roses. Brew yourself a cup of your favorite herbal tea and drink it in your favorite chair, even if you vex the cat. Turn on Mozart or Isaac Hayes, Kenny Rogers or the Moody Blues, even if your teenagers claim terminal eardrum pain. This half-hour is for you alone. Thumb through a joke book or a shamefully sentimental collection of love poems. Read a biker magazine. . . .

Take a steaming hot bath.

Go down for a nap.

Go romping with a pet.

Get a massage.

Watch an inane TV show, without apology.

Close the blinds and get involved in a game of solitaire.

Write a letter to your oldest friend.

Have sex.

Call someone who always cheers you up.

Get involved in your favorite hobby.

Well, okay . . . clean out a closet, if you insist.

Listen to a relaxation or meditation tape.

Now, if you have not been tempted by one of the above suggestions and you are still reading without any intention of stopping, you are in trouble.

"But reading this book is what I want to do right now," you object. "This is taking care of me."

Horsefeathers. Taking care of yourself means doing something just for yourself, not because you want to help someone else. You do something for yourself because you need a break from all the bad things worrying you about your good kid.

"But this is to help me. . . ."

Won't cut it. It's emotionally necessary for you to give yourself a period of pure pleasure, totally unrelated to your problems, to helping anyone else, or to improving your understanding of anyone else.

I know it isn't easy. We are a goal-oriented, competitive, hard-working people. To change yourself, you have to decide to change. If you can't, you are dangerously focused on your kid's difficulties. Good mental health requires that you take breaks, even if your child is in jail, in a psychiatric ward, or in the next room, sobbing uncontrollably after the biggest fight you two have ever had. Even if your child has run away, it's neurotic to refuse to give yourself pleasure because you assume the worst. Believing him dead is a way of punishing yourself and exacerbating your unhappiness. Assume he's all right, and take time out for pleasure. If something bad has happened, he will need a strong parent—one who has been taking care of herself. Even I, a proverbial worrier and caretaker and workaholic, devote a half-hour every day to myself and to fun. So does David. It keeps us both sane. It's also an important part of the ongoing search for serenity, which he, I, and most people need to pursue with some dedication.

Serenity

When you achieve serenity, your life will be forever changed. Begin with this prayer:

> God grant me the serenity
> To accept the things I cannot change,
> The courage to change the things I can,
> And the wisdom to know the difference.

Don't be put off if you're an atheist or an agnostic. Instead of "pray," think "hope." Consider God to stand for the Good Orderly Direction you seek in your life. This prayer, set down by the Roman philosopher-statesman Boethius almost fifteen centuries ago, contains all you need to know about gaining control of your life. (This famous classical writer's work about attaining serenity, *The Consolation of Philosophy,* was written in a dungeon as he awaited execution on an unjustified sentence of death; it was interrupted when he was taken off to be strangled.) The message is clear: Focus on changing what lies within your power to change, accept what cannot be changed.

Consider the numberless kinds of things you cannot control . . .

Earthquakes.

Someone else's behavior.

The future.

Tornadoes.

Someone else's feelings.

The past.

Hurricanes.

Someone else's thoughts.

The unknown.

The federal deficit.

Think about these things. Sure, you know you can't control hurricanes, but don't you believe that you can control the future? And control your kid's behavior, your spouse's feelings, or your best friend's thoughts about something? We all want to believe we're in control so that life can seem safer, more predictable. But you couldn't even control your kid when he was a newborn. You learned that you can't stop a colicky baby from crying, can't keep an active, healthy toddler sitting quietly in a chair for more than a few minutes, can't force a six-year-old to concentrate when she doesn't want to—not without committing abuse.

You learned in your first weeks and months as a parent that you do not control. You influence. Perhaps you tended to forget this lesson as your infant became a child. Youngsters like to please their parents, upon whom their survival depends, and they often do what you want. Perhaps you fell prey to the illusion that you were in complete control—until adolescence struck. Teenagers end your illusions. They resist control. You need to face the reality: You are not in complete charge of your adolescent and her behavior, or her feelings, or her thoughts.

With the illusion of control dissipated, how do you find serenity? The only way I've been able to let go of my fears for my sons and my efforts at control, particularly when they insisted on doing dangerous things, was to be certain that I had done all I could do. That is why, throughout this book, I have given you so many options in various troubling situations.

Letting go does not mean that you turn off. You keep on caring, as I've stressed again and again, but you turn over control of your child to a higher power—be it the power of a loving God, or the power of learning from mistakes, or any other power of your choice. It's easier to let go when you can let go to something larger than yourself.

Even so, you have to be strong. One woman told me about finally letting go of her drug-addicted son. He was in drug rehab but refusing to "work the program." He was wasting everyone's time and daily threatening to walk out. His mother faithfully attended twelve-step meetings as part of a concurrent family education and treatment program. One morning she was asked to read the meditation, which explored the implications of the sentence, "Death, like birth, is natural." Suddenly, she recognized what she feared most. She was afraid her son would die. How, she asked the other participants, could she let go when his life was at stake?

Toward the end of the meeting, a middle-aged man offered an answer. "This is my second time around," he began. "The first child I brought here four years ago is dead. Your fears are justified. But let me tell you what I learned. Like you, I was terrified of letting go. I believed I could somehow learn to control my son's drinking, but I couldn't. In the struggle, our relationship died. I hadn't seen my son for two years when the police called to say he'd been killed in a car accident. Maybe, if I'd been able to let go, to stop trying to control him, we could have healed our relationship. He might still have gone out drinking that night and been killed, but he would have known I loved him. I'm back here with my daughter, but if treatment doesn't work for her, I will do nothing to turn my back on our relationship. I may not let her live in my house, but I will never let her believe she has left my heart."

At a certain point, as this father learned, you have to forgo the controlling in order to preserve the caring.

Another mother put it this way: "Even in going to Al-Anon, I was trying to control my daughter. I hadn't let go. I worked the program hoping she would work it. I used the slogans and left the literature all over the house. As I saw it then, this was my last chance of saving my daughter's life. Yet the harder I worked my program for her, the less she worked hers for herself. Fortunately, I had a sponsor who slowly but surely brought me into the program for myself. She taught me to take care of my needs and turn my daughter's needs over to her higher power. I stopped trying to rescue her and started living my own life. She isn't working her program any harder, but I am at peace, and our relationship has improved."

How do you know that you have been able to let go? One simple answer: When you are no longer "rescuing" but responding responsibly. Probe your own feelings and actions to check for rescuing behavior. For example, are you doing something for your kid that he can and damned well should do for himself? Do you resent what you've done and eventually become furious with him? These are clues that you have not let go; you are still rescuing.

Of course, you might be a compulsive caretaker. . . .

Compulsive Caretaking

Welcome to the club. When I was raising Zach and Daniel and caring for our hundreds of foster children, I slipped from normal caretaking into compulsive caretaking. It didn't seem crazy at the time, but hindsight sees clearly that David and I both became increasingly nutty the longer we worked at it. Is it sane to spend fourteen years living twenty-four hours a day with an ever-changing group of slightly off-the-wall adolescents while trying to raise two sons as normally as possible? I'm grateful for those years, but I'm even more grateful they're behind us. Looking back, I realize we should have stopped four or five years earlier. We didn't, I see now, partly because of my compulsive caretaking.

As long as I can remember, I've been one of those people who has to rush in and fix things when someone else is angry, hurt, or dissatisfied. This behavior, as Jacqueline Castine argues in *Recovery from Rescuing,* is the specific type of addiction defined as compulsive in an effort to control one's own unsettling feelings. I'm an addict. When I see someone in pain, uncomfortable feelings are triggered in me; to control them, I race over and begin to caretake.

Castine's Rescuer's Quiz can indicate whether or not you suffer from the same condition. You can take it for yourself, but I've put down my own responses as an example of someone who definitely needed help learning to take care of herself.

RESCUER'S QUIZ

Question 1: Has the primary focus in your life been in serving the needs of others?

Levine: Yes. Since earliest childhood, I have seen my life as one of service.

Wounded animals, hurt children, tired parents—all called forth my caretaking instincts.

Question 2: Are you in or drawn to one of the service professions: teaching, nursing, social work, the ministry?
Levine: Yes. I am a social worker and teacher. I've been a foster parent.

Question 3: Have there been addicted people in your family?
Levine: Yes. My mother's father was probably an alcoholic. So were two of his children, and my mother was clearly a compulsive caretaker. She took in the family drunks and cared for them.

Question 4: Has your self-esteem been wrapped around your image of yourself as Super-Mom or Super-Neighbor or the guy who's last to leave the office?
Levine: Somewhat. I can certainly feel smug sometimes about all I've done and how hard I've worked. Knowing that my work is compulsive, however, has worn off some of the satisfaction.

Question 5: Are you the first one through the door with a casserole when someone dies?
Levine: No, but I'm usually the first one to offer tissues or support or a comforting word. And I always make the phone calls no one else wants to make.

Question 6: Are you the oldest child in the family? Are you the one everyone depends on, the one who can always be counted on to do the job and do it right?
Levine: I'm the youngest child, but the only daughter. I share being "the dependable one" with my oldest brother. I can certainly be counted on to do the job and do it right.

Question 7: When you attend a lecture or class, do you always think, "Oh, Mary should be here. She would really benefit from this." As you are reading this book, are you thinking about who else needs to read it?
Levine: Yes. Until I read this question, I had planned to buy twelve copies of Castine's book, and I knew exactly who was going to get a copy. I've whittled the list down to six. I may end up buying only one or two, if I work at it some more. Still, that is compulsive caretaking.

Question 8: Is it hard for you to take time for yourself and have fun?
Levine: Yes. I can have fun, but doing it just for myself and making time for it is hard. I spent all my vacations after college at home visiting my parents, until a therapist suggested I could take a fun vacation just for myself.

Question 9: Do you believe you are responsible for making other people happy?

Levine: Not happy, but comfortable. I know in my head that happiness is not mandatory, life is often painful and I'm responsible only for myself, but I feel very uncomfortable and guilty when I see someone hurting.

Question 10: Do you find yourself being resented when you were only trying to be helpful?

Levine: Yes. Not always, but very definitely at certain times.

Question 11: Do you find yourself giving advice that is not accepted?

Levine: As a social worker and teacher, I'm trained to be skilled at making advice palatable. Still, my advice is not always welcome or accepted.

Question 12: Do you think you know what is best for other people?

Levine: Sometimes. In my defense, let me say that I think most people can find what is best by looking within themselves. Of course, I know that others don't agree with that.

Question 13: Do you often feel, no matter what you do, that it isn't enough?

Levine: Yes.

Question 14: Has the former pleasure you used to get from loving and caring given way to feelings of exhaustion and resentment?

Levine: Not right now, but certainly at many points throughout my life.

Question 15: Are you especially critical of others who don't do their share?

Levine: Yes. Particularly when they are in positions of power.

Naturally, there are no right or wrong answers to this test. Mine tag me as a compulsive caretaker. Yours say the same for you, if they are similar. Also, defensiveness about your affirmative answers is another clue: Trying to explain away your caretaking is a symptom of doing too much. Finally, if you realize that you don't feel good about how much you do for others yet can't stop, face facts: you have the addiction. As with any other addiction—and I have not been using the word lightly—you need to be working one or another twelve-step program.

For the moment, we can begin with my hints for designing a program of self-help for compulsive caretakers. (Even if you don't have this problem, read on; I have some tips anyone can use.)

Find Support

When a friend suggested I join her and two other women for dinner, I stumbled upon my first step away from compulsive caretaking. Inspired by Robin Norwood's book, *Women Who Love Too Much,* my friend had decided that we should all form a support group; the title fitted all four of us only too well.

Two of the women came from families afflicted with alcoholism or drug abuse. As we met over the years, I realized how formative for me was the alcoholism in my mother's family and her role as the adult child of an alcoholic. I came to grips with these influences slowly enough. Nothing spectacular ever happened in our group, but the sharing, the empathizing, and the cheering on began the process of my learning to care for me.

Step 1 for you, then, should be to find a few people with the same problem and start meeting regularly. You don't need any professional guidance if you follow a few simple rules. Ours are basic:

We meet every three weeks.

We eat dinner.

We share the plusses and the minuses of our lives.

We cheer the good and sympathize with the bad.

We never criticize one another.

We offer no advice.

At most, when one member has a problem, another might recall her experience with a similar one.

Eventually, the growing strength of the process started in our meetings encouraged me to begin attending some twelve-step groups. At first I was interested primarily for professional reasons, I suppose, but gradually I found myself identifying with the other participants at the meetings, particularly at Al-Anon and Coda (Codependents Anonymous). I began actively working a program. First thing every morning, I get on my knees and repeat the serenity prayer. Then I read some affirming literature—a passage from Al-Anon's *One Day at a Time* or another spiritually oriented daily meditation book. (You can find such volumes in almost any bookstore, shelved near the Hazelden Meditation Books.)

Then, before getting into the daily swim, I plan the one specific thing I will do that day just for my own pleasure. A walk at the beach at sunset, a special phone call to a dear friend, more reading, or listening to music—whatever it is that day, it has to have only one salient characteristic: it lacks all purpose but giving me pleasure.

When, as a recovering compulsive caretaker, I sense myself growing anxious because someone else feels badly, I control my temptation with the serenity prayer or with one of the twelve-step slogans: "Turn it over." "Let go and let God." "Think." "Live and let live." "Easy does it." And, of course, "First things first." The last one, especially, reminds me to ask if I'm taking care of myself and my needs as much as I am those of other people. If you're having trouble letting go, use it often.

During the day, I monitor myself. When someone seems to be upset or in trouble, I don't make the compulsive caretaker's mistake of assuming that I need to do something. I ask what the person needs from me, if anything. Miracle of miracles, the usual reply is "Nothing." Fine. Once in the past, when a friend's purse was snatched just after she had cashed her paycheck, I instantly offered to give her half of mine. She laughed. It turned out her parents were seriously wealthy and she always deposited her pay into a vacation fund. All she needed from me was a quarter so that she could telephone her father's chauffeur to pick her up.

I still have to go to meetings and talk with my sponsor and others in a twelve-step program. I'm recovering, not cured. But my sense of serenity increases every day, as I learn to take care of me.

Perhaps you are reading this book and worrying about your good kid's bad behavior because you are compulsive about caretaking. Perhaps your addiction is not as strong as mine and twelve-step programs are not your answer but you might want to reread Chapter 16, "Getting Professional Help." You might need a support group, a therapist, or a religious advisor to help you ensure that you are caring but not rescuing. When you try to go it alone, when you ignore yourself and slavishly devote your energies to your teenager and her problems, we have come full circle, my friend: You are a good parent doing a bad thing.

Appendix

Where to Go for Help

Help is available from a variety of sources. If you can't find it in one place, look elsewhere, but keep looking until you find the group or individual counselor who clicks for you. The best place to start is with a self-help group. Members can provide you with emotional support as well as information about where to get more help if needed. For the name of a specific self-help group in your community as well as guidelines for evaluating a group, start your search by sending a self-addressed, stamped envelope, along with information about the kind of help you are looking for, to **The National Self-Help Clearing House, 33 West 42nd Street, New York, NY 10036; telephone: (212) 840-1259.**

There are also a number of toll-free hotlines that offer advice and information. The phone numbers often change, but this list is as up-to-date as I can make it.

FOR PROBLEMS RELATED TO CHILD ABUSE:

Child Help National Child Abuse Hotline   (800) 422-4453
Parents Anonymous   (800) 421-0353

FOR PROBLEMS RELATED TO DRUG AND ALCOHOL ABUSE:

Al-Anon	(800) 992-9239
Alcohol and Drug Counseling	(800) ALCOHOL
Cocaine	(800) COCAINE
Drug Abuse	(800) 662-HELP
Families Anonymous	(800) 736-9805

FOR SUICIDE PREVENTION:

Call the emergency room of your local hospital or your local suicide hotline. There is no national suicide hotline.

FOR HELP WITH RUNAWAY CHILDREN:

National Runaway Switchboard   (800) 621-4000

You can also check the White Pages of your telephone directory for a local phone number for most of the major self-help groups. Here is a list of the best-known groups and their national headquarters.

FOR PROBLEMS RELATED TO ALCOHOL OR DRUG ABUSE:

Adult Children of Alcoholics, Central Service Board, Box 3216, Torrance, CA 90505; telephone: (213) 534–1815.

Al-Anon Family Group Headquarters, Box 862, Midtown Stations, New York, NY 10018-0862; telephone: (212) 302-7240.

Ala-Teen is part of the Al-Anon Family Group. Information for Ala-Teen can be obtained through Al-Anon.

Alcoholics Anonymous (AA), Box 459, Grand Central Station, New York, NY 10163; telephone: (212) 696-1100; TDD for the hearing impaired: (212) 686-5454.

Children of Alcoholics Foundation, 200 Park Avenue, 31st Floor, New York, NY 10166; telephone: (212) 351-2680.

Narcotics Anonymous, Box 999, Van Nuys, CA 91409; telephone: (818) 780-3951.

Nar-Anon Family Groups, Box 2562, Palos Verdes, CA 90274; telephone: (213) 547-5800.

National Association for the Children of Alcoholics, 31582 Coast Highway, Suite B, South Laguna, CA 92677; telephone: (714) 499-3889.

FOR PARENTS FEARFUL OF BECOMING ABUSIVE AND FOR ABUSIVE PARENTS WHO WANT TO STOP:

Parents Anonymous, 6733 South Sepulveda Boulevard, Suite 270, Los Angeles, CA 90045.

FOR PARENTS IN NEED OF GENERAL SUPPORT:

Families Anonymous, World Service Office, Box 528, Van Nuys, CA 91408.
Tough Love, Community Service Foundation, Box 70, Sellersville, PA 18960.

FOR SINGLE PARENTS:

Parents Without Partners, 8807 Colesville Road, Silver Spring, MD 20910; telephone: (301) 588-9354. For single parents and their children.
Women on Their Own (WOTO), Box 0, Malaga, NJ 08328; telephone: (609) 728-4071. For single, divorced, separated, or widowed women who are raising children on their own.

FOR STEP-PARENTS:

Step Family Association, 28 Allegheny Avenue, Suite 1307, Baltimore, MD 21204; telephone: (301) 823-7570.

FOR ADOPTIVE PARENTS:

Adoptive Families of America, 3307 Highway 100 North, Minneapolis, MN 55422; telephone: (612) 535-4829.

FOR PARENTS OF MENTALLY ILL CHILDREN:

National Alliance for the Mentally Ill (NAMI), 1901 North Fort Meyer Drive, Suite 500, Arlington, VA 22209; telephone: (703) 524-7600.

FOR PARENTS OF CHILDREN WITH LEARNING DISABILITIES:

Association for Children with Learning Disabilities, 4156 Library Road, Pittsburgh, PA 15234; telephone: (412) 881-2253.

Foundation for Children with Learning Disabilities, 99 Park Avenue, New York, NY 10016; telephone: (212) 687-7211.

Resource for Children with Special Needs, Inc., 200 Park Avenue South, Suite 816, New York, NY 10003; telephone: (212) 677-4650.

I realize that groups are not for everyone. Some of you will prefer to seek help from an individual counselor. If you are financially able or have good insurance you can seek help from a psychotherapist, who could be a pastoral counselor, marriage counselor, family counselor, social worker, psychologist, or psychiatrist. The following organizations can refer you to a professional counselor. Some of these organizations will have local offices, which you can find in the White Pages of your telephone directory. If a local number is not available, you can contact these agencies at their national headquarters listed below.

American Association of Marriage and Family Therapy, 1717 K Street, N.W., Suite 407, Washington, DC 20006; telephone: (202) 429-1825.

American Association of Pastoral Counselors, 9508A Lee Highway, Fairfax, VA 22031; telephone: (703) 385-6967.

American Family Therapy Association, 1255 23rd Street, N.W., Washington, DC 20037; telephone: (202) 659-7666.

American Group Psychotherapy Association, 25 East 21st Street, New York, NY 10010: telephone (212) 477-2677.

American Nurses Association, 2420 Pershing Road, Kansas City, MO 64108; telephone: (816) 474-5720.

American Psychiatric Association, 1400 K Street, N.W., Washington, DC 20005; telephone: (202) 686-6000.

American Psychological Association, 1200 17th Street, N.W., Washington, DC 20036; telephone: (202) 955-7600.

National Academy of Certified Clinical Mental Health Counselors, 5999 Stevenson Avenue, Alexandria, VA 22304; telephone: (730) 823-9800.

National Association of Social Workers, 7981 Eastern Avenue, Silver Spring, MD 20910; telephone: (301) 563-0333.

Other sources of help include your pediatrician, your pastor or rabbi, your school guidance services, and many local agencies such as hospi-' tals, mental health clinics, family service agencies, YMCA, YWCA, YMHA, YWHA, boys' clubs, girls' clubs, and even your local Department of Social Service.

Suggested Reading

The books I've listed below were the most helpful to me in learning how to stop good kids from doing bad things. Browse through the list and see which titles speak to your current situation. As my comments upon each book explain more fully, some were not specifically written to address adolescent problems, but each one is full of ideas that parents of teenagers need to think about.

David Elkind, *All Grown Up and No Place to Go* (Reading, Mass.: Addison-Wesley, 1984). Elkind helped me understand the unique new pressures that are facing adolescents growing up today.

Robert DiGiullo, *Effective Parenting: What's Your Style?* (Chicago: Follett, 1980). One of the people who got me thinking about the differences between "tough love" and "soft love" parents, DiGiullo describes many other styles of parenting. I saw myself in three of them. This book is particularly valuable in helping you determine the fit between your parenting style and that of your child's other parent. I'm leary of the author's emphasis on his Style No. 7, which could promote guilt if you're not careful. Remember the indomitable Eleanor Roosevelt: "No one can make you feel inferior without your consent." That holds for guilt, too.

Haim G. Ginott, *Between Parent and Child* (New York: Avon Books, 1976), and *Between Parent and Teenager* (New York: Avon Books, 1982).

In both of these books, virtually the first to stress the importance of parental communication skills, Ginott helps us all by recognizing that socializing children is hard work, impossible to achieve without conflict. I found his insights very useful in coping with guilt.

Thomas Gordon, *Parent Effectiveness Training: The Tested New Way to Raise Responsible Children* (New York: McKay, 1970). Particularly effective for "tough love" parents who need to tone down a boot camp style, this book takes Ginott's work as foundation and further emphasizes the need for communication skills. Unfortunately, the author believes that parenting can be conflict-free if parents would only learn to speak like therapists. As I hope I've made clear in my own book, I believe that conflict comes with the territory and parents should speak in the language of parents.

Pauline Neff, *Tough Love* (Nashville: Abingdon Press, 1982). In contrast to Gordon, Neff teaches "soft love" parents how to get tougher, providing much sound advice and explaining how to build a support team. You will find her book especially helpful if your child's behavior makes it impossible for him to live with you. You will learn how to devise strategies that will maintain your relationship with your teenager even as you have to oust him from your home.

Dick Schaefer, *Choices and Consequences* (Minneapolis: Johnson Institute, 1987). Every parent needs to read this book, even though its main focus is teenage substance abuse. Schaefer explains how to manage confrontations that will help empower adolescents while at the same time help their parents let go of guilt. His behavior modification approach and contract system are the most effective I've encountered. (This is the source, by the way, of Tom Alibrandi and his magic words.) If you read only one book on this list, Schaefer's is the one.

Kenneth Blanchard and Spencer Johnson, *The One Minute Manager* (New York: William Morrow, 1982). Written for the business world, this shrewd little book is directly applicable to your most important job: raising children. The advice applies to parents dealing with teenagers as well as managers dealing with employees. You'll learn a lot about setting goals effectively and encouraging people to become their best. One-minute praising is a good corrective for parents who tend to gush too much. One-minute blaming should restrain those of us tempted to scold and scold and scold.

Roger Fisher and William Ury, *Getting to Yes: Negotiating Agreement Without Giving In* (New York: Penguin Books, 1983). When your adolescent does bad things, you definitely need to hone your negotiating skills. This clearly written book is one of the best primers for negotiating that I've found.

Manuel J. Smith, *When I Say No, I Feel Guilty* (New York: Bantam Books, 1985). This explanation of assertiveness training is required reading for dealing with any teenager who is into bad things. When that is the situation, hefty assertiveness training skills are necessary.

Robert E. Alberti and Michael L. Emmons, *Your Perfect Right: A Guide to Assertive Living* (San Luis Obispo, Ca.: Impact Publishers, 1986). If you are a "soft love" parent, you should read this excellent step-by-step guide to taking charge of your life.

Harriet Lerner, *The Dance of Anger: A Woman's Guide to Changing the Patterns of Intimate Relationships* (New York: Harper & Row, 1989). The "changing patterns" of the title, while not specific to teenagers, do indeed apply to all adolescents and parents dealing with each other in today's society.

Ginny NiCarthy, *Getting Free: A Handbook for Women in Abusive Relationships* (Seattle: Seal Press, 1986). Although this book focuses on the issues in abusive relationships between adults, it can help any reader understand exactly what abuse is and what must be done to stop it. You can learn whether or not a teenager you love is an abuser or a victim of abuse.

Daniel J. Sonkin and Michael Durphy, *Learning to Live Without Violence,* Revised Edition (Volcano, Ca.: Volcano Press, 1989). Although aimed toward a specific group, the clear advice outlined here has ramifications for anyone who is physically or verbally abusive.

Gayle Rosellini and Mark Worden, *Of Course You Are Angry* (New York: Hazelden/Harper & Row, 1986). These authors deal specifically with the anger associated with drug or alcohol abuse, but much that they say applies to all anger, no matter what the source.

David Treadway, *Before It's Too Late* (New York: Norton, 1989). Treadway explains in detail how to plan an intervention that will encourage a substance abuser to seek professional help.

Linda B. Francke, *Growing Up Divorced* (New York: Fawcett, 1984). If your teenager is a child of divorce, you need to read this very good explanation of the impact of divorce on children and adolescents.

Eric Rofes, *The Kids' Book About Divorce: By, for and About Kids* (New York: Vintage Books, 1982). From the source, the kids themselves, comes a wide range of practical advice for children who are dealing with the consequences of divorce.

Edith Atkin and Estelle Rubin, *Part-Time Father* (New York: Vanguard Press, 1976). Although written by women, this book does indeed have lots of good advice for fathers in the midst of a divorce, but divorced and divorcing mothers would be wise to take a peep, too.

Kathy McCoy, *The Teenage Body Book Guide to Sexuality* (New York: Pocket Books, 1984). Almost everything you and your child need to know about the physical changes of adolescence is clearly and accurately explained.

Caren Adams and Jennifer Fay, *Nobody Told Me It Was Rape: A Parent's Guide to Talking with Teenagers About Acquaintance Rape and Sexual Exploitation* (Santa Cruz, Ca.: Network, 1984). This is "must reading" for all moms, all dads, and all teenagers.

Lonnie Barbach, *For Yourself: The Fulfillment of Female Sexuality* (New York: Anchor/Doubleday, 1976). Definitely "must reading" for every woman from nine to ninety, this sensible book should also be read by men and boys.

Mary V. Borhek, *Coming Out to Parents: A Two-Way Survival Guide for Lesbians and Gay Men and Their Parents* (New York: Pilgrim Press, 1983). The title says it all, for this book really does offer a wealth of advice and support to everyone involved in dealing with same-sex love.

Judith Schaffer and Christina Lindstrom, *How to Raise an Adopted Child* (New York: Crown, 1989). This excellent account of the complexities faced by adoptive families is "must reading" for all who have adopted, are contemplating adoption, were adopted, or desire a deeper understanding of the subject.

Jerry Johnston, *Why Suicide?* (Nashville: Oliver-Nelson, 1987). Both the startling facts about teenage suicide today and suggestions for preventing it are covered in this book.

Ram Dass, *How Can I Help? Stories & Reflections on Service* (New York: Knopf, 1985). Because adolescence is often a time of loss and suffering, this guide to comforting someone can be very helpful in dealing with your teenager.

Larry LeShan, *How to Meditate: A Guide to Self-Discovery* (New York: Bantam Books, 1984). My first introduction to meditation, this thoughtful, welcoming guide remains one of my favorite books on the subject.

Jacqueline Castine, *Recovery for Rescuing: The Cure for Co-Dependency* (Deerfield Beach, Fla.: Health Communications, 1989). As readers of my book know, I tend to do more than I should for others, but Castine's approach has helped me restrain myself. If you have the same problem, she can help you take better care of yourself.

Robin Norword, *Women Who Love Too Much* (Los Angeles: Jeremy P. Tarcher, 1985). Inspired by this book, I formed my first personal support group the same year it was published. We are still meeting regularly.

Fredda Bruckner-Gordon and Barbara K. Gangi, *Making Therapy Work* (New York: Harper & Row, 1988). Everything you need to know about finding the right therapist and making good use of her is contained in this fine guide.

Otto Ehrenberg and Miriam Ehrenberg, *Psychotherapy Maze: A Consumer's Guide to Getting In and Out of Therapy* (Northvale, N.J.: Jason Aronson, 1986). You can gain a good basic understanding of the different types of therapy from this survey.

Index